NOVELL'S

Guide to NetWare® Printing

NOVELL'S

Guide to NetWare® Printing

J. D. MARYMEE AND SANDY STEVENS

NOVELL
PRESS®

Novell Press, San Jose

Novell's Guide to NetWare® Printing

Published by
Novell Press
2180 Fortune Drive
San Jose, CA 95131

Library of Congress Catalog Card No.: 96-78232

ISBN: 0-7645-4514-0

Printed in the United States of America

10 9 8 7 6 5 4 3 2 1

1X/RV/RQ/ZW/FC

Distributed in the United States by IDG Books Worldwide, Inc.

Distributed by Macmillan Canada for Canada; by Contemporanea de Ediciones for Venezuela; by Distribuidora Cuspide for Argentina; by CITEC for Brazil; by Ediciones ZETA S.C.R. Ltda. for Peru; by Editorial Limusa SA for Mexico; by Transworld Publishers Limited in the United Kingdom and Europe; by Academic Bookshop for Egypt; by Levant Distributors S.A.R.L. for Lebanon; by Al Jassim for Saudi Arabia; by Simron Pty. Ltd. for South Africa; by Pustak Mahal for India; by The Computer Bookshop for India; by Toppan Company Ltd. for Japan; by Addison Wesley Publishing Company for Korea; by Longman Singapore Publishers Ltd. for Singapore, Malaysia, Thailand, and Indonesia; by Unalis Corporation for Taiwan; by WS Computer Publishing Company, Inc. for the Philippines; by WoodsLane Pty. Ltd. for Australia; by WoodsLane Enterprises Ltd. for New Zealand. Authorized Sales Agent: Anthony Rudkin Associates for the Middle East and North Africa.

For general information on IDG Books Worldwide's books in the U.S., contact our Consumer Customer Service department at 800-762-2974. For reseller information, including discounts and premium sales, contact our Reseller Customer Service department at 800-434-3422.

For information on where to purchase IDG Books Worldwide's books outside the U.S., contact our International Sales department at 415-655-3078 or fax 415-655-3281.

For information on foreign language translations, contact our Foreign & Subsidiary Rights department at 415-655-3018 or fax 415-655-3281.

For sales inquiries and special prices for bulk quantities, contact our Sales department at 415-655-3200 or write to the address above.

For information on using IDG Books Worldwide's books in the classroom or for ordering examination copies, contact our Educational Sales department at 800-434-2086 or fax 817-251-8174.

For authorization to photocopy items for corporate, personal, or educational use, contact the Copyright Clearance Center, 222 Rosewood Drive, Danvers, MA 01923, or fax 508-750-4470.

For general information on Novell Press books in the U.S., including information on discounts and premiums, contact IDG Books at 800-434-3422 or 415-655-3200. For information on where to purchase Novell Press books outside the U.S., contact IDG Books International at 415-655-3021 or fax 415-655-3295.

John Kilcullen, *President & CEO, IDG Books Worldwide, Inc.*
Brenda McLaughlin, *Senior Vice President & Group Publisher, IDG Books Worldwide, Inc.*
The IDG Books Worldwide logo is a trademark under exclusive license to IDG Books Worldwide, Inc., from International Data Group, Inc.

Rosalie Kearsley, *Publisher, Novell Press, Inc.*
Novell Press and the Novell Press logo are trademarks of Novell, Inc.

Welcome to Novell Press

Novell Press, the world's leading provider of networking books, is the premier source for the most timely and useful information in the networking industry. Novell Press books cover fundamental networking issues as they emerge—from today's Novell and third-party products to the concepts and strategies that will guide the industry's future. The result is a broad spectrum of titles for the benefit of those involved in networking at any level: end-user, department administrator, developer, systems manager, or network architect.

Novell Press books are written by experts with the full participation of Novell's technical, managerial, and marketing staff. The books are exhaustively reviewed by Novell's own technicians and are published only on the basis of final released software, never on prereleased versions.

Novell Press at IDG Books is an exciting partnership between two companies at the forefront of the knowledge and communications revolution. The Press is implementing an ambitious publishing program to develop new networking titles centered on the current version of NetWare and on Novell's GroupWise and other popular groupware products.

Novell Press books are translated into 12 languages and are available at bookstores around the world.

Rosalie Kearsley, *Publisher, Novell Press, Inc.*
David Kolodney, *Associate Publisher, IDG Books Worldwide, Inc.*

Novell Press

Publisher
Rosalie Kearsley

Associate Publisher
David Kolodney

Market Development Manager
Colleen Bluhm

Communications Project Specialist
Marcy Shantii

Managing Editor
Terry Somerson

Acquisitions Editor
Anne Hamilton

Development Editor
Jim Sumser

Copy Editors
Michael D. Welch
Suki Gear
Tracy Brown

Technical Editor
Jeff Rosinski

Editorial Assistant
Sharon Eames

Production Director
Andrew Walker

Production Associate
Christopher Pimentel

Supervisor of Page Layout
Craig A. Harrison

Project Coordinator
Katy German

Graphics & Production Specialists
Vincent F. Burns
Laura Carpenter
Stephen Noetzel
Mark Schumann
Dale Smith

Media/Archive Coordination
Leslie Popplewell

Proofreader
Michael Hall

Indexer
Anne Leach

Cover Design
Archer Design

Illustrator
Dave Puckett

Cover Photographer
Jay B. Grant

For Kyle.
What a pleasant surprise.

To C. W. Rogers.
Yes, J. D. does have socks that match his suits these days.

And to Audrey Pine.
Had you not adopted J. D. at such a late age,
he might still not be in the computer industry.

About the Authors

J. D. Marymee, Master Certified Novell Engineer and Certified Novell Instructor, has worked for Novell since 1988 and is currently a Corporate Integration Manager.

Sandy Stevens, Enterprise Certified Novell Engineer and Certified Novell Instructor, is the former Product Marketing Manager for Novell's Printing Services and Novell Directory Services. She is currently a freelance writer based in Sandy, Utah.

Both J. D. and Sandy have consulted with thousands of NetWare customers in the design and implementation of their networks. Together they have over 25 years of combined networking experience.

Foreword

When we look at the evolution of network computing, the changes are astonishing. PC networks that once were just for the workgroup have expanded to enterprise and even global networks. But, through all this change, one thing remains constant—the need to print information. NetWare has long been the leader in providing unsurpassed network printing services.

With the evolution of PC networks, printing has grown from stand-alone printing environments to enterprise network printing environments with a multitude of shared network printers scattered throughout an organization. Network administrators today are finding that, as their networks grow, they are spending countless hours managing network printing. To minimize the time spent managing network printing, administrators must have a good understanding of NetWare's printing services and have the tools necessary to troubleshoot network printing problems.

In their book, *Novell's Guide to NetWare Printing*, J. D. Marymee and Sandy Stevens have provided a comprehensive guide to both NetWare 3 and NetWare 4 printing services. Administrators will find this book to be *the* single resource they need to understand NetWare's printing architecture, how to set up network printing, and how to manage a NetWare printing environment. This book is an exceptionally thorough reference that should be on every NetWare administrator's shelf! Enjoy.

Rob Whittle
Product Line Manager
NetWare Printing Services

Preface

Since the beginning of the PC era, the need to share printing resources has catalyzed the evolution of PC networks. As printers have become more sophisticated, powerful, and expensive, the desire to share printers has grown. Many of today's printers are specifically designed to be shared between multiple users, including such features as imbedded network interface cards that enable a direct connection to the network. As more and more printers are being shared on the network, the printing support challenges have increased. And though NetWare's printing services are unsurpassed in the industry, reference material on the NetWare print system has been too scarce.

Novell's Guide to NetWare Printing seeks to correct that problem. This book represents the first authoritative guide on NetWare 3 and NetWare 4 printing ever available from Novell Press.

What You'll Learn from Reading this Book

We've designed this book to provide a practical reference for network administrators, printing administrators, consultants, resellers and any others who are responsible for the configuration and support of a NetWare 3 or NetWare 4 printing environment. Because of the lack of reference material available on NetWare printing, this book was written to provide you with all the information you will ever need about NetWare printing.

This book presents detailed information about the NetWare printing system architecture, providing you with a solid foundation to assist you in the configuration and support of a NetWare printing environment. The book also takes an in-depth look at the utilities used to create and manage NetWare printing, giving you a single source reference for any printing task. Also covered in detail are the upgrade procedures from NetWare 3 to NetWare 4, managing a mixed NetWare 3 and NetWare 4 environment, and third-party printing solutions.

How We've Organized this Book

We've organized this book in two main parts: Part I, "NetWare Printing Theory and Operations," and Part II, "NetWare Printing Swift Track Guide."

Part I: NetWare Printing Theory and Operations

The first part of the book covers the way the NetWare printing system works and the configuration and management of NetWare printing services.

Chapter 1, "NetWare Printing Theory," discusses how network printing works and describes the NetWare printing system architecture. It covers print queues, print servers, and printers, and each of their roles in the NetWare print system. It also describes the process of sending print jobs to the network and how to simplify that process though the use of job configurations.

Chapter 2, "NetWare 3 Print Services—Theory of Operations," describes how printing works specifically in the NetWare 3 environment. It covers in detail the creation of print queues, print servers, and printers, as well as the creation of print job configurations.

Chapter 3, "NetWare 4 Print Services—Theory of Operations," introduces the reader to printing with NetWare Directory Services. It also details the creation and configuration of NetWare 4 printing objects and job configurations.

Chapter 4, "Print Services Migration," provides a guide to migrating printing from NetWare 3 to NetWare 4. It covers in detail the various migration options as well as the steps involved in moving printing services to NetWare 4.

Chapter 5, "Coexistence," is designed for those with a mixed NetWare 3 and NetWare 4 printing environment. It covers the considerations necessary when managing printing on a network that has both NetWare 3 and NetWare 4 print services. It also provides tips on making the mixed environment transparent and easy for users to use.

Chapter 6, "Managing NetWare 3 Print Services," provides a complete reference for managing a NetWare 3 printing environment with the PCONSOLE utility. This chapter details the tasks involved in managing print queues, printers, and print servers.

Chapter 7, "Managing NetWare 4 Print Services," covers the management of print queues, printers, and print servers in a NetWare 4 environment. Novell Directory Services management utilities for both Windows administrators (NWAdmin) and DOS administrators (PCONSOLE) are covered in detail.

Chapter 8, "Integrating Third-Party Solutions," discusses some of the most popular third-party network printing solutions and how those solutions fit into a NetWare environment. Solutions from Hewlett-Packard, Lexmark, QMS, and Intel are discussed.

Part II: NetWare Printing Swift Track Guide

The second part of this book provides a quick reference for network administrators, printing operators, and users who need easy access to the basic steps involved in setting up and administering network printing. Step-by-step instructions walk the reader through all of the tasks presented in Part I.

Appendix A: Troubleshooting

In Appendix A you will find a valuable troubleshooting matrix. This matrix includes many of the most common network printing problems, their possible causes, and recommended solutions—along with cross-references to chapters in this book where you can find more information. This matrix is a useful reference for anyone responsible for solving network printing problems.

Appendix B: Disk Installation Instructions

Just what you'd expect—instructions on installing the disk that comes with this book.

Special Features in this Book

This book contains a disk that we've filled with information and utilities that will enhance your NetWare printing system. Included on the disk are various Novell Application Notes and papers that have been written on managing and configuring both NetWare 3 and NetWare 4 printing. Also included are utilities that make it easier to manage and use NetWare printing.

Acknowledgments

When we began writing this book, we didn't realize that we were in for the time of our lives! You don't realize what a major effort is involved in the production of a book like this until you find yourself right in the middle of it. Though we put many hours into writing the manuscript, this book wouldn't have been possible without the hard work and sacrifices of many other people.

We'd first like to thank Jim Sumser at IDG Books for his patience and perseverance. Without his constant encouragement and guidance, we probably would have never completed this book. Jim, you said once you would make our lives a living hell but instead, you became an anchor and a much-needed guide. Thanks for keeping your sense of humor when the pressure was on.

We also thank Anne Hamilton at IDG Books for taking care of the logistical aspects of producing this book. Thanks Anne for your punctuality and being there when we needed you.

We thank Michael Welch at IDG Books who meticulously edited the pages of this book. Mike, your attention to detail is excellent. Thanks for helping to make an awesome finished product. And thanks to Suki Gear and Tracy Brown for helping at crunch time.

We would also like to extend special thanks to Jeff Rosinski who painstakingly provided a technical review of this book. Jeff's knowledge of NetWare and the NetWare print system is unsurpassed. Thanks for the time and effort you dedicated to this project.

A big thank you to Rob Whittle at Novell for his assistance throughout this project. Rob, you've always been a tremendous help and a pleasure to work with. Thanks for being there for us.

To Rose Kearsley and Colleen Bluhm at Novell Press, thank you for making this book possible. Your pursuit of excellence continues to put quality information in the hands of our readers.

And to all the others who were directly or indirectly responsible for making this book happen, you may not be mentioned but are certainly appreciated. Thank you.

J. D. & Sandy

Contents at a Glance

Table of Contents

Part II: NetWare Printing Swift Track Guide   283

Appendixes

PART I

NetWare Printing
Theory and Operations

About this Guide

We've designed Part I of this book to provide you with all the information you need to create, configure, and manage both NetWare 3 and NetWare 4 printing services. If you are managing a NetWare 3-only environment, the following chapters will benefit you:

- ▸ Chapter 1: NetWare Printing Theory

- ▸ Chapter 2: NetWare 3 Print Services—Theory of Operations

- ▸ Chapter 6: Managing NetWare 3 Print Services

- ▸ Chapter 8: Integrating Third-Party Solutions

If you are managing a NetWare 4-only printing system, the following chapters will benefit you:

- ▸ Chapter 1: NetWare Printing Theory

- ▸ Chapter 3: NetWare 4 Print Services—Theory of Operations

- ▸ Chapter 7: Managing NetWare 4 Print Services

- ▸ Chapter 8: Integrating Third Party Solutions

For those of you who will be upgrading a NetWare 3 print system to NetWare 4, Chapter 4 provides you with all the information you need to determine which upgrade method to use and the steps necessary to complete the upgrade.

If you will be managing a mixed NetWare 3 and NetWare 4 printing system, you will find all the chapters in this book useful. Chapter 5, "Coexistence," presents everything you need to be aware of when managing a mixed environment.

Where to Go for More Information

If you need more information on creating and managing your printing system, Part II of this book provides a practical step-by-step "Swift Track Guide" that walks you through the process of creating, configuring, and managing your printing system. If you require additional information, the disk included with this book contains a wealth of Novell Application Notes and other documents to assist you.

CHAPTER 1

NetWare Printing Theory

If you ask an administrator of any network, large or small, to identify his or her number one support issue, you'll generally get the same response: "Printing." But why is network printing such a problem? Is it the printing system design? Is it a weakness in the network operating system itself? Or is it a lack of understanding of how network printing works? The answer is probably some of each, but network printing problems most often result from a poor understanding of the underlying printing architecture and how network printing *really* works. Fortunately, this misinformation can be corrected. That's exactly what this book is for.

To help you more effectively install and maintain your NetWare printing system, we want to start with the basics of printing. As with any computer-related problem, you can't effectively troubleshoot or support something you don't fully understand, right? This chapter focuses on the NetWare printing architecture and helps you learn how printing in a NetWare environment actually works. The topics covered here pertain to both NetWare 3.x networks and NetWare 4.x networks. Let's dive right in.

Printing Locally

Before you can understand how printing on a network works, it helps to understand how *local* printing works. The term *local printing* refers to a PC—stand-alone or connected to a network—with a printer directly attached to it. Printing happens locally without going through the network, as shown in Figure 1.1:

FIGURE 1.1

Printing locally

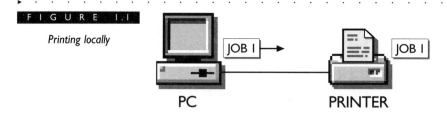

PC   PRINTER

If you are a seasoned printing pro and already understand how local printing works (if you know the mechanics, the difference between parallel and serial printing, how data is sent to the printer, redirecting data to a printer port, and so on), feel free to skip to the next major part of this chapter, "Capturing Print Output to the Network." But if printing is even somewhat of a mystery to you, then read on.

In a local printing scenario, a printer is generally attached to one of the computer's parallel ports. A parallel (LPT) port is a one-way communication channel specially designed to send information to a printer. Though a parallel port is referred to as a one-way channel, it's not totally one way because the printer can send certain signals to your computer, such as an out-of-paper signal.

When printing to an LPT port, the computer sends data to the printer over several wires instead of one (as in a serial port). Using several wires allows the parallel port to transmit data to a printer more quickly than a serial connection does. Most computers have at least one, but sometimes two or more, physical parallel ports. By default, these ports are matched to the logical DOS channels labeled LPT1, LPT2, LPT3, and so on. A parallel port generally has a 25-pin connector, as illustrated in Figure 1.2

F I G U R E   1.2

A 25-pin parallel port connector

In some cases, you may encounter a specialized printer or plotter that has a serial connector. These devices are connected to one of the computer's available serial ports—also known as COM ports. Most of today's printers with serial connectors also provide the option of a parallel connection. In this case, we recommend that you use the parallel option whenever possible. Here's why:

First, as already mentioned, serial printing is much slower than parallel. The reason for this is that a serial interface operates by sending one bit of data at a time to the printer, unlike a parallel interface that transmits eight bits simultaneously.

Second, serial ports were developed to support devices requiring a two-way communication channel that allows the computer to send and receive information from an input/output device such as a mouse or a modem. Because printers operate very differently from these devices, special serial cables are generally required to connect a printer to a serial port. To make matters more complicated, in the past each printer manufacturer seemed to treat serial ports a little differently, resulting in a specially wired cable for each printer type.

Finally, if we haven't given you enough reasons yet, serial printers can be very difficult to configure. Because of the transmission method used with serial printing, the computer and printer must agree on a number of settings for data to transmit correctly. These settings include the following:

- The rate at which data is transmitted (baud rate)

- The number of data bits per character (data bits)

- The number of bits signaling the end of a character (stop bits)

- Error checking used (parity)

- Software handshaking (XON/XOFF)

Guess who gets to configure all of this? Hopefully not you . . . but, because you're reading this book, it probably will be.

If you have a printer with only a serial connection option, the connector will either be a 25-pin as shown in Figure 1.2 previously (don't be fooled by the connector; serial cables are wired very differently than parallel) or a nine-pin connector as shown in Figure 1.3.

FIGURE 1.3

A nine-pin serial connector

Now that we've discussed the two methods of connecting local printers, let's take a look at how printing data is actually sent to the printer. The following are the most common ways data can be sent to a printer:

- Printing from an application

- Using the DOS PRINT command

► Copying a file to a printer port

► Redirecting output to a printer port

► Printing screen displays

PRINTING FROM AN APPLICATION

Sending printing data from a software application is the most common printing method. Whether you are using a Windows or a DOS application, generally all that is required to print is to tell the application what type of printer you are using and what printer port it is attached to. This is normally done by selecting the appropriate *driver* for your printer type.

Most applications provide drivers for all major printers on the market. In addition, if you are using Windows, you can choose to use the print drivers provided with Windows instead of the application's drivers. If you are using a clone printer for which an application or Windows doesn't have a specific driver, chances are likely that your printer emulates a brand-name printer such as an HP LaserJet or an Epson. Check your printer manual if you are not sure which printer yours emulates.

When printing, most applications default to redirecting printing output to LPT1. If you wish to send a print job to a printer attached to a different LPT port, you need to configure the application accordingly; otherwise you will not be able to print.

For example, let's assume your computer has two parallel ports that, by default, map to the DOS channels LPT1 and LPT2, respectively. A printer is attached to the second parallel port. A print job is sent but nothing happens on the printer. Why? Because, by default, the application is directing output to LPT1, but the printer is attached to the second parallel port (LPT2). The solution is to change the application's configuration to direct output to LPT2 instead of LPT1.

If the application you are using only redirects data to parallel ports, and you wish to send printing output to a printer attached to a serial port, you can use the DOS MODE command to redirect data from the parallel port to the serial port. Refer to your DOS reference manual for the exact syntax, but the command looks something like the following:

```
MODE LPT1:=COM1:
```

Once you enter this command, any data sent to LPT1 by an application or otherwise is redirected to COM1 instead.

· · · · ·

USING THE DOS PRINT COMMAND

If you want to print from the DOS command line or if you aren't a Windows user, the DOS PRINT command may be useful to you. PRINT allows you to print text files or other files you have created on disk. PRINT runs in the background, leaving your computer free so you can continue to work while your files are printing. DOS alone does not support multitasking, so this command can save non-Windows users a lot of time.

Again, check your DOS reference manual for the PRINT syntax for the version of DOS you are using, but a basic PRINT command looks something like this:

```
PRINT /D:LPT1 CHAP1.DOC
```

PRINT provides the option to have many files print at once; if you wish to do this, a queue size must be specified when you load the memory resident portion of PRINT the first time the command is issued. Your DOS manual provides details on how to do this.

COPYING A FILE TO A PRINTER PORT

Another method of printing text files from the DOS command line is to use the DOS COPY command to copy the file directly to an LPT or COM port. You can do this by using the standard COPY syntax but specifying the desired printer port in place of the destination path. For example, to copy the file AUTOEXEC.BAT directly to LPT1, the syntax is as follows:

```
COPY C:\AUTOEXEC.BAT LPT1
```

The term "PRN" is also used to indicate the first parallel port. So, an option for the preceding syntax would be as follows:

```
COPY C:\AUTOEXEC.BAT PRN
```

Copying files directly to printer ports is also an excellent method of troubleshooting printing problems. If, for example, you cannot print from within an application, copying a file directly to your printer port from DOS can help you determine if the problem is with the application or with the printer or printer connection.

REDIRECTING OUTPUT TO A PRINTER PORT

Information that would normally be displayed on your computer screen can be sent directly to a printer. You can do this using the DOS redirection symbol, ">". For example, if you want a directory listing of C:\WINDOWS to be sent directly to the printer attached to LPT1, you can enter the following command from the DOS command line:

```
DIR C:\WINDOWS >LPT1
```

Again, you can use "PRN" in place of LPT1 to indicate the first parallel port.

Redirecting output to a printer port can also help you troubleshoot printing problems. However, this option may cause your computer to hang if no printer is attached or if the printer is improperly attached to the printer port.

PRINTING SCREEN DISPLAYS

Every keyboard, all the way back to those of the original IBM PC, is equipped with a Print Screen key. Some keyboards require that you also hold down the Shift key, and others do not, but when you press the Print Screen key, any information on your screen at the time is sent to the printer attached to LPT1.

Using the Print Screen key is always useful for printing out error messages that may come across your screen while you work. Sometimes (but not always) when your computer hangs, if you're really lucky, you can press Print Screen before rebooting to have a record of what was on your screen just before you computer locked up. This is especially useful if you hadn't saved your file in a while.

Capturing Print Output to the Network

Now that we have reviewed some of the ways you can send print output to a local printer, let's take a look at how print output is sent to the network.

Directing print jobs to the network is a function of the NetWare DOS Requester—the NetWare workstation software responsible for directing service requests to the network—and is enabled through the CAPTURE command. CAPTURE is a NetWare workstation utility that, when executed, instructs NetWare to redirect print output from an LPT port to the network for printing. You can enable CAPTURE in three ways, as follows:

▸ From the DOS command line

▸ Through a login script

▸ From within Windows using NetWare's NWUser

▸ From Windows 95 Network Neighborhood

Whichever method of capturing you use, once CAPTURE is executed the application sending the print job is completely unaware that the printing is taking place on the network. It simply sends the print output to the LPT port specified; as far as it knows, the job is printed on a locally attached printer. However, NetWare "fools" the application and captures the print data from the LPT port and redirects it to the network for printing. Figure 1.4 illustrates this process.

▸ · ◂

F I G U R E   1.4

*Capturing print output to
the network*

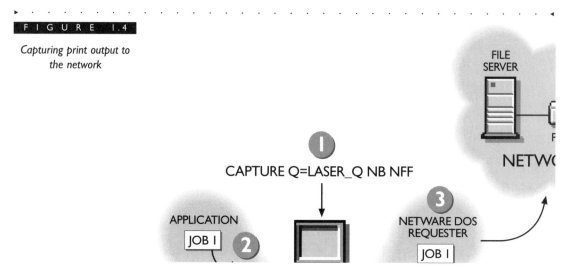

To better understand how print output is sent to the network, let's follow the process step by step. Refer to Figure 1.4 through each step.

1 • The CAPTURE command is entered at the workstation.

2 • The application directs the print job to the LPT port specified.

3 • The NetWare DOS Requester *captures* the print output and redirects it to the network for printing.

4 • The print job is printed on a network printer.

How the print job is handled by the network is determined by the parameters specified when the CAPTURE command was entered. Because of the minor differences between NetWare 3 and NetWare 4 printing, the available parameters for CAPTURE vary between the two operating systems. Tables 1.1 and 1.2 show the CAPTURE parameters for both NetWare 3 and NetWare 4. These parameters are covered in depth in Chapter 2 for NetWare 3 printing and Chapter 3 for NetWare 4 printing. To show you how to use the parameters in either case, here's a model of the CAPTURE syntax:

```
CAPTURE [parameter(s)]
```

TABLE 1.1	SYNTAX	OPTION	DESCRIPTION
NetWare 3 CAPTURE parameters	SH	Show	Displays current CAPTURE status.
	NOTI	Notify	Notifies user when the print job is complete.
	NNOTI	NoNotify	Does not notify user when the print job is complete.
	TI	Timeout	Specifies a time-out period for ending CAPTURE.
	A	Autoendcap	Specifies an automatic ENDCAP.
	NA	No Autoendcap	Specifies that no automatic ENDCAP is desired.
	L	Local	Specifies the local printer port to capture.
	S	Server	Specifies the file server to capture to.
	Q	Print queue	Specifies the print queue to capture to.
	CR	Create	Specifies a file in which to print data.
	J	Job configuration	Specifies the PRINTCON job configuration to use.
	F	Form	Specifies the PRINTDEF form to use.
	C	Copies	Specifies the number of copies to print.
	T	Tabs	Specifies the number of characters in one Tab stop.

(continued)

TABLE 1.1

NetWare 3 CAPTURE
parameters
(continued)

SYNTAX	OPTION	DESCRIPTION
NT	No tabs	Specifies that all tab characters are defined by the application.
NB	No banner	Specifies that no banner page will be printed.
NAM	Name	Specifies the text that appears on the upper part of the banner page.
B	Banner name	Specifies the text that appears on the lower part of the banner page.
FF	Form feed	Specifies that a form feed is desired at the end of a print job.
NFF	No form feed	Specifies that no form feed is desired at the end of a print job.
K	Keep	Specifies that the file server should keep all print data if the workstation hangs or loses power while data is capturing.
?	Help	Lists available capture options.

TABLE 1.2

NetWare 4 CAPTURE
parameters

SYNTAX	OPTION	DESCRIPTION
SH	Show	Displays current CAPTURE status.
NOTI	Notify	Notifies user when the print job is complete.
NNOTI	NoNotify	Does not notify user when the print job is complete.
TI	Timeout	Specifies a time-out period for ending capture.
AU	Autoendcap	Specifies an automatic ENDCAP.
NA	No Autoendcap	Specifies that no automatic ENDCAP is desired.
EC	End capture	Ends the capture of data to the LPT port specified, and returns to local printing.
ECCA	Cancel and end capture	Ends the capture of data to LPT ports and discards data that was being captured.
ALL	All	Used with EC (End capture) to end capture of all LPT ports.
L	LPT port	Specifies the local printer port to capture from.
S	Server	Specifies the file server in which to capture data.
Q	Print queue	Specifies the print queue to capture to.

	SYNTAX	OPTION	DESCRIPTION
TABLE 1.2 *NetWare 4 CAPTURE parameters (continued)*	P	Printer	Specifies which printer the job should be sent to.
	V	Verbose	Displays information about the specified printer, print queue, and print job configuration options.
	CR	Create	Specifies a file in which to print data.
	J	Job configuration	Specifies the PRINTCON job configuration to use.
	F	Form	Specifies the PRINTDEF form to use.
	C	Copies	Specifies the number of copies to print.
	T	Tabs	Specifies the number of characters in one Tab stop.
	NT	No tabs	Specifies that all tab characters are defined by the application.
	NB	No banner	Specifies that no banner page will be printed.
	NAM	Name	Specifies the text that appears on the upper part of the banner page.
	B	Banner name	Specifies the text that appears on the lower part of the banner page.
	FF	Form feed	Specifies that a form feed is desired at the end of a print job.
	NFF	No form feed	Specifies that no form feed is desired at the end of a print job.
	K	Keep	Specifies that the file server should keep all print data if the workstation hangs or loses power while data is capturing.
	?	Help	Lists available capture options.

NetWare Printing Components

The workstation side of network printing seems simple enough. You enter the CAPTURE command at each workstation, send a print job from your application, and, like magic, your print job is printed on a network printer. . . . Nice try. In a perfect world, maybe, but in this not-so-perfect world it gets a bit more complicated—there might be multiple users sending jobs to many different printers across the network, some printers might be attached to file servers and some to workstations. After a while it becomes confusing where local printing ends and network printing begins. To help minimize some of that confusion, let's now look at the network side of printing and explore the various components of the NetWare print system.

Regardless of whether you're running NetWare 3 or NetWare 4, the components of the NetWare print system are the same, although they may vary slightly in name or location.

For example, in NetWare 3 a print server can either run as a stand-alone device or be loaded as an NLM (NetWare Loadable Module) at the file server. In NetWare 4, print servers run only at the file server. However, a print server is a print server, so, regardless of where it may be running, it provides the same function in the NetWare print system.

The basic NetWare print system consists of three components:

▸ Print queues

▸ Print servers

▸ Printers

PRINT QUEUES

To describe how the network print process works, let's use an analogy of a typical airport experience. The first thing you do when you arrive at the airport is stand in line at the ticket counter to check in for your flight. This line is analogous to a print queue. A print queue is basically a holding place on a file server for print jobs waiting to be serviced by a print server, just as the check-in line at the airport is a holding place for passengers waiting to check in for their flights.

Physically, a print queue is simply a file server subdirectory. The location of that subdirectory varies depending on the version of NetWare you are running. NetWare 3 print queue subdirectories are always located in the SYS:SYSTEM directory and are assigned a unique hexadecimal number for the subdirectory name. NetWare 4 print queue directories can be placed on the volume of choice (this is a great improvement over NetWare 3 . . . we'll talk about why later) and are placed in a directory called QUEUES. The print jobs themselves are simply temporary files that are deleted after the print job is sent to the printer.

Now, back to our airport analogy. At every airport, you'll find a number of different airline ticket counters. How do you know which line to stand in? Well, that's simple: if your ticket is for a Delta flight, you get in the Delta line; if your ticket is for a Quantas flight, you get in the Quantas line.

But how does a print job know which queue to go to at the file server? Actually, the print job doesn't know—or even care, for that matter. It's the NetWare DOS Requester that is responsible for placing the job in the proper queue. Well, then, how does the Requester know which queue the job is intended for? That is based on the parameters specified when the CAPTURE command was entered at the workstation. The CAPTURE command instructs the network exactly how to handle the print job—which print queue to go to, how many copies to print, whether or not to enter a form feed at the end of the job, and so on.

Back in line at the airport. . . . Just as with any line for service, people are assisted on a first-come, first-served basis. So, when the ticket agent finishes helping one customer, he or she can help the next person in line. You wait patiently because you know your time will come. Then all of a sudden, out of the corner of your eye, you see a woman with a crazed look in her eye running up and yelling "I'm late! My flight leaves in ten minutes!" She has no time to wait in line, so a customer service agent escorts her to the front of the line. And then you see some wise guy run through a practically empty line labeled "first class" and he gets immediate service too.

Like the airport check-in line, print jobs in a queue are serviced on a first-in, first-out basis. If a "rush" job needs immediate printing, a *Print Queue Operator* (in most cases this is the network administrator) can move that job ahead of all others in the queue.

If rush jobs frequently need to be serviced immediately, it is a good idea to set up a special print queue (like the first class line) for those instances. When a print queue is created it is assigned a priority level from 1 to 10. Priority 1 print queues have the highest priority and are serviced immediately. When planning network print queues, consider setting the day-to-day queues at priority 2 or lower, and create a priority 1 queue for special rush jobs.

The NetWare queue system, known as QMS (Queue Management Service) is designed to provide more than just support for printing. For example, any application that requires a queuing mechanism—a Fax server, for example—can take advantage of the queue API (Application Programming Interface) to service Fax requests.

PRINT SERVERS

As a print job accumulates in the queue, it is ready for printing when the user signals that he or she is done sending data. This is done in one of three ways:

▸ When the user exits his or her application

▸ Through the CAPTURE *time out* parameter

▸ When the user issues an ENDCAP to end the CAPTURE

Once a user finishes sending print data to the queue, the print data file is closed and the job is labeled as "ready." The *print server* can now service the job from the print queue.

A print server is a device that is configured to service one or more particular print queues. When it sees a job waiting to be serviced, it opens the print job, starts reading from it, and routes the print job to the appropriate printer. Which printer the job is sent to is based on the print server's configuration.

Generally, a print server has one or more printers assigned to service a particular print queue. Those printers can be either directly attached to the print server or attached to workstations across the network. Figure 1.5 illustrates how a print server works.

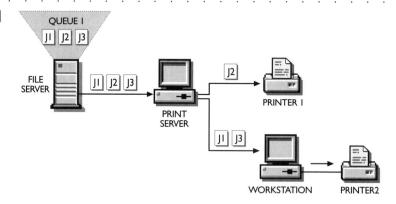

F I G U R E   1.5

Print servers route print jobs from print queues to printers across the network.

In Figure 1.5, the print server and file server are shown as different devices. This may be the case if you are using NetWare 3 print services. If you are using NetWare 4 print services, the print server software will always run as an NLM on a file server.

Once a print server is created, the print server software must be loaded. Table 1.3 illustrates the various options for loading a print server for NetWare 3 and NetWare 4.

TABLE 1.3	PRINT SERVER OPTION	NETWARE VERSION	LOCATION
Print server loading options for NetWare 3 and NetWare 4	PSERVER.EXE	NetWare 3 only	Dedicated workstation
	PSERVER.NLM	NetWare 3 and NetWare 4	File server

Print servers and their creation and configuration are covered in depth in Chapter 2, "NetWare 3 Print Services—Theory of Operations," and in Chapter 3, "NetWare 4 Print Services—Theory of Operations."

PRINTERS

Traditionally, one of the main reasons companies first installed local area networks was to enable employees to share expensive printers scattered throughout an organization. Today, while network operating systems provide many more compelling features than just printing, print sharing still tops the list of reasons why companies install networks.

Though print queues and print servers play a key role in network printing, network printers are truly the crux of the NetWare print system. The system provides extreme flexibility when it comes to connecting shared printers to the network. Printers can be attached to the network in four ways:

▸ File server attached

▸ Dedicated print server attached

▸ Workstation attached

▸ Network attached

File Server Attached

When printers are directly attached to the file server, the file server in most cases acts as a print server as well. In other words, the print server software,

PSERVER.NLM, is loaded on that file server. The only exception to this is an option available with NetWare 4 print services only. This option allows an NLM called NPRINTER to be loaded at a file server not acting as a print server. NPRINTER.NLM is the NetWare print driver that controls file server attached printers in the NetWare 4 environment. In the NetWare 3 environment, this driver is part of the Print Server software. Figures 1.6 through 1.8 illustrate the options for file server attached printers.

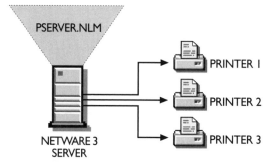

FIGURE 1.6

NetWare 3 file server/print server attached printers

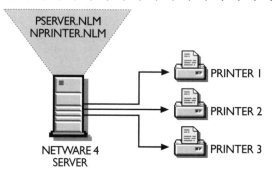

FIGURE 1.7

NetWare 4 file server/print server attached printers

When printers are directly attached to the file server/print server, they are referred to as *local* printers. *Local* indicates that they are local to the file server/print server.

If you recall, we also use the term *local* to refer to printing in a stand-alone environment (not printing through the network). This similar terminology can be confusing at times, but it helps to look at the context in which the term *local* is used. For example, if you see *local* when you are viewing the print server configuration screen, it is referring to a print server attached printer.

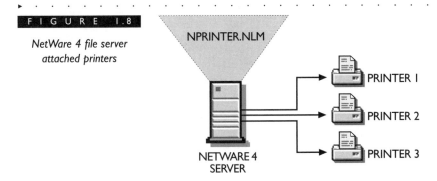

FIGURE 1.8

NetWare 4 file server attached printers

File server attached printers often deliver a good solution for organizations that wish to centralize their network printers but do not want to dedicate a PC to act as a print server. However, file server attached printers present a possible security breach. This is because the number one rule in securing the file server is to keep it locked up and inaccessible to uninformed persons—or informed persons with roguish intentions.

Locking up a file server that has shared network printers attached to it is close to (but not entirely) impossible. There are ways to secure a file server that is not physically locked up—a software lock at the console, or removing the keyboard and monitor—but the best policy to follow when securing a file server is "out of sight, out of mind." In other words, keep it in a locked room that only administrators have access to. So, how can you have a public shared printer attached to a file server in a locked room? A *really* long cable with the file server in one room and the printer in another. Don't laugh; though we don't recommend it, it's been done.

Dedicated Print Server Attached

Dedicated print server attached printers are only an option if you are using NetWare 3 printing services. With the release of NetWare 4, dedicated print servers were replaced with an improved and more reliable method of attaching printers to workstations.

Dedicated print servers are PCs running PSERVER.EXE. They can have as many printers attached as the hardware physically supports. Figure 1.9 illustrates dedicated print server attached printers.

F I G U R E   I.9

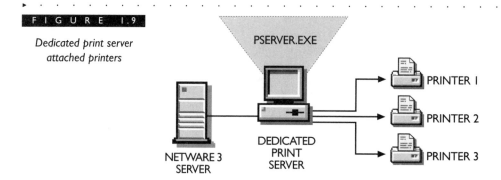

Dedicated print server attached printers

If an excessive number of printers are attached to a dedicated print server, the result may be a reduction in printing performance. Again, this is a hardware limitation more than a NetWare software limitation. Dedicated print server performance issues are covered in depth in Chapter 2.

Workstation Attached

In many cases, companies wish to turn printers already attached to a workstation into shared network printers. NetWare's printing services provide this ability by loading a small TSR (terminate-and-stay-resident) program at the workstation with the printer attached. For NetWare 3 print services this TSR is RPRINTER.EXE. For NetWare 4 print services, NPRINTER.EXE is used.

Workstation attached printers are defined as *remote* printers when configuring a print server. They are termed this way because they are remote from the print server itself.

The remote printer TSR is loaded in workstation memory and runs in the background so the workstation's operation is not affected by any network printing taking place on the attached printer. The workstation does not need to be logged in to the network for the printer to be shared; however, the NetWare DOS Requester must be loaded for the printer to show up on the list of network printers. Figure 1.10 illustrates workstation attached (remote) printers.

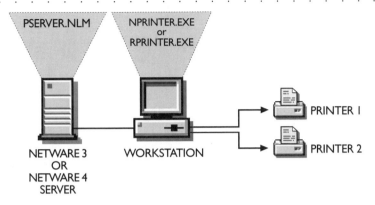

FIGURE 1.10

Workstation attached (remote) printers

Normally, while a workstation attached printer is being shared, anyone using that workstation needs to submit print jobs to the network for printing. Though it is possible to print directly to the attached printer, doing so may cause a conflict with print jobs being sent from the network. Most users aren't thrilled with having to send a print job through the network just to print on the printer sitting right next to them, so it may be necessary to take measures to avoid any possible conflicts.

If the person using the workstation isn't computer savvy, he or she may not even know the difference, but just as a precaution, you may want to place the following command in the workstation's NET.CFG file:

```
LOCAL PRINTERS=0
```

This command tells the Requester that no local printers are attached to this workstation, preventing the user from printing directly to it. Once the TSR is loaded, however, the printer becomes a network printer and can be accessed by submitting a job to the appropriate network print queue.

Another solution to avoid conflicts with network printing is to use the PSC command to make the printer *PRIvate* prior to sending a local print job to that printer. Assuming that the printer is configured as remote printer three on the print server PSERVER1, the PSC syntax is as follows:

```
PSC PS=PSERVER1 P=3 PRI
```

Once this command is entered, the printer is removed from the available list of network printers and other network users cannot print to it. To make the printer available to other network users again, PSC needs to be entered a second time with the following syntax (the SH indicates that the printer is once again a shared network printer):

```
PSC PS=PSERVER1 P=3 SH
```

This command syntax is a bit cryptic to the average user, so if printing locally to a shared network printer is absolutely necessary, you may want to create batch files to simplify the process for the user.

Network Attached

Many printers manufactured today are intelligent, network-aware printers. These printers provide an option to connect directly to the network instead of attaching to a PC. Whenever this is an option, it is generally the most hassle-free way of installing a network printer. It won't generate the user problems that develop with workstation attached printers, or the security issues that crop up with file server attached printers, and, in some cases, you won't have to dedicate a PC to act as a print server.

Network-aware printers generally have a network interface card that can be purchased as an add-on and installed in an available printer slot. They are then attached to the network just like a workstation would be. The configuration of a network interface card is illustrated in Figure 1.11.

Network attached printers are called *intelligent* printers because they generally have a processor, memory, and sometimes even hard disks. These attributes give them the ability to participate as an intelligent device on the network. Network attached printers vary in functionality depending on the manufacturer, but most have the ability to be configured as a NetWare remote printer. In this case, the printer would use its own remote printer software but use a standard NetWare queue and print server.

If the printer has a hard disk, it may also have the ability to queue its own print jobs. In this case, jobs would be submitted to the printer's queue as opposed to a standard NetWare queue.

Network attached printers and their options are covered in depth in Chapter 7, "Integrating Third-Party Printing Solutions."

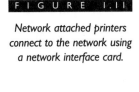

FIGURE   1.11

Network attached printers connect to the network using a network interface card.

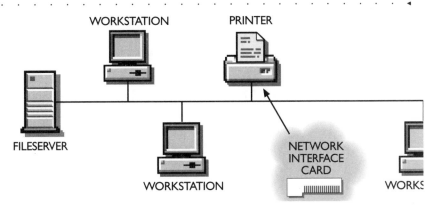

WORKSTATION   PRINTER

FILESERVER

WORKSTATION

NETWORK
INTERFACE
CARD

WORKS

Printing on the Network

As with printing in a stand-alone environment (non-network printing), print data can be sent to the network for printing in a number of ways. These include all of the methods we discussed at the beginning of this chapter under "Printing Locally." To quickly review, those methods were as follows:

▶   Printing from an application

▶   Using the DOS PRINT command (printing text files)

▶   Copying a file to a printer port

▶   Redirecting output to a printer port

▶   Printing screen displays

NOTE

If you skipped the "Printing Locally" section earlier in this book and are not familiar with one of the preceding printing methods, you may want to go back and read about them now.

Though these methods are still valid for network printing, you need to be aware of a few matters. First, once the CAPTURE command has been activated at a workstation, any time data is directed to the captured LPT port that data is then redirected to a network print queue. Some additional considerations when printing from applications and printing text files are discussed next.

PRINTING FROM AN APPLICATION

When it comes to network printing there are three kinds of applications:

1 • The application that knows *nothing* about network printing

2 • The application that *thinks* it knows how to print to the network

3 • The application that *really* knows how to print to the network

Unfortunately, most applications that you encounter fall into the first category—they know nothing about network printing. To print to the network from these applications, you need to issue the CAPTURE command before starting the application. As we mentioned when we discussed capturing print data to the network, these applications simply send data to the printer port specified and NetWare "captures" the data and redirects it to the network for printing.

The second type of application is one that *thinks* it knows how to print to the network. These applications were written to support earlier versions of NetWare and send print jobs to network printer numbers rather than print queues. You will probably never encounter one of these applications, but in case you do, it's important to understand the implications.

These applications send print jobs to printer numbers 0 to 4 to correspond to the printer numbers of early versions of NetWare. These printer numbers *do not* correspond to the printer numbers used by a print server. To support these applications, you must set up spooler assignments at the file server console so when an application tries to send a print job to a printer number, the spooler can intercept the job and put it into a print queue. The topic of creating spooler assignments is covered in Chapter 2.

The third type of application is completely compatible with the NetWare print system. With this type of application it is not necessary to use the CAPTURE command, because the application has the ability to send a print job directly to a NetWare print queue.

PRINTING TEXT FILES

When printing in a stand-alone environment, the DOS PRINT command is one method of printing text files. When printing to a network printer, the NetWare NPRINT command is a better option.

NPRINT was designed for network printing and has the capability of submitting a file directly to a print queue. When using NPRINT, capturing is not necessary. Many of the same parameters used with CAPTURE are used with NPRINT as well. Tables 1.4 and 1.5 show the available NPRINT parameters for both NetWare 3 and NetWare 4.

TABLE 1.4	SYNTAX	OPTION	DESCRIPTION
NetWare 3 NPRINT command options	NOTI	Notify	Notifies the user when the print job is complete.
	NNOTI	NoNotify	Does not notify when the print job is complete.
	S	Server	Specifies the file server to print the job to.
	Q	Print queue	Specifies the print queue to send the print job to.
	PS	Print server	Specifies the print server to service this job.
	J	Job configuration	Specifies the PRINTCON job configuration to use.
	F	Form	Specifies the PRINTDEF form to use.
	C	Copies	Specifies the number of copies to print.
	T	Tabs	Specifies the number of characters in one tab stop.
	NT	No tabs	Specifies that all tab characters are defined by the application.
	NB	No banner	Specifies that no banner page will be printed.
	NAM	Name	Specifies the text that appears on the upper part of the banner page.
	B	Banner name	Specifies the text that appears on the lower part of the banner page.
	FF	Form feed	Specifies that a form feed is desired at the end of a print job.
	NFF	No form feed	Specifies that no form feed is desired at the end of a print job.
	D	Delete	Specifies that the file should be erased after it is printed.
	?	Help	Lists available NPRINT options.

TABLE 1.5

NetWare 4 NPRINT command options

SYNTAX	OPTION	DESCRIPTION
NOTI	Notify	Notifies the user when the print job is complete.
NNOTI	NoNotify	Does not notify the user when the print job is complete.
P	Printer	Specifies the printer on which the job should be printed.
Q	Print queue	Specifies the print queue to send the print job to.
S	Server	Indicates which server to send the print job to.
V	Verbose	Shows detailed information about the printer, print queue, and print job configuration.
J	Job configuration	Specifies the PRINTCON job configuration to use.
F	Form	Specifies the PRINTDEF form to use.
C	Copies	Specifies the number of copies to print.
T	Tabs	Specifies the number of characters in one tab stop.
NT	No tabs	Specifies that all tab characters are defined by the application.
NB	No banner	Specifies that no banner page will be printed.
NAM	Name	Specifies the text that appears on the upper part of the banner page.
B	Banner name	Specifies the text that appears on the lower part of the banner page.
FF	Form feed	Specifies that a form feed is desired at the end of a print job.
NFF	No form feed	Specifies that no form feed is desired at the end of a print job.
?	Help	Lists available NPRINT options.
ALL	All	Used in conjunction with ?; displays all available online help options.

PUTTING IT ALL TOGETHER

So far, we have discussed all of the various components of the NetWare print system and covered the role each component plays in the network printing process. We've also looked at the different ways to submit print jobs to the network. To summarize, let's put all of these components together and follow a print job through the entire network printing process. Refer to Figure 1.12 as we work through each of these steps.

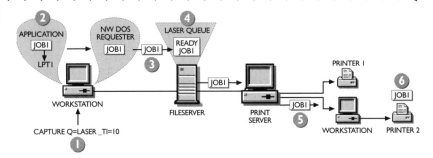

Network printing—
putting it all together

I • If a non-network-printing-aware application is being used, the CAPTURE command is entered at the workstation. For example:

```
Capture TI=10
```

2 • The application sends a print job to LPT1.

3 • The NetWare DOS Requester "captures" the print data and redirects it to the Laser queue at the file server.

4 • Ten seconds (TI=10) after the application finishes sending data to the print queue, the print file is closed and marked as "Ready."

5 • The print server then routes the job to the printer assigned to service the Laser queue.

6 • The job is printed.

Print Job Configurations—Simplifying Network Print Redirection

As you can tell from the printing options covered so far, as the number of users on your network increases, the amount of setup required also increases. Each user may have his or her own printing needs. For example, one user may need to print reports on a dot-matrix printer and letters on a high-quality laser printer. Another user may need to print in landscape mode for one application and print to a plotter for another. The bottom line is that each user may require a unique printing configuration. To ease the process of setting up users for network printing, Novell provides *print job configurations*.

Print job configurations are groups of print job options that simplify printing setup. Each user can have his or her own database of print job configurations that can be used when sending a print job. Instead of manually entering all of the print job specifications with CAPTURE or NPRINT each time they want to print, the user simply chooses the job configuration that meets his or her needs for that specific print job. This control not only makes it easier for the users, but the administrators have far fewer support calls for network printing issues.

Print job configurations are created for each user using the PRINTCON utility for NetWare 3 and NetWare 4 print services or, the NWAdmin utility for NetWare 4 print services.

Each user can have one of their print job configurations set as the *default* configuration. This enables CAPTURE or NPRINT to be issued without any parameters, using the options defined in the default job configuration.

Print job configurations also allow custom-defined forms and print devices to be used as described in the next section.

USING PRINT FORMS

Anyone who has spent any time at all printing on a network has probably run into the following scenario: You're late for a meeting and you need to print a document on company letterhead before you can go. You rush to the printer, put the letterhead in the manual feed tray, run back to your desk, send the print job, only to return to the printer to find someone else's job printed on the letterhead intended for your job. This situation not only irritates the user, it can also be expensive.

For example, a user may inadvertently print a 20-page report on three-part invoices that cost 30¢ apiece.

To prevent this headache, printer *forms* can be defined to tell the print server that a different form may need to be loaded at the printer. When a job is submitted to a print queue, the print server checks the form number requested (by CAPTURE or NPRINT) for that job. If the form number is different from the one currently mounted at the printer, by default the print job is not serviced until you mount the proper form in the printer. Print servers service different form types based on the *form service mode* defined when the printer is configured. Form service modes are covered in Chapters 2 and 3.

Printer forms are defined using the PRINTDEF utility for NetWare 3 and NetWare 4 print services or the NWAdmin utility for NetWare 4 only.

Using Nonstandard Print Devices

On rare occasions, you may encounter an application that does not have a print driver for the printer or the printer function that you wish to use. To allow for this, NetWare supplies what are known as *print devices*. Print devices are essentially printer drivers that can be selected with the CAPTURE *job configuration* option. By doing this, printer commands are sent to your printer prior to the actual print data. To better understand this process, it helps to understand the anatomy of a NetWare print job. See Figure 1.13.

F I G U R E   1.13

The anatomy of a NetWare print job

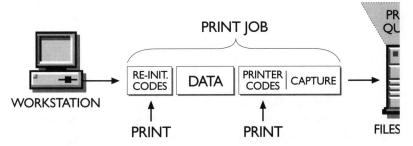

Every NetWare print job consists of three parts:

▸ A print header

▸ Print data

▸ A print tail

The print header consist of the CAPTURE parameters, which tell NetWare how to handle the print job, and any printer definitions that were selected through a print job configuration.

The print data is the data generated by an application. If the application you are using has a driver for your printer, the printer commands are included in the data portion of the print file. If this is the case, you will *not* (this is emphasized because it is important that you read this part carefully) need to use a NetWare-defined print driver. NetWare-defined drivers are only provided in case your application doesn't have a driver for your printer.

The final part of a print job is the print tail. This includes any reinitialize codes necessary to reset the printer if codes were sent in the print header. If you are using an application-provided driver, the print tail will be empty.

During a NetWare server installation, printer definitions are copied to the SYS:PUBLIC directory. NetWare 3 includes definitions for 30 printers and NetWare 4 includes 59 definitions. These printer definitions are files with a .PDF extension and are accessed using the PRINTDEF utility for NetWare 3 and NetWare 4 or the NWAdmin utility for NetWare 4 only. Importing and using printer definitions is covered in depth in the following chapters.

Summary

Though printing often seems to be the most frustrating part of the network, when you form a good understanding of the underlying printing architecture, setting up and maintaining your printing environment is less of a hassle. Our intent for this chapter was to develop a good foundation to help you understand the chapters to come and make your life in administering network printing a bit easier.

Now that we have the basics out of the way, let's get into some of the nitty-gritty of NetWare 3 and NetWare 4 printing. If you have a NetWare 3 network or a mixed NetWare 3 and NetWare 4 environment, move on to Chapter 2, "NetWare 3 Print Services—Theory of Operations." If you deal with NetWare 4 only, skip Chapter 2 and move right on to Chapter 3, "NetWare 4 Print Services—Theory of Operations."

CHAPTER 2

NetWare 3 Print Services— Theory of Operations

THE RELEASE OF NETWARE 3.0 INTRODUCED A REVOLUTIONARY NEW FEATURE FOR NETWARE OPERATING SYSTEMS—A MODULAR DESIGN. THIS DESIGN ENABLED THE OPERATING SYSTEM TO BE CONFIGURED OR RECONFIGURED ON THE FLY, WITHOUT EVER HAVING TO TAKE THE FILE SERVER DOWN. THIS WAS A GREAT IMPROVEMENT OVER THE NETWARE 2.X LINE OF OPERATING SYSTEMS.

Prior to the release of NetWare 3, to make a change to your network configuration, let's say just to add a printer, the server not only needed to be taken down but the operating system had to be relinked. This process was never easy because it required you to do the "floppy shuffle" (swapping floppy disk after floppy disk until the system was reconfigured), sometimes for as long as an hour or more!

NetWare 3 introduced the concept of print servers, print queues, and printers, and along with the modular operating system design, adding a printer can be done in minutes.

With that bit of history out of the way, let's jump right into the NetWare 3 print services.

Print Queues

In the previous chapter, we learned that print queues are holding places at the file server for print jobs waiting to be serviced by the print server. Physically, print queues in a NetWare 3 print system are subdirectories located on the SYS:SYSTEM directory that have a .QDR extension. The queue subdirectory name is the print queue's bindery ID number. This is a system-assigned number that NetWare uses to keep track of the queue rather than a name. This ID number can be viewed using the PCONSOLE utility under the Print Queue Information/Other Information menu option. Figure 2.1 shows a print queue ID number in PCONSOLE.

F I G U R E   2 . I

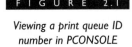

*Viewing a print queue ID
number in PCONSOLE*

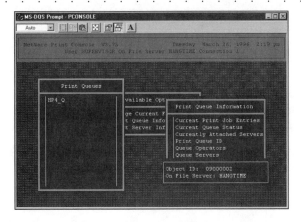

When print jobs are waiting to be serviced, they appear in the print queue sub-directory as temporary files. Once a print job is complete, the file is deleted from the print queue directory.

Also in the print queue directory are two printing control files. These files are NetWare *system* files that are flagged as hidden. These types of files can only be viewed with the NetWare NDIR command. Figure 2.2 displays the contents of the print queue directory.

F I G U R E   2 . 2

*NDIR can be used to
display the printing control
files in a print queue.*

Any files in a print queue directory with a *.Q extension are print jobs in the queue waiting to be serviced by the print server. As mentioned previously, these are temporary files and are deleted once the print job has printed. The *.SRV and

*.SYS files are the printing control files. The *.SYS file keeps track of the print jobs in the queue, maintaining information such as the job owners and job service orders. The *.SRV file indicates the print server and printer assigned to service this print queue.

PLANNING PRINT QUEUES

In Chapter 1 we used the analogy of an airport check-in line to describe how a print queue works. Let's go back to that analogy for a moment. . . . Let's say that the airport is extremely busy on the day you are traveling. As more and more people arrive at the airport, the check-in line gets longer as well as the wait. What can the airline do to expedite the check-in process? Well, they can create a second line, or they can bring in additional ticket agents to service the existing line. NetWare's print queues work much the same way. The more printers you have servicing a single print queue, the faster the print jobs will be serviced. Adding additional queues and printers also improves printing performance.

In the NetWare print system, printers can be assigned to service print queues in the following ways:

- ▸ One printer to one print queue

- ▸ Multiple printers to one print queue

- ▸ One printer to multiple print queues

- ▸ Multiple printers to multiple print queues

Which queue configuration option you choose largely depends on the number of printers available in your organization and the location of those printers. Let's take a look at when and why each configuration would be used.

ONE PRINTER, ONE PRINT QUEUE

This is probably the most common and the most simple configuration. In this environment, each print queue is serviced by a single printer, as illustrated in Figure 2.3.

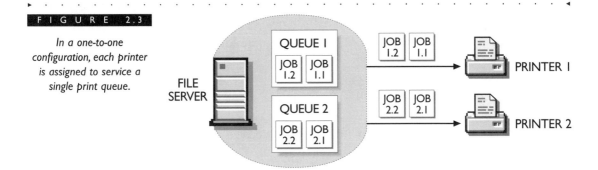

In a one-to-one configuration, each printer is assigned to service a single print queue.

The time required for a job to print depends on how fast each printer can service the jobs in its assigned queues.

MULTIPLE PRINTERS, ONE PRINT QUEUE

Multiple printers servicing a single print queue is a good solution if you have a number of identical printers in a common location and if users don't care which printer their job is printed on. For example, a pool of secretaries with a high volume of print jobs may have two or three laser printers in a single location. In the multiple-to-one configuration, all print jobs are submitted to a single queue and are serviced on a first-in/first-out basis by whichever printer is available. This configuration is shown in Figure 2.4.

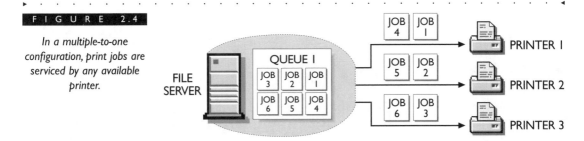

In a multiple-to-one configuration, print jobs are serviced by any available printer.

This configuration provides optimal printing throughput, as multiple printers are working to empty jobs out of the queue as soon as they are submitted. The time it takes for jobs to print is highly minimized with this configuration.

ONE PRINTER, MULTIPLE PRINT QUEUES

In our airport analogy, the airline had a special line set up for first class, "priority" passengers. These were the folks that received immediate service, regardless of how long the general check-in line was. The configuration of one printer to multiple print queues achieves the same result for print jobs.

When a print queue is created, it is assigned a priority level from 1 to 10. Priority 1 queues are of the highest priority and are serviced immediately. If special "rush" print jobs are required, or if you as the administrator feel that your jobs should always be printed first (you wouldn't do that, would you?), it is a good idea to set up a high priority print queue. In this case, the queue for rush jobs would be configured as priority 1 and all general print queues would be configured as priority 2 or lower. Lower priority queues are serviced after all high priority queues, regardless of how long jobs have been waiting.

In the example shown in Figure 2.5, JOB1, JOB2, and JOB3 are submitted at the same time. JOB3 is serviced first because it was submitted to a priority 1 print queue, followed by JOB1 and JOB2 from the priority 2 queue. While the jobs are printing, JOB4 and JOB5 are submitted. JOB5 is serviced before JOB4 because it was submitted to the higher priority queue. Regardless, though, the currently printing job finishes before any other jobs begin printing. In other words, the currently printing job will be completed even if a job with a higher priority is submitted.

F I G U R E   2.5

In a one-to-many configuration, all high-priority queues are serviced first.

MULTIPLE PRINTERS, MULTIPLE PRINT QUEUES

In this configuration, two or more printers service two or more print queues. At first, this configuration may seem like it would be rarely used, but it is quite useful in environments that have occasional large jobs or jobs that take a long time to print—as with graphics. This configuration enables you to make the most efficient use of identical printers at all times, without sacrificing printing performance.

For example, as shown in Figure 2.6, both PRINTER1 and PRINTER2 are assigned to service QUEUE1, which is a priority 1 queue. PRINTER2 is also assigned to service QUEUE2, which is a low-priority queue. PRINTER1 and PRINTER2 services the jobs in QUEUE1 first, and PRINTER2 services QUEUE2 as it is available.

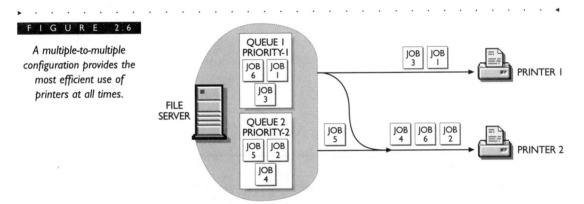

FIGURE 2.6

A multiple-to-multiple configuration provides the most efficient use of printers at all times.

By submitting time-intensive print jobs to a lower-priority print queue, this configuration ensures that printing continues even if a large graphics file is submitted. It also ensures that the printer assigned to time-intensive jobs doesn't sit idle even if jobs have not been submitted to the lower-priority queue.

CREATING PRINT QUEUES

NetWare 3 print queues are created using the PCONSOLE utility. To create a print queue, you must be logged in as SUPERVISOR or a SUPERVISOR-equivalent. PCONSOLE is a C-Worthy utility that is run from the DOS command line by simply typing the following:

```
PCONSOLE
```

Figure 2.7 shows the PCONSOLE main menu.

FIGURE 2.7

The PCONSOLE
main menu

The menu options of PCONSOLE are very self explanatory. However, if you are working in a multiserver environment, it is important to note the file server and user name at the top of the screen.

If you are attached to more than one file server, check the drive from which you execute PCONSOLE. If the drive is mapped to a directory on server HANGTIME, for example, any printing configuration done at this point is for that server.

To change servers, simply select Change Current File Server. A list of servers you are attached to appears, as seen in Figure 2.8.

FIGURE 2.8

Changing your current file
server in PCONSOLE

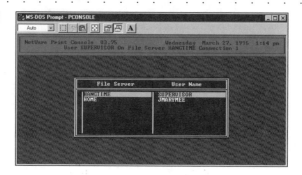

If you are not currently attached to a server that you'd like to configure printing on, pressing the Insert key provides a list of available servers. This enables you to log on to the desired file server and create printing components.

To create a new print queue, select Print Queue Information from the PCONSOLE main menu. A list of the existing print queues appears. Pressing the Insert key enables you to enter the name of the new print queue you are creating. This is shown in Figure 2.9.

FIGURE 2.9

Creating a new print queue in PCONSOLE

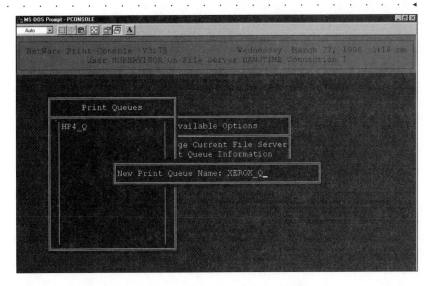

Print queue names can be any hexadecimal name, up to 47 characters in length. To make printing easier on both you and your users, print queue names should describe the type of printer that is assigned to service the queue or describe the type of printing that is being done. For example, as previously shown in Figure 2.9, if the printer servicing this queue is a Xerox, a name of XEROX_Q is sufficient. If the queue is set up specifically for printing graphics, GRAPHICS_Q is a good descriptive name. Though names such as GODZILLA and MOTHRA are fun, they have very little meaning to the average user.

Creating print queues is simple. Print queues, however, are only one component of the entire printing system. To have a functional printing system, at least one print server and one or more printers must be created and configured.

Print Servers

In Chapter 1 we learned that a print server's sole purpose in the NetWare print system is to monitor print queues and direct print jobs to the appropriate printers across the network. In a small local area network, print servers don't require a lot of planning. In most small networks, one print server is sufficient. When you are dealing with larger networks, planning print servers becomes a bit more important. The factors that need to be considered include the following:

▸ The number of print servers required

▸ The print server software location

▸ The physical print server placement

To design an efficient printing system, you need to look at the big picture, evaluating each factor individually and then together as a whole. For example, the number of print servers required depends on where the print server software is running and where each print server is physically located relative to the rest of the network.

NUMBER OF PRINT SERVERS REQUIRED

First, let's look at some of the factors that help you determine how many print servers you actually need. These factors are determined by your network configuration, including the number of printers, file servers, and routers on the network. The limitations of the print server software can also impact the number of print servers required in a given network.

Each NetWare 3 print server can support up to 16 printers. Those printers can either be directly attached to the print server or attached to workstations across the network. Because there probably isn't a PC in existence with 16 printer ports, the number of directly attached printers is limited to the number of physical printer ports of the print server PC. This is normally no more than two or three. The remainder of the printers will be attached to workstations across the network.

The easiest print server configuration is one print server per file server. However, this may not be the most efficient use of the print server because most file-server-based workgroups do not have more than 16 printers. In a multiserver environment, NetWare 3 ensures efficient use of print servers by allowing a single print server to be configured to service print queues and printers defined on other file servers. We'll cover how to do this later in the chapter.

For optimal printing performance, you may also want to consider any routers on the network when determining the number of print servers required. This is important because printing performance may suffer if, for example, a print server is on one side of the router and the printer and file server are on the other. We discuss this topic in greater detail when we cover physical print server placement.

Before you can determine exactly how many print servers your network requires, you need to look at the other two factors as well.

PRINT SERVER SOFTWARE LOCATION

In NetWare 3, print servers can run in three different locations:

▸ At the file server as an NLM.

▸ As a stand-alone device on a dedicated workstation.

▸ Embedded on a network-attached printer (such as Intel's NetPort or HP's JetDirect).

If the print server is running as an NLM at the file server, the print server is created and configured in PCONSOLE and then loaded using PSERVER.NLM. If you choose to run your print server as a stand-alone device, PSERVER.EXE is used to start the print server at a workstation. Once PSERVER.EXE is loaded, the workstation becomes dedicated as a print server and cannot be used for anything else.

When creating a NetWare print server in PCONSOLE, no special configuration is required for either option. Once created, a print server can be loaded as an NLM one day and as an EXE on a dedicated workstation the next.

If you are using a network-attached printer that is also acting as a print server, this device will have print server software embedded in it. If this is the case, you will not need to use a NetWare-defined print server for that printer.

So, which of the three options should you choose? That depends on your individual situation—whether or not you have network attached printers or an extra machine available to act as a print server, and so on. Strictly from a printing performance standpoint, it helps to review how a print server works:

1 • A user submits a print job to a queue at the file server.

2 • When the user is finished sending print data to the queue, the print job is closed and marked as "ready."

3 • The print server polls the print queue, opens the print job, and routes it to the appropriate printer.

Keeping these steps in mind, let's look at the performance-related issues of each print server option.

PSERVER.NLM

Running the print server as an NLM at the file server has pros and cons. On the positive side, if the print server and the file server that contains the print queue are the same device, a print job has a shorter route to the printer. Performance is improved even more if the printer is directly attached to the file server.

For example, in Figure 2.10, JOB1 has a shorter distance to travel because the printer is directly attached to the file server. JOB2 must go from the file server, across the network to the workstation with PRINTER2 attached.

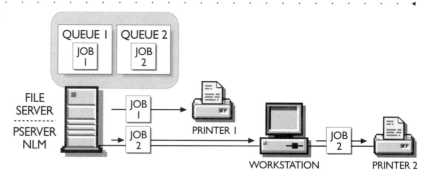

FIGURE 2.10

When using PSERVER.NLM, a print job has a shorter route to the printer.

The down side of running PSERVER.NLM at the file server is that additional file server resources (cycles, memory, and so on) are required when the file server is acting as a print server. In a situation where the file server is already heavily taxed, running the PSERVER.NLM just adds an additional burden.

PSERVER.EXE

Setting up a dedicated workstation as a print server reduces the burden on the file server, yet it does have an effect on printing performance. In Figure 2.11, print jobs now have an additional stop they must make before reaching their designated printers. As in the preceding example, print jobs going to print server attached printers have a shorter distance to travel than those going to workstation attached printers.

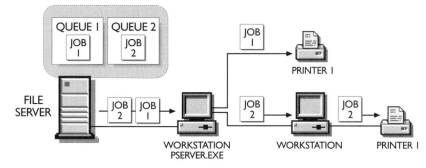

F I G U R E   2.11

Dedicated workstation-based print servers add an additional stop for print jobs.

Other PSERVER.EXE Performance Issues

In some cases an IS manager will pull an old computer out of storage and set it up as a print server. This computer is generally not only limited in processing power, but in memory as well (hard disk size doesn't matter because everything is done in memory on a print server). While this is an excellent use of an otherwise obsolete piece of hardware, be careful not to limit the overall performance of your printing system by using an 8088 with 640K of RAM. Obviously, it would be overkill to dedicate a P100 with 24 megs as a print server, so your best bet is to follow Novell's guidelines outlined in the *Print Server* manual. Those guidelines are as follows:

▸ Memory necessary for DOS and the NetWare DOS Requester

▸ 256K for PSERVER.EXE

▸ 10K for each printer

The manual also indicates that these figures will vary depending on buffer sizes, queues per printer, and notify objects per printer. Though it's not an exact formula, it can be used as a baseline. Once you have that baseline, add 2–4MB (or more if you can) just to be safe.

NETWORK ATTACHED PRINTER EMBEDDED PRINT SERVERS

From a printing performance perspective, print servers that are embedded on a network attached print device such as Intel's NetPort or HP's JetDirect offer the best performance. This is because the print server and the printer are the same device, so a print job goes from the file server queue directly to the printer. This process is illustrated in Figure 2.12:

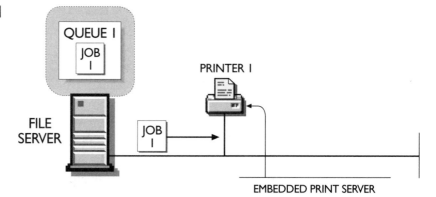

A network attached printer acting as a print server offers optimal printing performance.

QUEUE 1

JOB 1

PRINTER 1

FILE SERVER

JOB 1

EMBEDDED PRINT SERVER

For even better printing performance, some printers have hard drives that enable the printer to queue print jobs. In this case, the print job can be sent directly to the printer without having to be queued at the file server first. This would be the case with a large printing system such as a Xerox DocuTech or similar device. However, the average laser printer usually doesn't have an embedded hard disk.

PHYSICAL PRINT SERVER PLACEMENT

The final factor in print server planning is where to physically place your print servers on the network. The main issue to keep in mind when determining placement is how far print jobs have to travel to reach the printer. As we saw earlier, if a dedicated print server is being used, print jobs have to go through the print server before they can be routed to the printer. If the print server is on the opposite side of a router from the user or printer, an additional stop is added. This increases the amount of time it takes to print the print job, especially if the job must be routed across a busy network segment.

There is no hard and fast rule available for determining how many print servers you need and where those print servers should be placed. Consequently, you need to look at all of the factors discussed previously and analyze which choices provide the best performance for your network.

CREATING PRINT SERVERS

As with print queues, NetWare 3 print servers are created using the PCONSOLE Utility. From the PCONSOLE main menu, select Print Server Information; a list of the currently defined print servers appears. Adding a new print server can be done by pressing the Insert key and entering the new print server name, as shown in Figure 2.13.

FIGURE 2.13

Adding a new print server in PCONSOLE

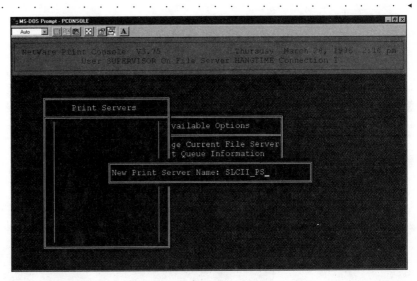

Once the print server is created, printer support needs to be added. We discuss this matter next.

Printer Support

As mentioned earlier, each print server can support up to 16 printers; these printers can be either directly attached to the print server or attached to workstations across the network. To complete the configuration of a print server, you must define the printers it supports and their locations. A print server's configuration can be modified at any time, but an active print server must be taken down and restarted before the changes take effect.

PRINT SERVER ATTACHED PRINTERS

Print server attached printers are referred to as *local* printers. They are called local printers because they are attached to one of the print server's local LPT or COM ports. To define a local printer, select the desired print server in the PCONSOLE Print Server Information menu and then select Print Server Configuration. The menu options shown in Figure 2.14 appear.

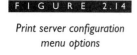

Print server configuration menu options

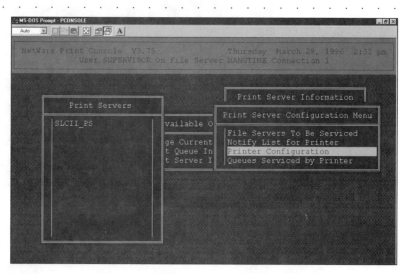

By selecting Printer Configuration you are presented with a list of the 16 available printers—printer numbers 0 through 15. Select the printer number you wish to configure and assign a printer name. Printer names can be from 1 to 47 characters in length but should describe the printer being configured.

Once you enter the name, the printer type can be configured. Pressing Enter provides a list of available printer types. The available printer types are listed in the menu shown in Figure 2.15.

F I G U R E   2.15

Configuring local printers in PCONSOLE

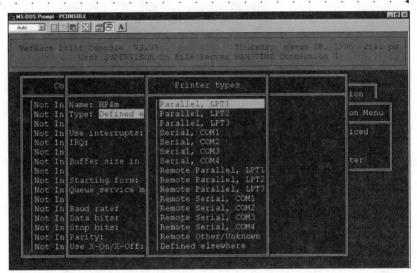

The first seven options listed—Parallel, LPT1 through Serial, COM4—are used for configuring local or print server attached printers.

Once you select the printer type, you are provided with a list of configuration options. These options vary depending on whether you are configuring a parallel or serial printer. If you are configuring a parallel printer, you are presented with the options shown in Figure 2.16.

▶ . . . . ◀

F I G U R E   2.16

Parallel printer configuration
options

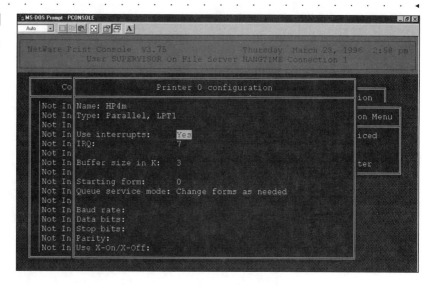

In many cases, you can use the defaults shown on this screen. In the event you
wish to customize the configuration, refer to Table 2.1, which defines each option.

T A B L E   2.1

Parallel printer configuration
options

OPTION	DEFINITION
Use interrupts	Tells the print server whether the printer port should be interrupt-driven or polled. Using interrupts can improve printing performance. Don't use interrupts if another device in the computer might conflict with the interrupt required.
IRQ	If interrupts are being used, this is the interrupt used by the printer port. LPT1 generally defaults to IRQ 7. COM1 generally defaults to IRQ 4.
Buffer size in K	This is the size of the print server's buffer for this printer. If the printer stops and starts during printing, this number may need to be increased.
Starting form	This is the PRINTDEF form number that is mounted for this printer when the print server starts.
Queue service mode	Tells the print server how to service print jobs with different form numbers.

If a serial printer is being configured, the screen shown in Figure 2.17 is presented:

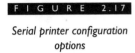

FIGURE 2.17

Serial printer configuration options

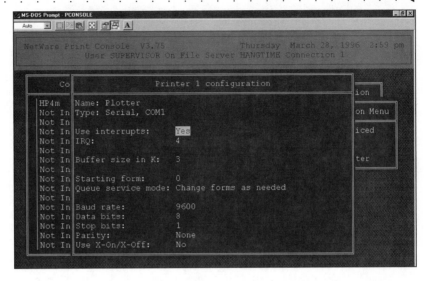

Serial printers require more configuration than parallel printers because the computer and printer must agree on a number of factors for printing to be successful. Table 2.2 defines each option for configuring serial printers.

OPTION	DEFINITION
Use interrupts	Tells the print server whether the printer port should be interrupt-driven or polled. Using interrupts can improve printing performance. Don't use interrupts if another device in the computer might conflict with the interrupt required.
IRQ	If interrupts are being used, this is the interrupt used by the printer port. LPT1 generally defaults to IRQ 7. COM1 generally defaults to IRQ 4.
Buffer size in K	This is the size of the print server's buffer for this printer. If the printer stops and starts during printing, this number may need to be increased.

TABLE 2.2

Serial printer configuration options

(continued)

TABLE 2.2	OPTION	DEFINITION
Serial printer configuration options (continued)	Starting form	This is the PRINTDEF form number that is mounted for this printer when the print server starts.
	Queue service mode	Tells the print server how to service print jobs with different form numbers.
	Baud rate	Specifies the baud rate at which the printer operates. Baud rate options include 300, 600, 1200, 2400, 4800, and 9600.
	Data bits	Defines the number of data bits in a character. Options range from 5 to 8.
	Stop bits	Defines the number of stop bits signaling the end of a character. Options are 1, 1.5, and 2.
	Parity	Specifies the error checking used by the printer. Options are none, even, or odd.
	Use X-On/X-Off	Specifies whether the printer uses the X-On/X-Off handshaking protocol.

To complete the printer configuration, each printer must be assigned to service one or more print queues. We'll cover how to do this a bit later.

REMOTE PRINTERS

Remote printers are printers that are attached to workstations across the network. Configuring a print server to support a remote printer is accomplished by taking the same steps as described previously for local printer configuration, except that the printer type selected in Figure 2.15 should be preceded with the word "Remote." For example, if the printer being configured is attached to a workstation's first parallel port, the Remote Parallel, LPT1 option should be chosen. The screen in Figure 2.18 shows a remote printer configuration.

F I G U R E   2.18

Workstation attached printers are configured as "remote" printers when setting up a print server.

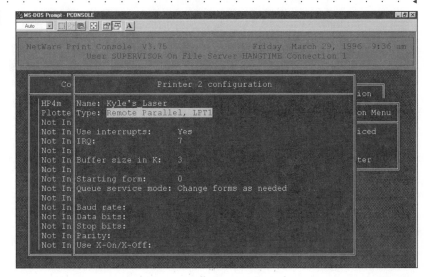

As with local printers, the remote printer configuration is not complete until one or more queues have been assigned to service this printer. This process is described next.

ASSIGNING QUEUES TO PRINTERS

The final step in configuring a print server is to assign print queues to be serviced by the printers. Again, this is done through the PCONSOLE Print Server Information menu. To make the print queue assignments, select Queues Serviced by Printer. A list of the currently defined printers is then displayed, as shown in Figure 2.19:

F I G U R E   2.19

Currently defined printers in PCONSOLE

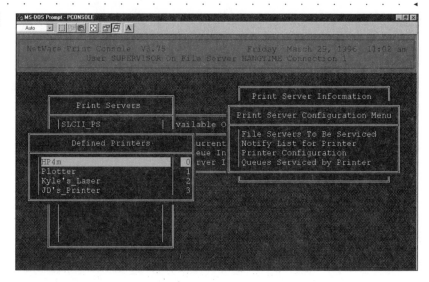

Select the printer you wish to configure and press the Insert key. A list of available print queues is presented. Select the print queue that this printer should service and press Enter. You are then prompted to assign a priority to this print queue. Print queue priorities range from 1 to 10, with priority 1 being the highest. Figure 2.20 shows a print queue priority being assigned.

F I G U R E   2.20

Assigning a print queue priority

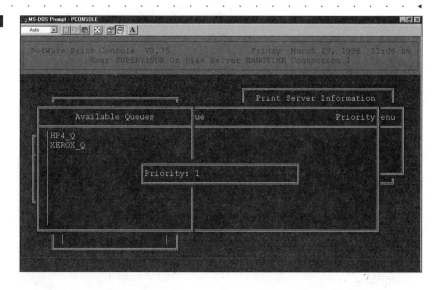

This process needs to be completed for each of the printers you are configuring; then you can bring up the print server.

Loading the Print Server

After the print server configuration discussed previously is complete, you are ready to bring up the print server. As we discussed earlier, you have two options for loading the print server software, as follows:

▸ On a dedicated workstation

▸ On a NetWare server

LOADING THE PRINT SERVER ON A DEDICATED WORKSTATION

Before the print server software can be loaded on a workstation, the workstation must have access to the following files:

IBM$RUN.OVL

PSERVER.EXE

SYS$ERR.DAT

SYS$HELP.DAT

SYS$MSG.DAT

These files can either be copied to a local subdirectory on the workstation's hard drive or accessed by logging in to the file server. These files are copied to the SYS:PUBLIC directory when NetWare is installed.

If the preceding files are copied to the workstation's hard drive, they do not need to be logged in; however, the NetWare DOS Requester must be loaded.

NOTE

The NetWare DOS Requester must be loaded because the print server will log in to the file server in order to service the queues. Because of this, it is also a good idea to configure a password for the print server during creation and supply it when loading a print server.

Before loading the NetWare DOS Requester, the following syntax must be entered in the workstation's NET.CFG file:

```
SPX CONNECTIONS = 60
```

The NET.CFG file is a workstation configuration file that is normally located in the same directory in which the NetWare client software is located. If the default directory was accepted when the client software was installed, the file will be located in C:\NWCLIENT.

After you complete the preceding steps, the print server software can be loaded. This is done using the following command syntax:

```
PSERVER [fileserver] printserver
```

If the workstation is already logged in to the file server on which the print server is defined, it is not necessary to specify the file server name when loading the print server.

Once the print server is loaded, the print server screen is presented. This screen looks similar to the print server screen shown in Figure 2.21:

FIGURE 2.21

Dedicated workstation print server screen

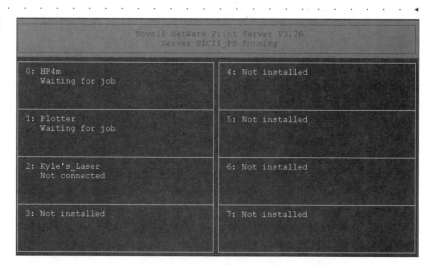

Once the print server software is loaded, the workstation becomes a dedicated device; thus this screen is displayed until the print server is taken down. Downing a NetWare 3 print server is covered in Chapter 5, "Managing NetWare 3 Print Services."

LOADING THE PRINT SERVER ON A FILE SERVER

To load the print server software on a file server, go to the server console and enter the following command:

```
LOAD PSERVER [printserver name]
```

Once loaded, a screen similar to the one already shown in Figure 2.21 is displayed. However, unlike a dedicated workstation print server, the print server screen can be exited. This is done by pressing Alt-Esc.

Supporting Multiple File Servers

As we discussed earlier, each print server can support up to 16 printers. What we haven't talked about yet is the fact that a single print server can support queues on up to eight different file servers. You're probably wondering, "Why would I want to do that?" The main reason is to make it easier on users to use printers defined on file servers other than their default server.

USING THE GUEST ACCOUNT

The traditional method of allowing users to use printers defined on other file servers is through the use of the GUEST account. When CAPTURE is entered at the workstation, the desired file server can be specified by using the following syntax:

```
CAPTURE S=servername Q=queuename [Other Options]
```

If the GUEST account exists, the user is transparently attached to the file server and can submit jobs to the print queue. If the GUEST account does not exist, the user is prompted for a valid login name and password.

The problem with this method of using printers on other file servers is that not only does the user have to have a valid user ID to log in, but, once logged in, the user is using a licensed connection. In some environments, these licensed connections are limited and administrators prefer to reserve them for other tasks, such as file access.

The *Defined Elsewhere* Option

NetWare 3 provides another method for users in a multiserver environment to share printing services. However, this method does not require the user to log in or attach to a second file server and thus does not use a licensed connection.

As we discussed in the "Printer Support" section earlier in this chapter, printer numbers 0 through 15 can be defined for any given print server. We covered how to configure these printers as local or remote printers. However, you may recall seeing another option in the printer configuration screen—a *defined elsewhere* option.

Printers configured as type "defined elsewhere" are logical printers linked to a queue on a local file server. The real printer is defined on a second file server somewhere on the network. When a user sends a print job to the queue linked to the "defined elsewhere" printer, the job is automatically serviced by a print server defined on the second file server. The result is that users can send print jobs to printers defined on file servers other than their default, without ever having to log in or attach to those servers.

Figure 2.22 illustrates how NetWare 3 print servers can service queues on multiple file servers.

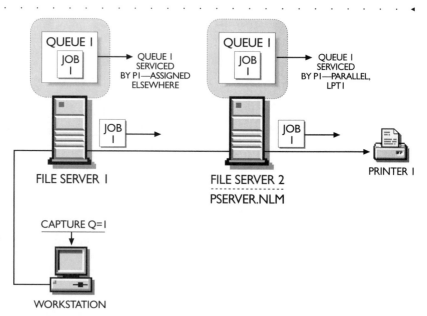

F I G U R E   2.22

NetWare 3 print servers can service queues on up to eight file servers.

To set up a print server to service queues on multiple file servers, do the following:

1 • Create print queues on each file server.

2 • Create print servers on each file server with identical names. Choose one print server as the "real" print server; the others will be "logical" print servers.

3 • Define the printers on the "real" print server. These printers will be defined as local or remote, depending on whether they are connected directly to the print server or connected to a workstation running RPRINTER.EXE.

4 • Assign a queue to service each printer.

5 • Define printers on the "logical" print servers. These printers must have exactly the same names and printer numbers as the printers defined on the "real" print server. Specify the printer configuration as type "defined elsewhere."

6 • Assign the "defined elsewhere" printers to service queues on the file server containing the "logical" print server.

7 • On the "real" print server add the additional file servers that will be serviced to the "File Servers to be Serviced" list.

8 • Bring up the "real" print server by loading PSERVER.NLM at the file server or by running PSERVER.EXE at a workstation. It is not necessary to load the "logical" print servers.

Once the preceding tasks are completed, users will send print jobs to the queues defined on their default file server. Those queues are serviced by the "real" print server. Again, the benefit to configuring your print services in this manner is that users with different default file servers can all share the same printers without logging in to multiple servers.

Connecting Remote Printers

To make a workstation attached printer available as a network printer, work-station software must be loaded. This software is a TSR (terminate-and-stay-resi-dent) program called RPRINTER.EXE. When RPRINTER is loaded, it runs in workstation memory in the background. Because of this, the workstation's opera-tion is not affected by any network printing taking place on its attached printer. RPRINTER requires very little workstation memory—only 9K. This amount includes all the buffer space necessary to use the printer as a network printer.

PREPARING TO RUN RPRINTER

Before RPRINTER can be loaded at a workstation, a few preparatory steps need to be taken. First, the workstation's NET.CFG file must be modified to include the following line:

```
SPX CONNECTIONS = 60
```

The NET.CFG file is a workstation configuration file that is normally located in the same directory in which the NetWare client software is located. If the default directory was accepted when the client software was installed, the file will be located in C:\NWCLIENT.

The workstation does not need to be logged in to the network for the printer to be shared. However, the NetWare DOS Requester must be loaded for the printer to show up on the list of network printers. In addition, the print server must be up and running before RPRINTER can be loaded at the workstation.

If the workstation is not logged in to the network when RPRINTER is loaded, it must have access to the following files:

```
IBMRUN.OVL

RPRINTER.EXE

RPRINTER.HLP

SYS$HELP.DAT

SYS$MSG.DAT

SYS$ERR.DAT
```

These files are copied to the SYS:PUBLIC directory when NetWare is installed and can be accessed by any logged-in user. To make them available to a workstation not logged in, you need to copy these files to a subdirectory on the workstation's local hard drive. You also need to make sure the subdirectory is included in the workstation's PATH statement in the AUTOEXEC.BAT file.

Once you take these steps, RPRINTER can be loaded in one of two ways:

▶ Using the Remote Printer Utility

▶ From the DOS command line

Loading RPRINTER from the Remote Printer Utility

When RPRINTER is loaded at a workstation, the appropriate print server and printer number must be specified. This can be done using command line parameters or by simply typing RPRINTER at the workstation's DOS command line. When you type RPRINTER without any parameters, the Remote Printer utility is loaded as shown in Figure 2.23.

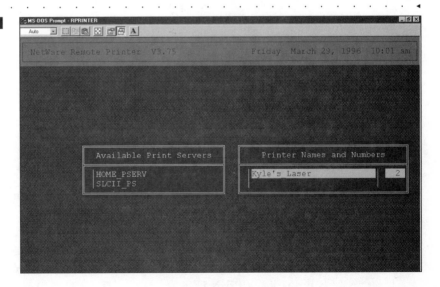

FIGURE 2.23

Loading RPRINTER from the remote printer utility

As you can see, this utility provides a list of the currently available print servers and the remote printer names and numbers.

This makes it very easy to run RPRINTER without having to know the proper command-line syntax. The downside of this utility is that there is no way to automate it. In other words, each time the workstation comes up, the print server and printer must be selected.

Loading RPRINTER from the DOS Command Line

In many cases, it is not realistic to require users to run a utility and select a print server and printer each time they turn their workstations on. Most users don't care for the extra hassle and are probably not crazy about the fact that they have to share their printer with other users. So, to automate the loading of RPRINTER, command line parameters can be used. This allows RPRINTER to be loaded from an AUTOEXEC.BAT file or a login script.

The RPRINTER command line format is as follows:

```
RPRINTER [printserver printernumber]
```

So, to load remote printer number 2 on print server SLCII_PS, the syntax would be:

```
RPRINTER SLCII_PS 2
```

Once you enter this command, you receive a message indicating that the remote printer has been installed.

If you have more than one shared network printer attached to a workstation, you need to run RPRINTER for each printer.

Unloading RPRINTER

RPRINTER can be unloaded by either rebooting the workstation or by using the following command line option:

```
RPRINTER [printserver printernumber] -r
```

If RPRINTER has been removed from memory successfully, you receive a message indicating that the remote printer has been deinstalled.

NOTE

RPRINTER cannot be unloaded successfully if you attempt to unload it while running Windows. Be sure to exit from Windows before unloading RPRINTER.

Capturing to the Network

Before we jump in to the NetWare 3 CAPTURE parameters, let's do a quick review of CAPTURE from Chapter 1.

CAPTURE is a NetWare workstation utility that, once executed, instructs NetWare to redirect print output from an LPT port to the network for printing. Once CAPTURE is executed, an application sending a print job is completely unaware that the printing is taking place on the network. It simply sends the print output to the LPT port specified and, as far as it knows, the job is printed on a locally attached printer. NetWare "fools" the application, however, and captures the print data from the LPT port and redirects it to the network for printing. This trickery is illustrated in Figure 2.24.

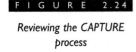

F I G U R E   2.24

Reviewing the CAPTURE
process

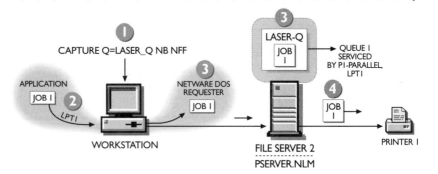

The CAPTURE process goes as follows:

1 • The CAPTURE command is entered at the workstation.

2 • The application directs the print job to the LPT port specified.

3 • The NetWare DOS Requester *captures* the print output and redirects it to the queue at the file server.

4 • The print server routes the job to the appropriate network printer.

USING CAPTURE

How a print job is handled by the network is determined by the options used with CAPTURE. The CAPTURE syntax is as follows:

CAPTURE [Option...]

The NetWare 3 CAPTURE options are given in the Table 2.3.

TABLE 2.3			
NetWare 3 CAPTURE options	**SYNTAX**	**OPTION**	**DESCRIPTION**
	SH	Show	Displays current CAPTURE status.
	?	Help	Lists available capture options.
	NOTI	Notify	Notifies user when print job is complete.
	NNOTI	NoNotify	Does not notify user when print job is complete.
	TI	Timeout	Specifies a time-out period for ending CAP-TURE.
	A	Autoendcap	Specifies an automatic ENDCAP.
	NA	No Autoendcap	Specifies that no automatic ENDCAP is desired.
	L	Local	Specifies the local printer port to capture.
	S	Server	Specifies the file server to capture to.
	Q	Print queue	Specifies the print queue to capture to.
	CR	Create	Directs spooled output to a designated file instead of the network printer
	J	Job configuration	Specifies the PRINTCON job configuration to use.
	F	Form	Specifies the PRINTDEF form to use.
	C	Copies	Specifies the number of copies to print.
	T	Tabs	Specifies the number of characters in one tab stop.
	NT	No tabs	Specifies that all tab characters are defined by the application.
	NB	No banner	Specifies that no banner page will be printed.
	NAM	Name	Specifies the text that appears on the upper part of the banner page.

T A B L E 2.3	SYNTAX	OPTION	DESCRIPTION
NetWare 3 CAPTURE options (continued)	B	Banner name	Specifies the text that appears on the lower part of the banner page.
	FF	Form feed	Specifies that a form feed is desired at the end of a print job.
	NFF	No form feed	Specifies that no form feed is desired at the end of a print job.
	K	Keep	Specifies that the file server should keep all print data if the workstation hangs or loses power while data is capturing.

The options used with CAPTURE vary depending on what task you wish to accomplish. Some common printing tasks and the command options used are covered next.

Viewing CAPTURE Status

If you wish to view the current status of a workstation's LPT ports, you can enter the following at the DOS command line:

CAPTURE SH

This option provides the following information:

▶ Whether CAPTURE is enabled

▶ Which CAPTURE options have been used

▶ Whether data is printed to a printer or file

The screen shown in Figure 2.25 is an example of the information provided by CAPTURE SH.

F I G U R E   2.25

CAPTURE SH provides information about a workstation's current CAPTURE status.

Selecting a Printer

NetWare 3 does not support capturing directly to a printer number (this functionality was added in NetWare 4), so, to select a printer with the NetWare 3 CAPTURE command, the print queue assigned to service the printer must be selected. As mentioned in the print queue section, it is a good idea to assign print queue names that are descriptive of the printer assigned to service the queue. This makes capturing much easier for both the user and the administrator. The following is an example of selecting the print queue to capture to:

```
CAPTURE Q=HP4_Q [Other Options]
```

If the printer you wish to capture to is on a file server that the user is not currently attached to, the file server name must be specified as follows:

```
CAPTURE S=HANGTIME Q=HP4_Q [Other Options]
```

If a GUEST account exists on the server specified, the user is automatically attached as GUEST. If the GUEST account has been deleted or renamed, as is sometimes done for security reasons, the user is prompted for a login name and password.

Specifying the Port to Capture

By default, NetWare redirects data from LPT1 to the network if a port is not specified when CAPTURE is executed. If you wish to capture another LPT port, LPT2 for example, you need to indicate this in the CAPTURE statement. The following is an example:

```
CAPTURE L=2 Q=HP4_Q [Other Options]
```

NetWare 3 supports capturing of up to three LPT ports—LPT1, LPT2, and LPT3. Because LPT ports are logical DOS channels, an LPT port can be captured even if it is not mapped to a physical printer port. For example, a workstation may have only one physical parallel port, but can have three capture statements issued. This provides different network printing options depending on the LPT port that data is directed to. As a result, LPT1 may be captured to a laser printer on the network, LPT2 to a color printer, and LPT3 may direct data to a file.

Printing to a File

The CAPTURE command can be used to send print data to a file for later printing. When sending data to a file, you must specify the path and filename you wish to print to. This is shown in the following CAPTURE statement:

```
CAPTURE L=3 Q=HP4_Q CR=SYS:USERS\KYLE\PRINT.JOB
```

When printing to a file, data accumulates in the file until an ENDCAP is issued. If an *Autoendcap* is being used, the file is rewritten with each print job. If you would like to send multiple print jobs to the file, be sure to use the *NoAutoendcap* parameter when CAPTURE is executed. Here's an example:

```
CAPTURE L=3 Q=HP4_Q CR=SYS:USERS\KYLE\PRINT.JOB NA
```

When *NoAutoendcap* is used, a manual ENDCAP must be entered when you are ready to write the accumulated print jobs to the file. Autoendcap and NoAutoendcap are covered later in this section.

Once print jobs are written to a file, the file can be printed using the NPRINT command.

Notifying Users that Jobs are Complete

How often have you made a trip to the printer to see if your job has printed, only to find it still stuck behind others in the queue? In a environment with busy network printers, a print job may wait behind other jobs in the queue for quite some time before being serviced. CAPTURE can be used to notify users when their print job has finished printing, saving unnecessary trips to the printer.

CAPTURE provides two options for notification:

▶ NOTI

▶ NNOTI (Default)

Unless specified in the CAPTURE statement, NNOTI is enabled, indicating that users will not be notified when their print jobs are complete. To enable notification, use the NOTI option, as in this example:

```
CAPTURE Q=HP4_Q NOTI [Other Options]
```

Specifying the Number of Copies to Print

The CAPTURE command can be used to define the number of copies to print of each print job. NetWare can print 1 to 255 copies of each print job. The following example specifies five copies of every print job sent to LPT2.

```
CAPTURE L=2 C=5 [Other Options]
```

Use caution when using this option along with the option to print multiple copies within an application. For example, if you request five copies of a print job from an application as well as entering the preceding CAPTURE statement, NetWare prints five copies of every copy sent by the application. The result would be 25 copies of a single print job!

Using Multiple Form Types

If different form types are used on the same printer—for example, invoices and letterhead—the PRINTDEF utility can be used to define form numbers. These form numbers allow the print server to check the form currently mounted for that printer, preventing inadvertent printing on an incorrect form type. To use forms, specify the form number or name in the CAPTURE statement. An example of this is as follows:

```
CAPTURE Q=HP4_Q F=2 [Other Options]
```

Or,

```
CAPTURE Q=HP4_Q F=LETTERHEAD [Other Options]
```

Printing With and Without Tab Translations

When printing from an application, most applications send printer codes with print jobs that format the job. This code indicates such things as the font to be used and other formatting information, including the number of characters in one tab stop or *tab translations*. NetWare provides two options for tab translations:

▶   NT

▶   T=n (Default)

If you are printing from an application, you want to be sure to allow the application to define its own tab stops. The NT option of CAPTURE indicates no NetWare defined tabs are desired. Use of this option is shown in the following example:

```
CAPTURE Q=HP4_Q NT [Other Options]
```

If you are using an application that does not have a print formatter or if you are printing ASCII text files, you may need to have NetWare define the tab stops. This can be done with the T= option. If NT is not specified, the default is T=8. The following example sets the NetWare defined tab stops to ten spaces:

```
CAPTURE Q=HP4_Q T=10 [Other Options]
```

Controlling Banner Pages

A banner page is a single page that, by default, prints out before each user's print job. This banner page makes it easy to separate one user's job from another in a busy printing environment. The following CAPTURE options are provided to control the banner page.

▶   NB

▶   NAM=name (Default)

▶   B=banner (Default)

As mentioned before, banner pages are enabled by default. To turn off the banner page, use the NB capture option. Here's an example of specifying no banner page:

```
CAPTURE Q=HP4_Q NB [Other Options]
```

If you choose to use banner pages, the job owner's name is printed on the top half of the page and the filename appears on the bottom half. You can control what is printed on the banner page by using the NAM= and the B= options. For example, to print a banner page with "Payroll" at the top and "Confidential" at the bottom, the CAPTURE statement would look something like the following:

```
CAPTURE NAM=PAYROLL B=CONFIDENTIAL [Other Options]
```

Controlling Form Feeds

By default, NetWare prints a form feed after each print job. This is useful if you are printing text files or if you are using an application that doesn't automatically issue a form feed at the end of a job. In most cases, applications do issue a form feed, so the extra NetWare form feed is just a waste of paper. The two options for controlling form feeds are:

- ► FF (default)

- ► NFF

To disable the NetWare form feed at the end of each job, use the NFF option as follows:

```
CAPTURE Q=HP4_Q NFF [Other Options]
```

Using the K (Keep) Option

If a workstation hangs or loses power while capturing data to the network, by default the file server discards all data that it has received from that workstation. The K option can be used to ensure that the file server saves any data received from the workstation. Consequently, if the workstation hangs while sending data to a queue, the server prints the data instead of discarding it. The following shows an example of using the K option:

```
CAPTURE Q=HP4_Q K [Other Options]
```

Using Job Configurations

Now that we've covered all of the CAPTURE options, you can see that CAPTURE statements can be cumbersome. For example, to capture LPT2 to the print queue LASER_Q, printing two copies on form two, with no banner, no form feed, and no tabs, the CAPTURE statement would look like the following:

```
CAPTURE L=2 Q=LASER_Q C=2 F=2 NB NFF NT
```

To simplify capturing to the network, PRINTCON can be used to create a database of print job configurations for each user. These job configurations contain CAPTURE options users frequently require. So, rather than entering long capture statements like the one just given, a job configuration can be created and the J option can be used with CAPTURE, as follows:

```
CAPTURE J=Laser
```

Ending the CAPTURE

As mentioned in Chapter 1, when a print job accumulates in the queue, it is ready for printing when the user signals that he or she is done sending data. This is done by issuing an ENDCAP to end the capture. Once an ENDCAP has been issued, the print data file is closed and the print server sends the job to the appropriate printer.

NetWare provides the following CAPTURE options to control how and when the ENDCAP is issued.

▶   A

▶   TI=

▶   NA

The default is A or Autoendcap. This option indicates that an automatic END-CAP is issued but not until the user exits his or her application. Though exiting the application works, most users don't want to have to do this to make their jobs print. To solve this problem, use the *time out* (TI=) option.

TI specifies the number of seconds that NetWare waits after an application last writes to a print file before issuing an Autoendcap. For most applications, a TI of 15 seconds is sufficient, as specified in the following example:

```
CAPTURE Q=HP4_Q TI=15 [Other Options]
```

Using the A option with TI does not reset the capturing of LPT ports. Consequently, the capturing of data continues after the Autoendcap is issued.

The NoAutoendcap (NA) option can be used if you wish to send multiple print jobs to the queue for later printing. Here's an example:

CAPTURE Q=HP4_Q NA TI=0 [*Other Options*]

When the NA option is used, a manual ENDCAP must be entered before the print jobs are printed. Then ENDCAP syntax is as follows:

ENDCAP [Option . . .]

Table 2.4 shows the NetWare 3 ENDCAP options.

T A B L E 2.4	SYNTAX	OPTION	DEFINITION
NetWare 3 ENDCAP options	L=*n*	Local	Ends the capture of the LPT port specified.
	ALL	All	Ends the capture of all LPT ports.
	C	Cancel	Ends the capture of LPT1 and discards all data without printing it.
	CL=*n*	Cancel local	Ends the capture of the LPT port specified and discards all data without printing it.
	C All	Cancel all	Ends the capture of all LPT ports and discards all data without printing it.

When ENDCAP is issued, the LPT port specified is automatically set back to local mode. For data to be captured to the network once again, a new CAPTURE statement needs to be issued.

· ◄

Supporting Applications that Print to Printer Numbers

On rare occasions, you may encounter network applications that were designed to support the printing services of earlier versions of NetWare. These applications send print jobs to printer numbers 0 through 4 to correspond to the printer numbers of early versions of NetWare rather than print queues. These printer numbers *do not* correspond to the printer numbers used by a print server. To support these applications, you must set up spooler assignments at the file server console. With spooler assignments, when an application tries to send a print job to a printer number, the spooler can intercept the job and redirect it to a print queue.

Spooler assignments are set up using the file server console command SPOOL. The SPOOL syntax is as follows.

```
SPOOL n [TO] queue name
```

So, suppose you are using an application that is sending print jobs to printer number 1. You need to create a spooler mapping to send those jobs to a valid print queue. To do this, go to the file server console and enter a SPOOL command similar to the following:

```
SPOOL 1 TO HP4_Q
```

If you wish to see the existing spooler mappings, you can enter SPOOL alone without any parameters, as follows:

```
SPOOL
```

Print Job Configurations

As mentioned previously, capturing data to the network can be simplified by using print job configurations. Print job configurations are groups of print job options that simplify printing setup. Instead of manually entering all of the print job specifications with CAPTURE or NPRINT each time users want to print, they simply choose the job configuration that meets their needs for that specific print job. This not only makes it easier for users, but administrators have far fewer support calls for network printing issues.

Print job configurations are created for each user using the PRINTCON utility. Figure 2.26 shows the PRINTCON main menu.

F I G U R E   2.26

PRINTCON can be used to
create custom print job
configurations for users.

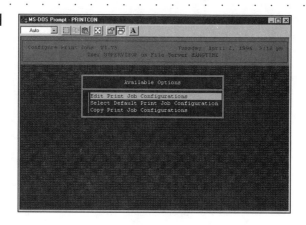

The first thing to notice when looking at the PRINTCON main menu is the user name shown at the top of the screen. In this case it is user SUPERVISOR on server HANGTIME. The importance of noticing this information is described below.

In NetWare 3, print job configurations are user-centric, meaning each user has his or her own print job configuration database. This database is stored in a file called PRINTCON.DAT, which is located in each user's individual mail directory under SYS:MAIL. User mail directories correspond to the user ID numbers found in SYSCON. The PRINTCON.DAT file is created when the first job configuration is created in PCONSOLE.

CREATING PRINT JOB CONFIGURATIONS

To create a print job configuration select Edit Print Job Configurations from the PRINTCON main menu. Using the Insert key enables you to enter a job configuration name. Once you have assigned a name to the job configuration, the screen shown in Figure 2.27 is displayed.

FIGURE 2.27

The print job configuration screen

Look closely at this screen. Notice that the options shown here are the CAP-TURE options we covered previously. The only exceptions are the Device and Mode fields at the bottom left column. These options enable the use of custom print drivers defined using the PRINTDEF utility. PRINTDEF is covered later in this chapter.

SETTING THE DEFAULT JOB CONFIGURATION

Each user can have a print job configuration set as the *default* configuration. This setting simplifies capturing even further by allowing CAPTURE or NPRINT to be issued without any parameters at all. When this happens, the options defined in the default job configuration are used.

Setting the default job configuration is simple. Just choose Select Default Print Job Configuration from the PRINTCON main menu, select the job configuration you wish to be the default, and then press Enter. Selecting a default job configuration is shown in Figure 2.28.

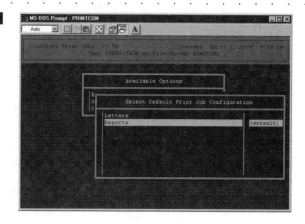

The default print job configuration is used if CAPTURE or NPRINT are issued without any parameters.

COPYING PRINT JOB CONFIGURATIONS

As mentioned earlier, print job configurations are user-specific. Unfortunately, NetWare 3 does not allow print job configurations to be assigned on a group or global basis, as with NetWare 4. So, to make creating job configurations for each user easier, NetWare 3 allows job configurations to be copied from one user to another.

To copy a print job configuration, select Copy Print Job Configurations from the PRINTCON main menu. You are prompted to enter the source user and the target user. NetWare then copies the PRINTCON.DAT file from the source user to the target.

Defining Print Forms

Earlier we discussed how NetWare's print forms prevent users from printing on incorrect paper types. To define a print form, run the PRINTDEF utility and select Forms from the main menu. A list of the existing forms is presented. To create a new form, simply press the Insert key and enter the form name and parameters. Figure 2.29 shows the form definition screen.

FIGURE 2.29

The print form definition screen

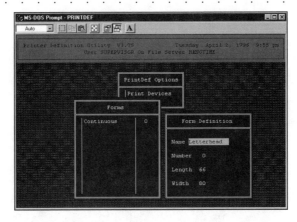

The length and width parameters are for information only and do not have any effect on the formatting of print jobs. Print jobs are formatted by the application being used. NetWare enforces the proper form type for these print jobs through the F= parameter of CAPTURE or NPRINT.

When a job is submitted to a print queue, the print server checks the form number requested for that job. If the form number is different from the one currently mounted at the printer, by default the print job will not be serviced until the proper form is mounted in the printer. Print servers service different form types based on the *queue service mode* defined when the printer is configured.

Creating Custom Print Devices

If you are using an application that does not have a print driver for the printer or the printer function that you wish to use, you can use PRINTDEF to define custom *print devices*. Print devices are essentially NetWare-defined printer drivers that can be selected using PRINTCON job configurations. Referring back to Figure 2.27, the Device and Mode fields are used to select print devices created in PRINT-DEF. Because this is the only way to select print devices, PRINTCON job configurations must be used if you wish to use custom print devices.

NetWare 3 includes definitions for 30 printers that are copied to the SYS:PUB-LIC directory during the NetWare installation. These printer definitions are files with a .PDF extension and are accessed using the PRINTDEF utility.

To use a NetWare print device definition, you must first import it to the PRINT-DEF database. This is done by selecting Print Devices from the PRINTDEF main menu and then selecting Import Print Devices. Enter SYS:PUBLIC as the source directory and a list of the available print devices will be displayed, as shown in Figure 2.30.

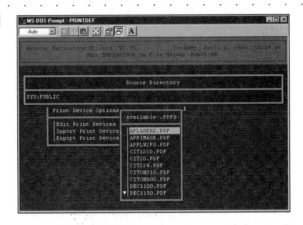

F I G U R E   2.30

Importing print devices from the SYS:PUBLIC directory

Use the arrow keys to select the print device you wish to import. To view or edit a print device once it has been imported, select Edit Print Devices from the Print Device Options menu. When a print device is selected, you will see two edit device options, as shown in Figure 2.31.

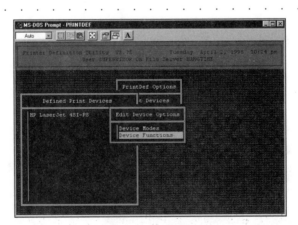

F I G U R E   2.31

Print devices consist of device functions and device modes.

Device functions are escape sequences that make up the printer specific codes. Device modes are combinations of device functions that result in a specific print type, such as landscape or duplex printing. Most printer manuals include the escape sequences necessary to accomplish certain printing types.

Though device functions and modes can be manually defined by using the Insert key and entering the codes, the process is quite unwieldy. Whenever possible, use a NetWare-defined print device. If you do not find a NetWare print device for your printer, check your printer's manual to see if it emulates another printer type before manually entering the printer codes.

Summary

Printing with NetWare 3 has been greatly improved over previous versions of NetWare. A new printer can be set up in minutes on the fly without having to take the file server down. Previous versions of NetWare not only required the server to be taken down but also required a complete relink of the operating system.

Though printing has improved with NetWare 3, it is still important to take the time to plan your printing services to ensure that printing is as simple as possible for both you and your users. This planning includes determining your print queue configurations, the location and number of print servers, and whether or not you should use print job configurations or custom print devices. Doing so makes the job of supporting a network printing system easy.

This chapter sought to provide you with the information necessary to make wise decisions when planning and configuring your NetWare 3 printing system. If you work in a mixed NetWare 3 and NetWare 4 environment, move on to Chapter 3, "NetWare 4 Print Services—Theory of Operations." In this chapter you will see that NetWare 4 introduces a number of improvements over the NetWare 3 printing services. If you work in a NetWare 3-only environment, feel free to skip the next three chapters and move on to Chapter 6, which covers managing a NetWare 3 printing system.

CHAPTER 3

NetWare 4 Print Services—
Theory of Operations

NetWare 4 is similar to NetWare 3.x printing, with some added new twists. In many ways, printing is more simplified than the traditional printing methods under NetWare. Most apparent is the integration with Directory Services for locating and using print resources. There are new objects to deal with in the tree, such as print servers, queues, and printer objects. Much of NetWare printing can still be administered from the DOS interface via the familiar PCONSOLE print tool, even though printing is coupled with Directory Services. Ideally the best way is to use NWAdmin, because it enables a more graphical method of viewing and manipulating objects in the printing system. In addition, it is a central area from which the administrator can manage the entire network.

Directory Services and Network Printing

Now we come to my favorite part. How does Novell's Directory Services simplify network printing? Well, in order to provide a clear understanding of that, a short NDS (Novell Directory Services) primer is necessary.

X.500 and Directories

Way back in the computer Stone Age (say, 1988), there was a group of people that put a specification together for a global directory that could be implemented in computer networks. The details aren't important so much as the concept. In most systems today, finding resources is half the battle of consuming network resources. A good example is printing. Which printer should you use? What driver do you need? Where is the printer you've printed to? These are issues that NDS attempts to address.

A Real-World Example . . . Well, Almost!

Imagine a sky diver accidentally lands on your house, leaving a hole in your roof in the shape of a sky diver, and scraping paint off the side of your house. Now, where would you go to find someone to fix the damage? You would let your fingers do the walking, as shown in Figure 3.1. In today's world, the following would be the scenario:

1 • You find the name of a reputable roofer.

2 • You call 411 to find the number.

3 • The operator says it's out of the area and gives you the area code for the city where the roofer lives.

4 • You call information within that area code and they confirm the number for you.

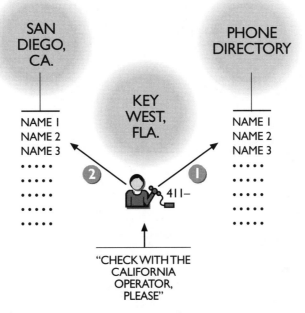

Figure 3.2 illustrates how it would be a bit different if this were an X.500 world:

1 • You call 411 and ask for a roofer with certain qualities (reputable, honest, cheap).

2 • The operator looks in his area and can't find one (let's say you live in Delta, Utah).

3 • While you wait, the operator calls another operator and asks him for a reference. If he does not have one, your operator keeps trying until *all* possibilities are exhausted.

4 • Your operator gives you the number.

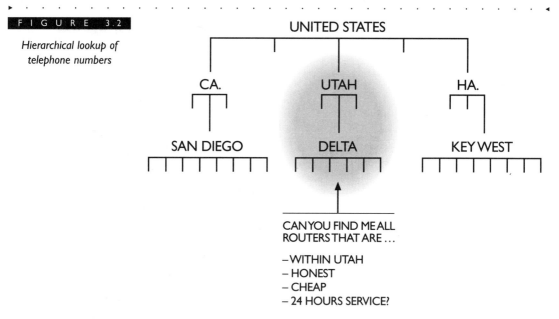

This would assume that we lived in a hierarchical world, where telephone operators and areas were divided into the following categories:

▸ Countries

▸ States

▸ Cities

▸ City areas

This would simplify searching for resources. Get the idea? But how does this relate to printing? What if you, as a user, could simply say, "Find me all of the printers that are faster than 16 pages per minute, support PostScript, are nearby, and can print graphics . . . and then print to it!" In a nondirectory network, the sticky pad method is frequently used. Sticky pads are usually tacked up on a monitor to enable quick access to resources within the network. In an NDS world, you can let NDS do the walking.

Printing Objects in NDS

NDS supports several of the same printing objects as 3.x—primarily, print server objects and queue objects. In addition, there is a new object called the *printer* object, shown in Figure 3.3.

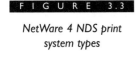

F I G U R E   3.3

NetWare 4 NDS print system types

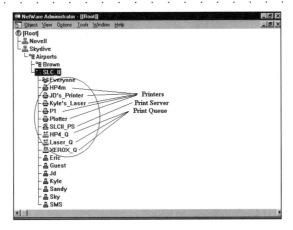

Although there was the concept of a printer definition in NetWare 3.x, the user *never* actually referred to it when printing. All captures were done explicitly to the queue. Now in 4.x, the printer object can be chosen by name when printing. This makes printing a little more intuitive than capturing to something as esoteric as a queue. Queues can still be captured for backward compatibility if necessary. When looking for a printer or queue, NDS can act as the broker of that information. Typically, the administrator sets up a default printer or a queue, enabling users to be network-ready once they've logged in. To be flexible, a user can be allowed to browse and use other printers via NDS. I'll have some examples of that later in the chapter.

Directory Support and Management

Imagine the military as it is today. At the very top you have generals and admirals, while down lower in the food chain you have chiefs and enlisted personnel. If something, such as a dress code, has been mandated from the top of the hierarchy (in a perfect world, that is!), then that change propagates down to *all* levels of the service, as is shown in Figure 3.4.

Military hierarchy

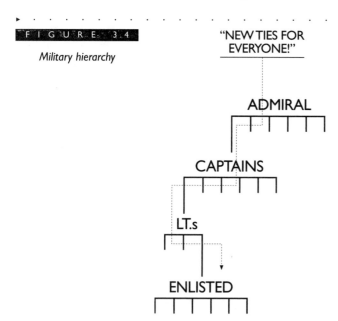

What if the military was organized as a federation of managers? Then any change would have to be communicated to *each* of the heads of each member of the federation, as Figure 3.5 shows. This would consume enormous amounts of time and be highly inefficient.

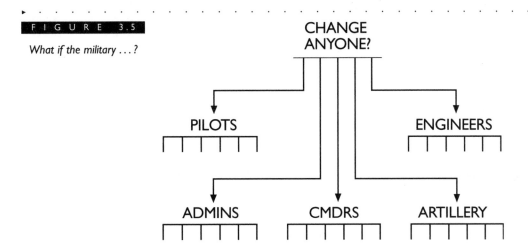

Another example of how the military benefits from a hierarchical organization is when a person is transferred. Within an area, people get access based on what department they're in. By access, we mean access to things such as printers, fax machines, copiers, and so on. When a transfer takes place, the person *loses* access to departmental machines, and *gains* access to machines in the new area, as Figure 3.6 illustrates. This is the way organizations typically work.

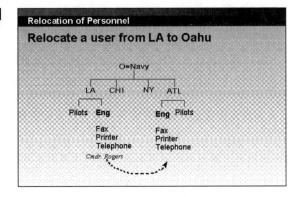

Does that mean NDS can do the same? Essentially, you have the same scenario when a device is created in the directory. A device might be a printer (as we'll create), a fax machine, or perhaps a new service. The administrator can grant access to users several ways, including the following:

> To an individual user

> To a group

> To any other object created in the directory

In this way, access to a printer can be given to a user, several users, a group of users, or an object, as is shown in Figure 3.7.

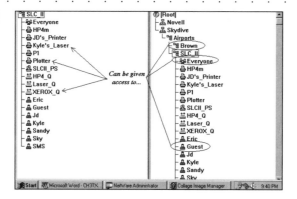

FIGURE 3.7

Granting access to printers and queues

An example where an object would be given rights is when a printer server needs access to a queue in order to service it. The administrator would then give rights to the printer server, allowing access to the queue. These kind of assignments typically are done by the application when it is installed. In other words, because *any* object can be given NDS access to *any other* object, associations between objects can be used for any purpose. Using this methodology, information about how a user gains rights resides in the network itself. Based on security assigned by the administrator, when users are moved, their new rights are based on the following:

> The new container they are moved to

> The groups they belong to

> Any individual rights that have been explicitly assigned

Naming and Directory Services

One key difference in a directory service is the capability of hierarchically naming network resources. If you think about it, this is stuff you use everyday. For example, when you introduce yourself to another person, you probably use your last name and first name:

Hi! My name is J. D. Marymee.

Note that *most* people use their first and last name when performing introductions. This implies some genealogy about the person. In this case, the conversation might go like this:

Oh. So are you related to Prosper Mérimé, author of the play *Carmen*?

And, in effect, the last name implied something about the person. When you get to know the person well enough, they will call you by your first name only, because they already know all about your full name. In directory services, naming works on a similar basis. If I reside in a part of the tree under Engineering, my name might be JMarymee.Brown.Airports.Skydive. This would be known as my *full name*. I usually only need to know my full name when logging in from a different workstation than normal. Usually, I just need to use the name jmarymee and the rest is implied. That is, of course, if I'm at my normal workstation. When printing, a similar situation may occur. Let's suppose that you have a printer in your area, Brown.Airports.Skydive (also known as *context*), that you normally print to. It is an old HP LazyJet II, adequate for normal purposes, but you *need* a faster printer for a large document. It so happens, in SLCII.Airports.Skydive there is a mega-fast new HyperJet Mega III (60 pages per minute), shown in Figure 3.8.

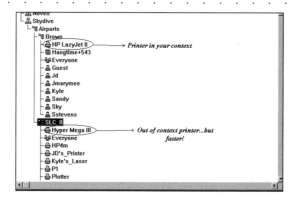

FIGURE 3.8

Out of context printers

How would you use it? Let's forget about searching for it for now. Instead, you know someone in sales who told you about this awesome new device. Remember that when printing to your local printer, you usually obtain access through one of the following ways:

▸ You are automatically *captured* to the printer when you log in.

▸ You choose the printer from a list of devices available to you. This list could have been presented to you via Novell's NWUser utility, Network Neighborhood (Windows 95), or a DOS utility.

If your friend in sales told you the name (in this case Hyper_Mega_III.SLCII. Airports.Skydive), then you could choose it manually and begin capturing to it. Notice that because the Hyper_Mega_III printer is not a member of your local area, you need to use its full name, Hyper_Mega_ III_.SLCII.Airports.Skydive. This is just like using your full name when being introduced to a new person.

Searching in Directory Services

Now that you know about naming, what about searching for objects such as printers when using the directory? This turns out to be relatively simple. The key to understanding searching is to apply a real-life example. Let's say you have the unhappy task of locating a person named Dilbert Smith, who is somewhere in Idaho. Note that the name Dilbert is not very common. Smith, unfortunately, is. So how do you determine the *scope* of the search? Number one, you would find out as much information as possible about *where* in Idaho Dilbert lives. You would probably not initiate a search encompassing the *entire* state, unless you had a *really* boring love life! Instead, you would limit the scope to the narrowest possible range. If you know Dilbert lives in Idaho Falls, the directory scope would probably be: Great Falls.Idaho.United States. However, what if we *did* want all the Smiths, but they needed to fit a range of attributes? Here's a possible query:

Find me all Dilbert Smiths who have blue eyes and red hair and are over the age of 21.

In this case, you might broaden the range of the scope to the full United States. Because there probably aren't many of this type of Dilbert, the scope can be wider. Now let's apply that example to printing services. Using the same example given earlier, Hyper_Mega_III, you decide that you need a faster printer for your report. You *could* just browse around and hope to find what you need. But to be really efficient, a search would be recommended, like the one shown in Figure 3.9. In this case, you would search for a printer that:

► Supports graphics

► Is faster than 16 pages per minute

► Is made by HP

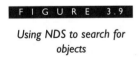

F I G U R E   3.9

Using NDS to search for objects

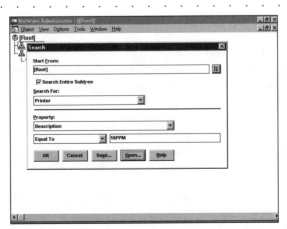

Then you would initiate the search. In NetWare 4, this utility is usually either NWAdmin or NLIST. What is returned is a list of printers matching the criteria, as shown in Figure 3.10.

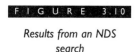

FIGURE 3.10

Results from an NDS search

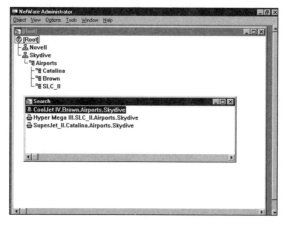

You could then select one and continue. Note that if you did *not* have rights to use the printer, you might not have seen it either. That depends on the administrator and how the system is set up. You'll learn more about that shortly.

Rights and Inheritance in the Directory

As we mentioned earlier, the hierarchy in Directory Services enables a greater flexibility when managing services such as printing. You have several ways to assign printing services rights in the directory.

Print Queue Access Rights

When a print queue is created under NetWare 4, two people automatically get access by default. They include the following:

▶ The user who created the queue

▶ The container (OU) in which the queue was created

Note that if an EVERYONE group exists, it also gets automatic access, as is the case in Figure 3.11.

Default queue access list in NWAdmin

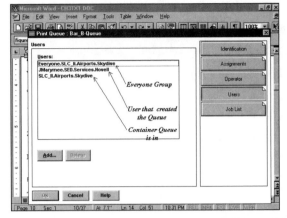

This ensures that the user creating the queue *at least* has access to it, and that users in the same area as the queue can use it. This concept (except for container membership) is similar to that of NetWare 3.x. In NetWare 3.x, as you remember, the EVERYONE group and SUPERVISOR were given default access. Because NetWare 4 doesn't have the concept of a SUPERVISOR (in the normal 3.x application, anyway!), the system assumes the creator is the logical first user. Access to the queue is paramount to printing, even under NetWare 4. If a user has queue access, nothing else is necessary if the rest of printing has been set up. To enable others to use printing under NetWare 4, simply add the user/group/container (OU) to the users property under NWAdmin, or PCONSOLE, as shown in Figure 3.12. As in NetWare 3, users/groups/containers typically *do not* need access as operators unless they need to manage the queue. This would include the capability of deleting jobs and setting holds on them.

Necessary access to use print system

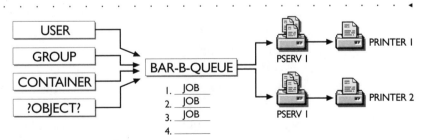

Another benefit to using the directory for assigning rights to queues is the global nature of assignments. When you assign a user rights to a queue, it applies to *that* user. When you assign rights to a group, it applies to *that* group. But, as Figure 3.13 illustrates, when you assign rights to a container, those access rights apply to the following:

▸ *All* users/objects within the container

▸ *All* users/objects below the container that was assigned

▸ *Any* other subcontainers that exist below

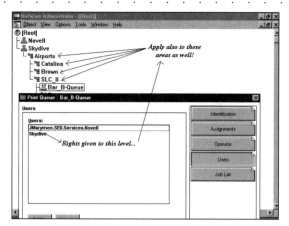

Beware the inheritance of NDS!

Remember, with great power comes great responsibility!

Directory access rights   The second half of print queue rights applies when working with the directory. Directory access controls the visibility of objects within the hierarchy. By default, the special group *public* has browse access to the root of the tree. This means that all objects can see all other objects once authenticated. As a result, you may see things, but you may not be able to access them. Because rights to objects can be given to any other object, visibility can be tightly controlled by the administrator. This means access can be given to the following:

▸ **User.** In this case, only the user and the administrator can see the chosen queue during a search or browse.

▸ **Group.** The same applies for a group as for a user.

▸ **Container.** Much like giving print access described earlier, if DS access is given to a container, it flows down to all lower layers. Again, with great power comes great responsibility!

In the printing arena, this means you may have default browse access to all queues, but when you actually try to capture to one of them (via NWUser in Windows 3.1, Network Neighborhood in Windows95, or CAPTURE in NETUSER or DOS), you will get a message similar to that shown in Figure 3.14.

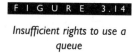

F I G U R E   3.14

Insufficient rights to use a queue

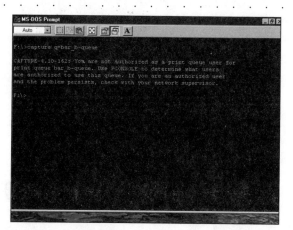

So why use user groups at all?   You may be wondering why you would use user groups at all, because it seems that containers cover a lot of access. In essence, containers can greatly simplify your printing life, at least as an administrator. However, one drawback to using a container also happens to be its greatest strength. If you move a user *out* of a container and into a new one, the user *loses* queue access garnered as a user of the old container and potentially gains new queue access by virtue of being in the new container. Note that the user might even retain old queue access and gain new rights. This may be the case if the queue access/DS rights were given high up in the tree. Because rights flow downward you may retain your old access privileges!

NetWare 4 Printing Objects

NetWare 4 contains several objects used for printing; print queue, network printers, and print servers. As stated earlier, they are very similar to NetWare 3 printing objects, but behave slightly differently.

Print Queues

The most fundamental part of NetWare printing is the print queue. NetWare 4 printing still requires a place to store data as it's being printed on a local or remote printer. This way, the client application stays free to complete other tasks. NetWare 4 print queues can be placed under any volume belonging to a server in the 4.x tree. Unlike NetWare 3.x, the queue is placed at the root of the file tree (for example, SYS:), instead of under the SYS:SYSTEM directory. When you do a directory of the root of SYS:, you will see a directory called Queues that the system will have created *after* you have created your first queue. The queue subdirectories will reside inside that directory, as shown in Figure 3.15. Like NetWare 3.x, the subdirectory name will be the unique Object ID generated by NetWare when the queue was created. If you ever accidentally delete this directory, you will need to re-create the queue from scratch because it is uniquely created at the same time as the queue.

F I G U R E   3.15

Queue storage areas on a NetWare volume

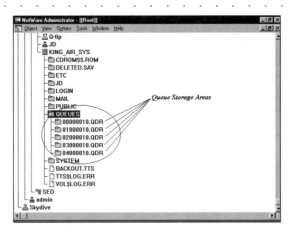

Network Printers

Two types of printers can be created when using the supplied PSERVER.NLM that comes with NetWare 4: NPRINTER.NLM (server based) and NPRINTER.EXE (workstation based). The difference is where the physical printer actually gets plugged into the network. NPRINTER.NLM is automatically loaded when the PSERVER.NLM is loaded, *provided* that you have configured a local printer. This is done with either PCONSOLE (DOS), or NWAdmin (Windows), when print services are created. It's also a bit tricky when you're looking for the specific option. As it turns out, print servers created under NetWare 4 *automatically* assume a remote printer (NPRINTER.EXE) when a new printer object is created, as shown in Figure 3.16. Therefore, if you will have server-attached printers, be sure to specify local printer port support! We'll cover how to do that shortly. Splitting the print server/port software is different from the NetWare 3 style of printing. In NetWare 3, the PSERVER.NLM encompassed both the print server itself and the local printer port support. So why the change? Primarily, Novell needed a way to abstract print server functionality (which does not need to be tied to hardware) from physical port access (which *is* highly hardware dependent). This feature became necessary for the implementation of SFT III NetWare (which is built into NetWare 4).

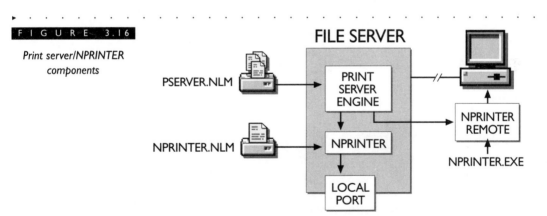

FIGURE 3.16

Print server/NPRINTER components

And those third parties! Another aspect of maintaining separate server/port software is the capability for third-party vendors to *hook in* from a printer perspective, as shown in Figure 3.17. In fact, hardware vendors such as HP Xerox have embedded software in their printers that can talk to a NetWare print server as a remote port. This simplifies the administrator's job, and reduces PC hardware requirements for remote printers. I'll discuss these aspects in more detail in Chapter 8.

Functionally, both NPRINTERS support the print server in the same fashion. The main difference is that additional traffic is generated when the NPRINTER.EXE is used. This is because the print job must go:

1 • From the workstation to the server-based queue

2 • From the server to the remote printer

FIGURE 3.17

Flow of a print job to a remote NPRINTER.EXE

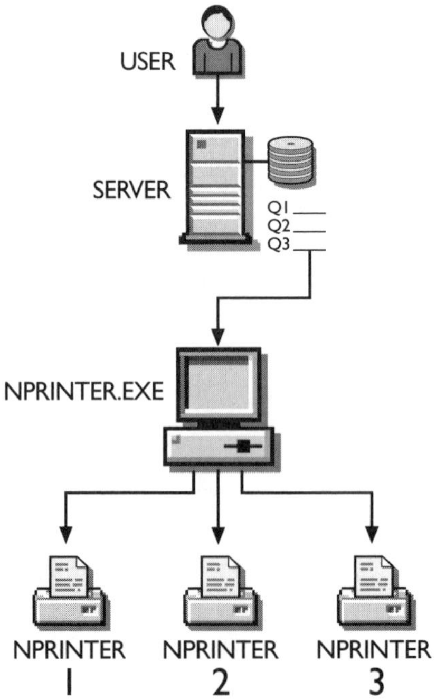

USER

SERVER

Q1
Q2
Q3

NPRINTER.EXE

NPRINTER 1   NPRINTER 2   NPRINTER 3

In essence, the job is traversing the LAN cabling twice! This may not be important in smaller LANs, but as the network grows, LAN traffic becomes more of an issue.

Print Servers

The queue is the repository of the jobs waiting to be printed, but the print server is the real workhorse of the printing system. The print server is responsible for polling jobs in the queue and directing them to an assigned printer when the printer or printers are available. Print servers under NetWare 4 can only run in the following two ways:

▸ As an NLM running at the server

▸ Inside a print device (such as Intel's NetPort or HP's JetDirect cards that can be embedded in HP printers)

NetWare 4.x comes with the software to run the print server in a server (NLM). A JetDirect card or NetPort will have the software already embedded on the device, as shown in Figure 3.18.

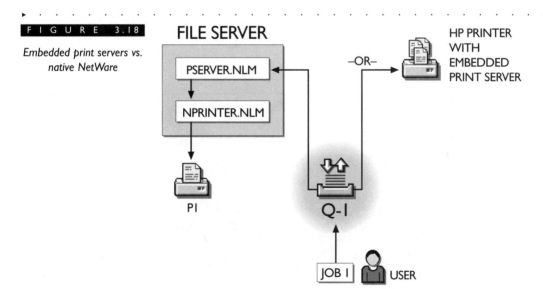

FIGURE 3.18

Embedded print servers vs. native NetWare

FILE SERVER

PSERVER.NLM

NPRINTER.NLM

P1

–OR–

HP PRINTER WITH EMBEDDED PRINT SERVER

Q-1

JOB 1   USER

Print Server Placement

So where do you run the print server? That depends on what the environment will be. Most networks end up with a combination of arrangements depending on what sort of printers and devices are available. First, let's look at the issue solely from a perspective of network traffic. In each scenario, the print job *must* first be spooled from the user to the queue. Once in a queue, the print server must then open the job and route it to an appropriate printer (locally or remotely attached). The printer then receives the job and prints it. Logically, you would assume that the more things there are between the user and the printer, the slower the printout will be and the more traffic that will be generated. And you would be right! Therefore, network administrators usually analyze the best combination in order to maximize printer availability and speed.

Server-Based Print Servers   Server-based print servers usually provide the best all-around support for printing, unless you have print devices on the network (such as a JetDirect). The server-based print server consists of two elements, PSERVER.NLM and NPRINTER.NLM.

PSERVER.NLM

PSERVER.NLM handles the routing of the print jobs from the queue to the local or remote printer port. This NLM can be loaded either manually from the console, remotely (using RCONSOLE), or automatically from AUTOEXEC.NCF, as shown in Figure 3.19. PSERVER.NLM automatically loads NPRINTER.NLM one or more times if printing output will be routed to a local server port (parallel or serial).

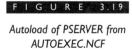

FIGURE 3.19

Autoload of PSERVER from AUTOEXEC.NCF

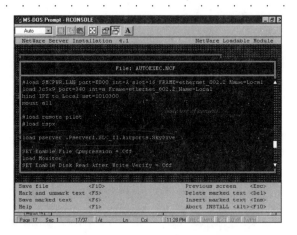

NPRINTER.NLM

This NLM works with PSERVER to provide local printer port support (parallel and serial port devices). As mentioned earlier, NetWare 3 encompasses both NLMs within the PSERVER.NLM module. In NetWare 4 they are broken out for reasons stated previously. Server-based printing flow goes something like this:

Step One: The user submits a print job to the queue. This generates network traffic, as the file/data is transferred to the subdirectory on the server where the queue is placed. Again, this is just a specially named directory that NetWare knows about. Once in the directory, the queue waits until a print server polls waiting jobs and attempts to serve a waiting job.

Step Two: The print server polls for new jobs and finds one waiting. It then opens the job, reads the print record (automatically created when the job was spooled), and attempts to print it on an available printer. If one of the configured printers supporting the print server is on the same server (NPRINTER.NLM), then the print data is sent directly to the hardware port. If not, then the data must be sent across the LAN again to the destination device.

Step Three: If the data is being sent by the print server to a remote printer (covered later), then the print data must be sent to the remote device for final servicing. This adds additional network traffic to the LAN backbone. For this reason, unless bandwidth is not an issue, server-based print servers with remote printers are not implemented as often.

Setting up NetWare 4.x Printing—The Basics

We'll first cover the basic steps needed to get printing up and running under NetWare 4. Later, we'll go into the more advanced steps (such as Job Definitions), and in the third-party section, we'll give you some guidance on integrating critters such as HP JetDirects, QMS, Lexmark printers, and the like.

Print Forms and Print Job Configurations

As described in Chapter 1, NetWare has the capability to create print job configurations. This is one of the most useful options under the printing system, one that enables the supervisor to set up automatic printing for users. In addition, setting up job configurations enables greater flexibility for choosing different printing options when a variety of applications are being executed. For example, a print job configuration can be created that sets up all the flags necessary for a graphics application. Another may be provided that is designed to set up optimal printing for a word processing program, and so on.

NetWare 4 Enhancements NetWare 4 adds a hierarchical twist to print job configurations. In NetWare 3, each user can be given a default print job configuration that is executed automatically when printing first begins. In addition, more configurations can be defined. However, these options are specifically designed for each user. Although the supervisor can copy an existing configuration to other users, he or she has no easy way to deploy a default or additional configuration to a group of users. NetWare 4 leverages the concept of *Organizational Units* as part of directory services to accomplish this. A user can still be given a default or additional print job configuration if desired, but the administrator can also deploy them at an OU, as shown in Figure 3.20. When assigned this way, any user who is contained within the specified OU is automatically given any print job configurations assigned to the OU. When you view a user without *any* assignments, you'll see a blank area under Print Job Configurations. When you look at the user again, after you have assigned a job configuration to the OU, you'll see a configuration available that was not there before. Click on the OU's configuration and make it *default*, re-view the user, and you'll see that the user will also reflect the change. See Figure 3.21.

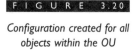

FIGURE 3.20

Configuration created for all objects within the OU

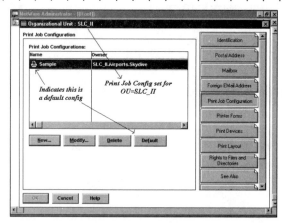

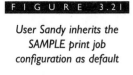

FIGURE 3.21

*User Sandy inherits the
SAMPLE print job
configuration as default*

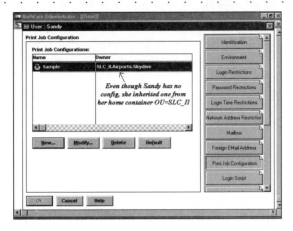

In addition, if the user is moved *out* of the container and into a different one, the user loses the configurations inherited as part of the container, and gains any new configurations assigned to the user's new OU. Another significant change is the location of the configuration files themselves. In NetWare 3, each user's configuration file was kept in the SYS:MAIL subdirectory in the user's personal mail area (something like 000003C7 or some obscure system-defined directory). Because everything the user did in NetWare 3 was server-centric, storing this information in the mail area made sense. In NetWare 4, that sort of information about the user is available in a much more global fashion. The user's print job configuration is kept in the directory service, where it can be globally found and used. This also means that the configurations for the user are protected if a server should go down, because the directory usually creates at least two replicas of the NDS database. Bear in mind that print job configurations only take effect when executing either CAPTURE or NPRINT from a command-line (DOS), or via a login script. If you are using Windows 95 or an NT workstation, the client may have a preconfigured setting for desired print options set when the client was installed or last configured. In that event, print job configurations will only be useful during a client session to the server. Novell's CLIENT32 architecture for Windows 95 *will* enable Login Script execution upon logging in. Therefore, users with Windows 95 and CLIENT32 deployed will still gain an advantage with Login Script directed captures. Novell's next NT client release should be the same.

Using the Print System under NetWare 4

Capturing to the printing system under NetWare 4 is extremely similar to all past versions of NetWare. In essence, you need to tell the system you are ready to send output. You have several ways to accomplish this, such as the following:

- ▸ Use the DOS-based CAPTURE command (same as in NetWare 3).

- ▸ Use the C-Worthy utility NETUSER.

- ▸ Use the tool *NWUser* under Windows (included when you install the VLM client.

- ▸ Use a network-aware application (such as WordPerfect).

- ▸ Create a printer under Windows 95 while using the Novell 32-bit client.

All in all, the easiest way, if your application supports it, is a network-aware application. Ideally, you (if you're a system supervisor) should set up a system that sets all the defaults for users that log in to the network on a daily basis. Exceptions, or more sophisticated users, can be allowed to exercise more extensive browsing privileges.

Printer Object versus Print Queue   As noted before, *everything* must ultimately be sent to a queue. It is most logical, at least to most users, that a person would send data to a *printer*. Therefore, NetWare 4 enables users to actually issue a capture against a NetWare 4 defined printer name. Printer objects are not an optional part of the overall print system. You *must* create at least one printer in order to create a fully functional printing system. When a printer is defined under NetWare 4, a *default queue* is also assigned. In essence, this tells the printing system *where* to send the data should a user capture to a printer name rather than a queue. See Figures 3.22 and 3.23.

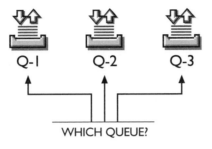

F I G U R E   3.22

Which queue does the user want?

WHICH QUEUE?

CAPTURE   P=MEGA LASER

F I G U R E   3.23

Assigning a default queue for a printer under NWAdmin

Remember, NetWare doesn't care which you use as long as the system can find a way to get the data to a queue, where you, as a user, have rights. A default queue would look something like this:

```
CAPTURE P=.HPLaser4.sales.Acme
```

Whereas a queue capture might look like this:

```
CAPTURE Q=HP-Queue.Sales.Acme
```

This is mostly a semantics exercise. It won't provide a performance advantage one way or the other. What it boils down to is the following:

> ▸ Can the users find resources when they need them?

> ▸ Is it fairly intuitive?

> ▸ Can change be introduced without creating major impact to the user?

Whichever approach you select, it should answer some of these questions.

Print Server Management Functions In the management section, you'll learn more about actively managing the printing system on a day-to-day basis. Managing the system as a whole can be relatively easy, depending on how well the system was planned and implemented. Print server management can be done from one of two locations: the server or a client, via tools such as NWAdmin. The main module that supports print server functionality under NetWare 4 is PSERVER.NLM. Although it is not designed as a full management tool, PSERVER. NLM has some options that you can work with to determine printing problems. This can be done remotely, via RCONSOLE, or at the server console directly. Primarily, the following options are used to view and manage via PSERVER:

> ▸ The health and status of the print server itself (this includes the capability of shutting down the print server and getting current revision information).

> ▸ The status of the individual printers defined under the print server. This includes the capability of stopping the printer, rewinding a printer, selecting a new printing form, aborting a job, and so on.

Most people tend to leave the PSERVER.NLM console resident at the server, and choose to manage the system view tools such as NWAdmin and PCONSOLE without having to take a walk and visit an offending server. Pretty much anything that you can do at the server under PSERVER.NLM can be done more graphically and easily using NWAdmin.

Printing Administration Tools

NWAdmin and PCONSOLE are the main tools used in creating the printing components.

NWAdmin   NWAdmin is the all-encompassing graphical tool for NetWare administration. Although no quick setup for printing is included in NWAdmin, creating the necessary components is relatively straightforward. We'll be using this tool first.

PCONSOLE   This DOS C-Worthy utility looks almost identical to the NetWare 3.x system, but there are some differences. PCONSOLE for 4.x includes the option to toggle to bindery support. This means the PCONSOLE tool can be used to administer printing services under NetWare 3.x and NetWare 4.x. This removes the need to use two separate DOS tools. If you have a mixed network, use the NetWare 4.x utilities. All of PCONSOLE's functionality is in NWAdmin. See Figure 3.24.

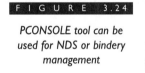

F I G U R E   3.24

PCONSOLE tool can be used for NDS or bindery management

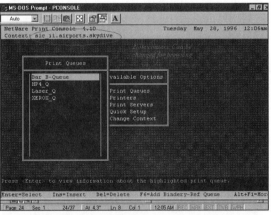

In case you're wondering, the DOS C-Worthy utility is so named because of the developer toolkit. C-Worthy screens, a longtime identifier of NetWare servers, are still used for DOS administration and user functions. These tools are used for both client and server applications today. Many third parties are now writing "snap-ins" for the graphical tool NWAdmin instead, mostly because of its simple interface and central location for managing all aspects of the network.

PRINTDEF   We'll cover this later, but PRINTDEF's function is to create system-supported form types and NetWare-supported print drivers.

PRINTCON   The PRINTCON tool enables customization of default parameters used when printing is initiated. In essence, if user Sam wants a banner printed when he submits a job but user Sandy doesn't, PRINTDEF can specify a print job configuration that can be customized for each. We'll create some of these later. All of this functionality as well is included in NWAdmin.

Starting with the Queue

Fundamental to the printing system is the queue. Even when supporting third-party printing systems, a queue must still be created. Whether it's created with NetWare utilities makes no difference. We'll be using NWAdmin first to create a basic queue.

For those of you who know NetWare 3.x printing, the elements are almost the same.

Step by Step

First, start NWAdmin. At this point, we're going to assume you have *some* NDS knowledge other than this book. Select a *context* (container, OU, and so on) where you wish the queue to exist. A lot of administrators place queues either in a separate OU or within the same context as a file server object. Reasons for this include the following:

> ▸ In a small office, it's the simplest way to find resources. Everyone accesses the printers/queues from the same area. This would be a nonhierarchical deployment of the directory.

> ▸ The server that is represented by the server object contains the volume that supports the printer/queue being created. It may be more logically appealing to keep those objects close to each other.

> ▸ Users can think about network resources the same way that they view *physical* office resources. The server and the printers/queues are located within the same area.

Again, there isn't a *technical* reason for locating the print resources within the same area, but they may be easier to use if the users can logically relate to them.

Creating the Queue The items that must be supplied when creating a new print queue are as follows:

Directory Queue versus Bindery Queue: If you are creating a regular queue (and we are), choose Directory Services Queue. A Bindery Reference Queue can service jobs out of a queue that resides on a 2.x or 3.x server. This can be useful if you have a mixed environment and need to support queues from a single location. In addition, you can submit a job to Bindery Reference Queue and it will automatically be sent to the referenced queue on the 3.x server.

Print Queue Name: Usually you want to give a queue a descriptive name. It is easier to find a queue named HPLaser4M_Q than just LaserJet.

Print Queue Volume: This is the physical space where the job will be stored as it is spooled and when it is serviced. Therefore, this *must* reference a volume somewhere in the 4.x tree. In addition, the container in which the queue is created must have rights to that volume in order to create print jobs there.

In previous versions of NetWare, the queue was *always* stored under SYS:SYSTEM in the volume SYS:. In NetWare 4, the NWAdmin utility creates a subdirectory off the root of the volume chosen (which can be other than SYS: now!) and calls it QUEUES. This is where the data is stored for the queue. See Figure 3.25.

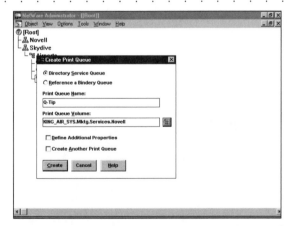

F I G U R E   3.25

Print queue create options

I • Press the Insert key with the chosen context selected. A list of potential object types will be listed. Choose the Print Queue object type and press Enter. Or, for NetWare 4.11 users, click the Print Queue button on the NWAdmin tool bar.

2 • Give the queue a descriptive name. NDS enables more than the standard DOS-limited eight character names. This way, the user or administrator can view resources without having to closely scrutinize information about the object. At this time, you have the option of choosing to add additional information to the queue. This could include information used to search for the object, as well as configuration options that affect how the queue is used. More on that information shortly.

3 • Select the print queue volume by clicking the Browse button to the right of the Print Queue Volume field and then browsing the directory tree to choose the volume on which you wish this print queue to be stored.

4 • Select Create to create the new queue object.

Now that the queue is created, the next step is to add some configuration data (see Figure 3.26). Note that, at this point, you *could* create the other components (print server and printer) and have a complete printing system. What we'll do instead is look at the other options available that can enable a more flexible environment. The following are some of these options:

▶ Queue operators

▶ Queue users

▶ Assigned print servers

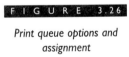

FIGURE 3.26

Print queue options and assignment

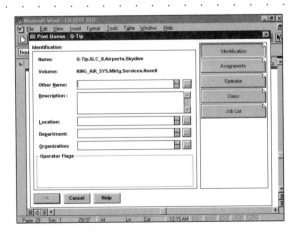

Remember that in order to print under NetWare 4, or even NetWare 3, you *must* have access to a queue. By default, whenever you create a print queue, the container containing the queue is given access. Now, the way that NDS works, *any user* who is contained within the same OU as the queue will be allowed access. Suppose now that this queue is being serviced by a high-capacity color printer. You may not wish to have just *anyone* submitting print jobs at $.30 apiece. Therefore, you'll need to control access to that resource. What you can do at this point depends on how you manage your network. You can also combine these options in the following ways:

▸ **Create a group and give it access to the queue.** Groups can be composed of users inside and outside the OU where the queue exists

▸ **Grant access to one or more OUs.** Allows departmental access to the queue. This puts the burden of how the user gains access to the queue on NDS. If the user is within one of these OUs, they have access. If they are moved (dragged and dropped) out of the container, they will lose those access privileges, unless they are moved into an OU with similar access.

▸ **Grant access to a user.** Allows very granular management of the queue down to the user level. This enables the administrator to say, "Only this or these users can print to this queue."

Another set of options that allow management of the queue after it is created are shown at this point (see Figure 3.27). These options are:

▸ **Allow users to submit print jobs**. This option allows the administrator to temporarily halt submission of new print jobs.

▸ **Allow print servers to service jobs**. This allows the administrator to prevent print servers servicing any new jobs.

▸ **Allow print servers to attach to the queue**. This option prevents allowed print servers from attaching to the queue and servicing jobs.

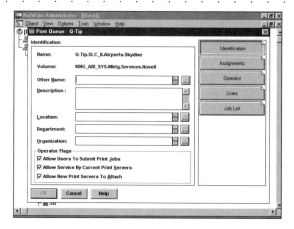

Operator flags options

We'll cover these options in more detail under management. Some of them are self-evident, but we'll spend some time working with the details in that section. Primarily, they are designed to make controlling the print system as flexible as possible. Keep in mind that the queue is the primary object that users need access to in order to print, even if a user selects a printer object as the target object (it is eventually sending the data to a default queue in the background).

Defining a Printer Object

Once the queue has been established, it is time to create at least one printer object. Note that the queue can be in a totally different part of the tree and still be serviced by the printer. The steps to create a printer are:

1 • To begin creating a printer object, you once again choose a container (context) in which you wish to create the object and press Insert (or choose Create from the File Menu). For NetWare 4.11 users, an alternate method is to click on the Object button on the NWAdmin toolbar. Then you can choose a descriptive printer name and choose Create.

2 • Next you can edit properties of the printer object. This can be done by choosing Define Additional Properties when the printer is created, or by double-clicking on the printer once it has been created.

3 • Next you can customize the items of the printer. The most important is Assignments, because it is where you assign a printer to service a particular queue.

The items that can be customized here are:

Identification   This section is relatively straightforward. These are the data that you can set when searching for printers in directory services. The key one tends to be *description*.

Assignments   Assignments is the most critical area for the printing operation. Here is where you assign a printer to service a particular queue. The following are the two most important items:

▸ **Priority**. When you add a queue, you can specify a priority as well. This enables an administrator to have certain queues serviced over others. Why? Well, let's say the engineering department has higher priority (over the printers) than does marketing. If the engineering queue has higher priority, 1 being the highest, then the engineering jobs will be serviced before the marketing jobs. If a job is in process, regardless of priority, it will be completed first before a new job is serviced. If all queues are added at equal priority, or you only have one printer servicing each queue, this option is ignored.

▸ **Default Print Queue**. Remember that a user can capture to either a printer or a queue in NetWare 4. Therefore, if a user specifies a queue, the system knows *exactly* where to send the job. If the user selects a printer name instead, which queue should the system send the job to? This is where you can assign that option. Note that by default, the first queue assigned becomes the Default Print Queue. See Figure 3.28.

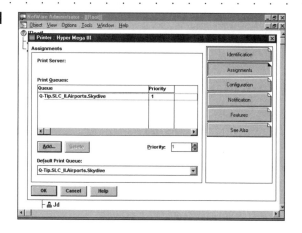

Configuration   As previously noted, this option is where you (as the Administrator) decide if the printer is local or remote and whether the system will use NPRINTER.NLM or NPRINTER.EXE. This is chosen under Communication in this detail page. Your choices in Communication include which port to use and interrupt service. Typically, the default of *polled* is adequate. Port number depends on the remote or local port you wish to use. The critical option here is whether to use *Manual Load* or *Auto Load*.

Manual Load: This option means you will remotely load NPRINTER.EXE and attach to this print server using the preceding specifications (interrupt, port, and so on). Another option here might be a printer with embedded remote printer software such as an Intel NetPort or Lexmark printer. They, in effect, act as an NPRINTER.EXE driver remotely when they load.

Auto Load: This means that PSERVER.NLM will load NPRINTER.NLM when the print server is loaded. Again, the options chosen will prevail as the port and interrupt. See Figure 3.29.

The following are some other options to enable further configuration of the printer:

Printer Type: This enables the selection of the protocol type you'll be using. Depending on what you choose, you'll need to specify some protocol-specific information. Most of these are self-explanatory.

Banner Type: This denotes the type of banner you'll be printing, if one is desired. This is either a standard text banner or a postscript one (if your printer can support postscript).

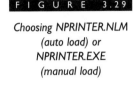

Choosing NPRINTER.NLM (auto load) or NPRINTER.EXE (manual load)

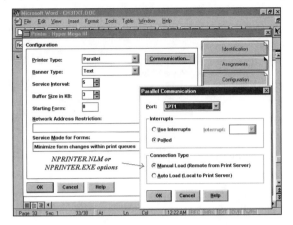

Service Interval: This is how often the print server checks the print queue for print jobs going to this printer. If you want to have jobs printed faster, you can decrease this amount at the added overhead of more polling.

Buffer Size: This specifies how much data can be sent to this printer at a time. Default is 3KB and usually need not be changed.

Starting Form: This option, as described in the general theory section, is where you can specify which form will be the default for this printer. If no forms are created, zero is the default.

Network Address Restrictions: For security reasons, you may not want just *any* station to become a remote printer. This option enables the administrator to select by hardware address which stations can support remote ports. Today, this means just IPX/SPX stations.

Service Mode for Forms: This option is how the printer knows to service a forms environment. If forms are created on the network, you may want to have forms mounting be a manual or semi-automated process. This option enables that selection.

Notification   When a problem snarls up the network, ideally someone would be notified, preferably the administrator in charge of the problem device. As with NetWare 3, NetWare 4 printers can send notification messages when situations such as "out of paper" occur. See Figure 3.30.

*Fault notification
configuration*

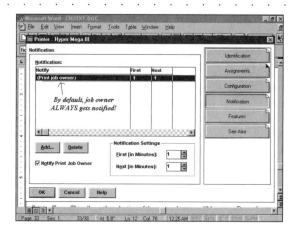

Features   The Features list enables other printer-specific information to be entered. Features can be used when searching for printers with certain options, such as special type faces or cartridges (such as a Tax Program forms cartridge).

See Also   As with most other objects, this field is used to place object specific data that the administrator wishes to track. Typically, this information is not used by users.

Defining Print Servers

Last but not least, a print server should be created to tie the other components together. Creating a print server in NetWare 4 is very similar to creating a print server in NetWare 3. Just assign the printers to the print server that will service them! To create a print server, much like creating the other two objects, choose a context and then press Insert or choose Create from the File Menu. Or, if you are using NetWare 4.11, you may click the Object button from the toolbar and then choose Print Server as the object you wish to create. The following are items used for print servers:

Identification   Identification is pretty self-explanatory. Again, populating these fields assists in doing directory-wide searches of specific objects. Most fields, as with the others, are optional.

Assignments   This is where it all ties together! To complete the assignments, merely choose one or more printers that this print server will service and you are complete! Note that you do *not* choose print queues. The printers themselves have been assigned to print queues.

Port numbers are usually only relevant to older style printing that required the use of a number instead of a printer name. You can usually leave these at a default. See Figure 3.31.

FIGURE 3.31

Assigning printers to be serviced by a print server

Users   Notice that here you can enable users to do "something" to the print server. This in no way grants access to a user/group/container to use a queue or any part of the printing system. So what does it do? Its only purpose is to enable users to view print server status information. This includes forms being serviced, percent of current job complete, and so forth. Normally, most users do not need this kind of access.

Operators   This option enables an administrator to subassign management rights of print servers to other users. This does not enable creation of new print servers. It enables a user to abort print jobs, mount new forms in the printer, notify the print server, and so on. Interestingly, you assign this right under the print server object, but it enables access under the printers that are being supported by the print server. In other words, to see the effect of this right, you double-click on printer objects in the tree and manage aspects of currently serviced print jobs after having been made a print server operator. Printers and print servers are related in this way.

Auditing   As part of NetWare's NCSC C2 Evaluation, significant auditing had to be enabled under NetWare. This option runs independently of the AUDITCON auditing functions, but falls under the same general guidelines. When enabled, the system tracks printing information in a permanent log stored under the SYS:SYS-TEM subdirectory. The log file is typically called PSERVER.LOG. The subdirectory under SYS:SYSTEM is the unique object ID assigned by the system when the print server was created.

Print Layout   This is a management/troubleshooting option that enables an administrator to see at a glance how components of the system are functioning. When you choose Print Layout, you can see an expanded view of the printing components and their relationship to each other (see Figure 3.32). By clicking on any one of the components and clicking the right-mouse button (or selecting Status from the menu), you can get a quick update of the status of the component (see Figure 3.33). This can be useful when determining network printing problems. We'll discuss this in more detail under the network management section of this book.

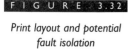

F I G U R E   3.32

*Print layout and potential
fault isolation*

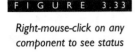

FIGURE 3.33

Right-mouse-click on any component to see status

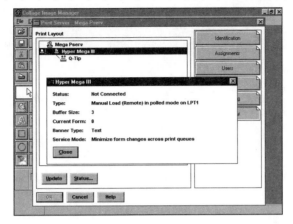

Printing Object Creation Made Easy with NetWare 4.11

NetWare 4.11 adds a feature to NWAdmin that makes creating and configuring print services quick and easy. This is an option found under the Tools menu called Print Services Quick Setup. Using this option, you can create a print queue, printer, and print server in a single action—*and* all necessary assignments are made automatically. This saves you immeasurable time when setting up NetWare 4 printing. Earlier versions of NetWare 4 provided this capability but only in the DOS-based utility PCONSOLE as described in the PCONSOLE section that follows. Because most NetWare 4 administrators prefer GUI administration over DOS-based, this option was seldom used.

Let's take a quick look at how Quick Setup works in NetWare 4.11. By selecting Print Services Quick Setup from the NWAdmin Tools menu, a dialog box similar to the one shown in Figure 3.34 is displayed.

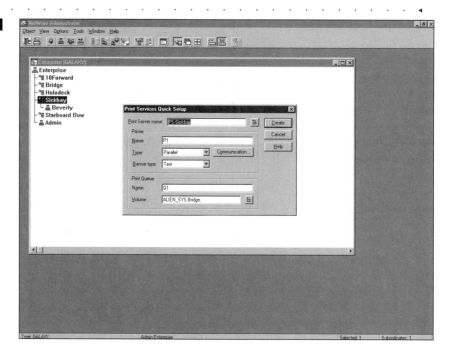

F I G U R E   3.34

Using the Print Services Quick Setup option of NWAdmin under NetWare 4.11

As you can see in Figure 3.34, this option provides basic defaults that you can either accept or customize to fit your printing environment. When you select Create, the print objects you define on this screen are automatically created and the necessary assignments for a fully functional print system are made. For each additional printer you would like in this context, simply repeat the process. Once a print server has been created in a context, that print server is used as the default for each subsequent printer you create. The best part about this option is that you are provided with a single location to configure your printing services, which is much easier than creating each object individually and then manually making the appropriate assignments.

Dealing with the DOS Side

The main tools, as previously noted for managing printing under DOS, are PCONSOLE, PRINTDEF, and PRINTCON. We'll touch on PCONSOLE only, as the functionality of each is extremely similar to that of NetWare 3.x.

PCONSOLE.EXE

The one redeeming feature that PCONSOLE has is that it provides a Quick Setup option for those of you who have not upgraded your NetWare 4 servers to NetWare 4.11. As described previously, in NetWare 4.11 this functionality has been added to the GUI administration utility, NWAdmin. In versions prior to NetWare 4.11, this functionality is only provided through PCONSOLE.

Quick Setup allows for a "quick setup" of printing, enabling all the associations and definitions to be completed with a minimum of user input. The following are the two main questions you need to consider:

> ▶ *Where* (within which context) do you wish to create the printing components?

> ▶ *Which* volume do you wish to use to store print server information?

The only drawback to using Quick Setup is that *all* the components will be created within the same context. This may or may not be an issue, depending on how decentralized your administration is. In a smaller scenario, this option is very workable.

To create the print system components, it is recommended that you first choose a context from the PCONSOLE main screen (see Figure 3.35).

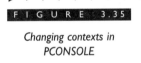

F I G U R E 3.35

Changing contexts in PCONSOLE

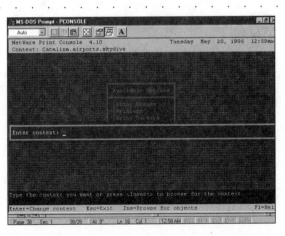

Note that you can use the Insert key and browse different areas of the NDS tree for a desired location. If you are browsing, note that you also need to select the new context with the F10 key instead of the Enter key. Once the context has been selected, choose Quick Setup from the main menu. Note that there are some default names for the devices. At this stage, you can modify them or take them as defaults. The only main choice you *may* have to make is the volume in which the queue will be stored. If you choose a context where a volume exists, it will select that volume as a default. If not, you will need to browse the tree and find a suitable volume. Remember, this will be the area where the data will be temporarily stored when users are sending print jobs. After these selections have been made, you can then select F10 and all three components will be created. At this point, you can run NWAdmin and check out the new print components. See Figure 3.36.

Submitting required Quick *Setup options*

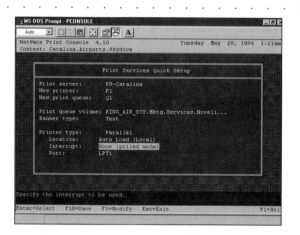

NDS versus Bindery Mode   You may notice in the main menu an option key (F4) that enables you to choose you PCONSOLE views print devices. The main difference between the two is the following:

- In Bindery mode, you *must* authenticate to *each* server with a separate name and password. To view resources, you merely switch which server you are viewing

- In NDS mode, you can browse the tree without further authentications. This means you will only log in once to manage, view, or use print resources.

The following are a few other advantages that PCONSOLE has over NWAdmin:

▸ You can submit existing files for print under PCONSOLE's Print Queues/Print Jobs option by using the Insert key. This can be handy for a quick print if you don't know the command line.

▸ You can identify the print queue's unique ID number (the one the system uses to create the print queue's subdirectory) under Print Queues/ Information. This is mostly handy if you are curious. Find the queue's home volume and look into its subdirectory. You can see the files and setup that NetWare uses to manage part of the printing system.

Summary

You should have a good grasp now on the general aspects of printing under NetWare 4. Although some of the visual aspects of printing are different from NetWare 3, the general printing philosophy remains the same. The tools are more global in scope and you can see that it's more important to view resources in a directory than individual servers as in the past. Printers are not an exception. How effective and easy they are to use still depends on good planning and management. That's where you, the administrator, can really add value.

CHAPTER 4

Print Services Migration

NetWare 4 and Novell Directory Services (NDS) add an entirely new dimension to NetWare print services—a global printing environment. Printers in NetWare 4 are no longer configured on particular file servers as with NetWare 3; they are now global network objects. As such, users can send a job to a printer without having to know the print queue or file server the printer is associated with. In addition, other components of the NetWare print system, which are user- or file-server specific in NetWare 3, are global in NetWare 4. These components are discussed in greater detail later in this chapter.

Chances are likely, if you are reading this chapter, that you have made the decision to upgrade your NetWare 3 file server or file servers to NetWare 4. Congratulations! This is a decision that not only makes printers easier to use but also easier to administer. This chapter provides you with the information necessary to ensure your printing objects in the NetWare 3 bindery are successfully upgraded to NetWare 4 NDS objects.

NOTE

If you have not yet read Chapter 3, "NetWare 4 Print Services— Theory of Operations," you may want to do so now. The information provided explains how NetWare 4 printing works. This information enables you to have a better understanding of the upgrade process.

NetWare 3 vs. NetWare 4 Printing

If you've read Chapters 2 and 3, you should have a pretty good understanding of how printing works under each version of NetWare. But, on the other hand, maybe your head is spinning with concepts that seem to make sense but aren't quite concrete. To make the transition from NetWare 3 to NetWare 4 printing easier, we thought it would be nice to include a quick summary of the differences. We've done this in Table 4.1, as follows.

*NetWare 3 and NetWare 4
printing differences*

COMPONENT	NETWARE 3	NETWARE 4
Printers	NetWare 3 printers are file-server specific and are defined at the time a print server is created. To use NetWare 3 printers, users must capture to the appropriate print queue and log in to the server that contains the print queue. This requires a valid login ID and password.	NetWare 4 printers are global objects that are created independently of file servers and print servers. Users can print to a NetWare 4 printer by simply selecting the printer and sending the print job. They are not required to know the print queue or file server. Because NetWare 4 printers are global objects, users only need to be logged in to the directory tree and have the *browse* right to the printer they wish to use. By default all users are granted the *browse* right to the entire directory tree.
Remote printers	NetWare 3 remote printers can be attached to workstations across the network. The remote printer software is a TSR program called RPRINTER.EXE.	NetWare 4 remote printers can be either workstation attached or file server attached. The remote printer workstation software is a TSR program called NPRINTER.EXE. The remote printer file server software is a NetWare Loadable Module called NPRINTER.NLM.
Print queues	NetWare 3 print queues are subdirectories that, by default, are created in the SYS:SYSTEM directory. The location of NetWare 3 print queues is not configurable, which sometimes causes problems if the SYS: volume is short on disk space. Users must capture to a NetWare 3 print queue in order to print to a desired printer. This requires a valid login ID and password on the file server that contains the print queue.	When a NetWare 4 print queue is created, the administrator can choose the volume location for the print queue subdirectory. Print queues are then created off the chosen volume in a subdirectory called QUEUES. Though users *can* capture to a print queue under NetWare 4, users are not required to know the print queue assigned to a desired printer in order to print to it. In addition, because user IDs are global in NetWare 4, as opposed to server-centric in NetWare 3, users are not required to have multiple user IDs if they wish to use printers serviced by queues on different file servers.
Print servers	Print servers in NetWare 3 are file-server specific. Each print server can support up to 16 printers. A NetWare 3 print server can run on either the file server, using PSERVER.NLM, or on a dedicated workstation using PSERVER.EXE.	Print servers in NetWare 4 are global objects, not associated with a single file server. Each print server can support up to 256 printers. NetWare 4 print servers run only at file servers through the use of PSERVER.NLM. Dedicated workstation print servers are not an option under NetWare 4.

(continued) |

TABLE 4.1

NetWare 3 and NetWare 4
printing differences
(continued)

COMPONENT	NETWARE 3	NETWARE 4
Job configurations	NetWare 3 print job configurations are user-specific and are stored in a database file called PRINTCON.DAT in each user's individual SYS:MAIL subdirectory. Print job configurations cannot be assigned on a global basis but can be copied from one user to another.	NetWare 4 print job configurations are part of the global NDS database and can be assigned on the user or container level. Configurations can be copied using the cut-and-paste feature of Windows.
Print devices	NetWare 3 print devices are file-server specific. If multiple file servers require the same device configuration, the device must be imported on each file server.	NetWare 4 print devices are part of the global NDS database. Device configurations must be imported for each container in which the device is to be used.
Print forms	NetWare 3 print forms are file-server specific and are defined on a per-file-server basis.	NetWare 4 print forms are part of the NDS database and are defined at the container level.

Migrating NetWare 3 Print Services to NetWare 4

Before we jump into a full discussion of upgrading printing, let's run though a quick overview of the how the upgrade from NetWare 3 to NetWare 4 works.

Included with NetWare 4.1 are two utilities that can be used to upgrade NetWare 3 file servers—INSTALL.NLM and MIGRATE.EXE. If you are upgrading to NetWare 4.11, it offers an additional utility, DS MIGRATE. INSTALL.NLM provides an option to perform what is known as an *in-place* upgrade. The in-place upgrade converts an existing NetWare 3 file server to NetWare 4 using the same file server hardware. If a NetWare 2.x file server is being upgraded, the 2XUP-GRDE.NLM is run first to reformat the server's NetWare 2.1x or NetWare 2.2 partition, without losing any data, and transform it into a NetWare 3.1x partition. The NetWare 4.1 installation program is then run to complete the upgrade.

MIGRATE.EXE performs what is known as an *across-the-wire* migration. This method migrates NetWare 3 bindery objects from the NetWare 3 file server, across the network, to a new or existing NetWare 4 file server. This method requires two file servers plus a workstation from which to run MIGRATE.EXE.

You can also use MIGRATE.EXE to perform what is known as a same-server migration. This method migrates bindery objects only. File server data is migrated by performing a backup of the data before the migration is started and then restoring the data after the migration is complete. This method requires only one file server and a workstation to perform the upgrade to NetWare 4. However, there are some risks involved. Specifically, after the backup is complete and the bindery is migrated to a working directory on the workstation, the NetWare 3 server is completely wiped out—yikes!!!—and NetWare 4 is installed in its place. Consequently, this method of upgrade is not commonly used.

NetWare 4.11 added a new upgrade utility, DS MIGRATE, that is a great improvement over previous versions of NetWare 4. If you are migrating your NetWare 3 file server across-the-wire to a NetWare 4.11 server, you should use DS MIGRATE instead of MIGRATE.EXE. The reason for this is that DS MIGRATE is a much more complete utility (it migrates all objects where MIGRATE.EXE does not) and it is much easier to use.

DS MIGRATE enables you to upgrade your NetWare 3 bindery by first modeling the bindery information through an easy-to-use graphical interface and then performing the actual migration. This process provides you with greater flexibility in determining where you want migrated objects to be placed in the directory tree.

Regardless of the upgrade method you use, when a NetWare 3 file server is upgraded to NetWare 4, all of the users and groups defined on that server are automatically upgraded to NDS objects. Printing objects are also upgraded. In some cases, however, additional steps may be required to fully upgrade the NetWare 3 printing system to NetWare 4. These additional steps vary depending on which NetWare upgrade method you use.

The following sections cover the upgrade of NetWare 3 printing services to NetWare 4 in greater detail.

IN-PLACE UPGRADE

When you use the in-place upgrade method to upgrade a NetWare 3 file server to NetWare 4, the NetWare 4 installation program performs the upgrade by replacing the existing NetWare 3 system files with NetWare 4 system files. It also copies NetWare 4 files (SERVER.EXE, LAN drivers, disk drivers, name space support modules, and so on) to the boot directory on the server's DOS partition. NetWare Directory Services (NDS) is then installed and the bindery database is upgraded to an NDS database.

During the upgrade process, a "server context" is selected. This is the location in the NDS tree in which the file server is placed. All bindery objects are placed in the same context as the server that is being upgraded. The following information is upgraded:

- ▶ Users

- ▶ Groups

- ▶ Print servers

- ▶ Print queues

- ▶ Trustee rights

- ▶ Security equivalencies

- ▶ MAIL directories

- ▶ User restrictions (for example, account, password, disk space, connection, and so on)

How Printing is Upgraded

Somehow it seems that printing is a second-class citizen when it comes to upgrades. Whichever upgrade method you choose, additional work always needs to be done when the upgrade utility is finished. When it comes to the in-place upgrade, printing is only partially upgraded.

As indicated previously, print queues and print servers from the NetWare 3 bindery are upgraded to NetWare 4 NDS objects. However, they are only partially upgraded. The print server objects are upgraded, but the print server configuration is not. This approach makes sense because printers are not automatically upgraded. In addition, PRINTCON print job configurations and PRINTDEF forms and devices are not upgraded.

Before you get too worried that you will have a ton of clean-up work to do before your printing is up and running after the upgrade, let's take a look at PUP-GRADE.

Running PUPGRADE   PUPGRADE is an NLM that must be run after the in-place upgrade is complete. It completes your printing upgrade. Specifically, PUP-GRADE does the following:

▸ Upgrades your PRINTCON database—NetWare 3 PRINTCON data-bases are user and file-server specific and are stored in each user's indi-vidual SYS:MAIL subdirectory. NetWare 4 PRINTCON databases are global and are stored as part of the Directory Services database.

▸ Upgrades your PRINTDEF database—As with PRINTCON, PRINTDEF databases in NetWare 3 are file-server specific and are stored in a file call NET$PRN.DAT in the SYS:PUBLIC directory. In NetWare 4, PRINTDEF databases are part of the Directory Services database.

▸ Upgrades your print servers and printers—As mentioned earlier, print servers are only partially upgraded. PUPGRADE converts the print servers to NDS objects and creates the defined printers as NDS objects. In addition, all printer, print queue, and print server assign-ments are reestablished.

To run PUPGRADE, type the following at your newly upgraded file server console:

LOAD PUPGRADE

Figure 4.1 shows the PUPGRADE main menu.

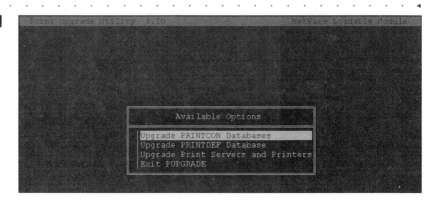

PUPGRADE enables you to complete the upgrade of your printing environment when you use the in-place upgrade method.

Before you are given access to the menu shown in Figure 4.1, you are prompted to log in as ADMIN. Once you provide the login ID and password, you can continue with the upgrade of your printing services.

Upgrading Print Servers and Printers   The first step in upgrading your printing environment is to complete the upgrade of your print servers and printers. When you select the Upgrade Print Servers and Printers option, a list of the print servers defined in the NetWare 3 bindery is shown. When you select the print server you wish to upgrade and press Enter, the upgrade begins. As the upgrade takes place, the upgrade status appears on your screen, as shown in Figure 4.2.

PUPGRADE Print Server Upgrade Status report

```
Print Upgrade Utility 4.10                          NetWare Loadable Module
          Print Server Upgrade Status (press any key to pause)
Print server SLCII_PS is being upgraded.
Printer file PRINT.000 has been found.
    Printer HP4m has been created.
    Print queue HP4_Q/.Hp4 Q.SLC_II.Airports.Skydive has been added.
Printer file PRINT.001 has been found.
    Printer Plotter has been created.
    Print queue PLOTTER_Q/.Plotter Q.SLC_II.Airports.Skydive has been added.
Printer file PRINT.002 has been found.
    Printer Kyle's_Laser has been created.
    Print queue XEROX_Q/.Xerox Q.SLC_II.Airports.Skydive has been added.
Printer file PRINT.003 has been found.
    Printer JD's_Printer has been created.
    Print queue QMS_Q/.Qms Q.SLC_II.Airports.Skydive has been added.
Printer file PRINT.IDX has been found.
    Warning: Printer HP4m renamed to HP4m0
    Printer HP4m0 has been created.
    Print queue HP4_Q/.Hp4 Q.SLC_II.Airports.Skydive has been added.
Printer file PRINT.004 has been found.
Press any key to continue ... ('C' for continuous)
```

If you don't catch all the information on this report while the upgrade is taking place, don't worry. The data is written to a file called *printserver_name.UPG* and is stored in the SYS:SYSTEM directory on your file server.

Because user ADMIN does not exist in NetWare 3, user ADMIN is not included in the list of authorized users for upgraded print queues. In addition, user ADMIN is not included as an authorized operator for upgraded print queues and print servers. Not to worry, though, ADMIN does have the necessary rights to modify the user and operator lists. So, all you need do to solve this is to log in as ADMIN, run NWAdmin, and add the user to the user and operator lists.

Upgrading PRINTCON and PRINTDEF Databases   Upgrading PRINTCON and PRINTDEF databases is just as simple as upgrading print servers and printers. When you select the Upgrade PRINTCON Database option, the upgrade takes place immediately. When you choose Upgrade PRINTDEF Database, you are prompted for a context that you wish for this database to be upgraded to.

As with upgrading print servers and printers, a status report appears on the screen during the upgrade of these databases. After the upgrade, the PRINTCON upgrade report can be viewed in a text file called PRINTCON.UPG, stored in SYS:SYSTEM. The PRINTDEF report can be viewed in a text file called PRINT-DEF.UPG, also stored in SYS:SYSTEM.

What to Do After the Upgrade   Once you've run PUPGRADE, you should verify that your printing environment was successfully upgraded. You should check the following list of items:

1 • Check that all print queues, printers, and print servers were upgraded.

2 • Verify assignments between print queues, printers, and print servers.

3 • Verify print devices at the container level.

4 • Verify print forms at the container level.

5 • Verify each user's print job configurations.

The first step is to verify that all print objects were upgraded. The easiest way to do this is to compare the printing structure on your NetWare 3 file server to what has been migrated to NetWare 4. Ideally, you should make note of your printing environment before the upgrade. Otherwise, you'll have to verify the upgrade based on memory.

To see that the objects were upgraded, log in to your NetWare 4 network as a user with administrative rights in the context the print objects were migrated to. Run the NWAdmin utility and verify that all print queues, printers, and print servers have been upgraded.

The second step is to verify the assignments between the printing objects. You can do this by selecting a print server object in NWAdmin and then choosing Details. In the details screen, you'll find an option called Print Layout. This option enables you to check the assignments with a quick glance. Figure 4.3 shows the print layout for a print server.

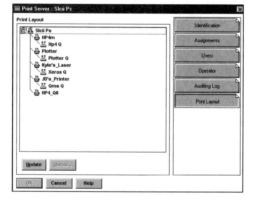

F I G U R E   4.3

The print layout option of a Print Server's details is a quick way to verify that all printing assignments were upgraded properly.

The next step is to verify print devices at the container level. Again this can be done in NWAdmin by selecting the container object the devices were upgraded to. Choose Details and then Print Devices. Print forms can be verified by choosing Print Forms in the Details screen.

The last step is to verify that all users' print job configurations were properly upgraded. You can do this by choosing each individual user in NWAdmin, selecting Details, and then selecting Job Configurations.

All of the preceding actions can also be done using the DOS-based PCONSOLE utility. For details on using the NetWare 4 version of PCONSOLE, refer to Chapter 7, "Managing NetWare 4 Print Services."

NOTE

ACROSS-THE-WIRE MIGRATION

When an across-the-wire migration is performed, data files are migrated across the network, from a source NetWare 3 server to a new or existing NetWare 4 server. Bindery information is migrated to a working directory on the workstation MIGRATE.EXE is run from. Once migrated to the workstation, the bindery is translated to NDS and copied to the NetWare 4 server. The objects are placed in the *bindery context* of the NetWare 4 server. This is illustrated in Figure 4.4.

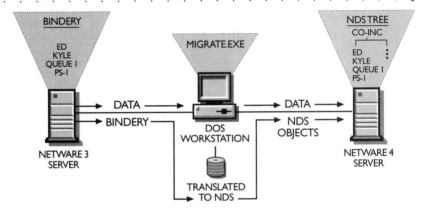

FIGURE 4.4

An across-the-wire migration migrates NetWare 3 file server data and bindery information across the network to a NetWare 4 server.

Before beginning the migration, the type of migration you wish to perform must be defined in the migration utility. The options include the following:

▸ The type of migration (across-the-wire or same-server)

▸ The server type you are migrating from (source LAN type)

▸ The server type you are migrating to (destination LAN type)

Once this information has been provided, the configuration screen shown in Figure 4.5 is presented.

FIGURE 4.5

Configuring the migration parameters in the migration utility

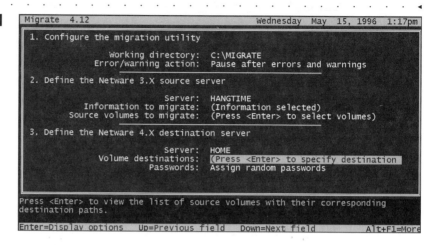

```
Migrate  4.12                           Wednesday  May  15, 1996  1:17pm
┌─────────────────────────────────────────────────────────────────────┐
│ 1. Configure the migration utility                                    │
│                                                                       │
│              Working directory:  C:\MIGRATE                           │
│           Error/warning action:  Pause after errors and warnings      │
│                                                                       │
│ 2. Define the Netware 3.X source server                               │
│                                                                       │
│                        Server:  HANGTIME                              │
│         Information to migrate:  (Information selected)                │
│      Source volumes to migrate:  (Press <Enter> to select volumes)    │
│                                                                       │
│ 3. Define the Netware 4.X destination server                          │
│                                                                       │
│                        Server:  HOME                                  │
│           Volume destinations:  (Press <Enter> to specify destination │
│                     Passwords:  Assign random passwords               │
│                                                                       │
└───────────────────────────────────────────────────────────────────────┘
 Press <Enter> to view the list of source volumes with their corresponding
 destination paths.
 Enter=Display options   Up=Previous field   Down=Next field      Alt+F1=More
```

This menu is used to define the parameters of the migration such as the source server, destination server, and the information to be migrated. To select a source and destination server, you must be authenticated to both as SUPERVISOR or the equivalent. Because the migration utility is bindery based, it requires a bindery connection to the NetWare 4 server.

Before running MIGRATE.EXE, log out of all servers and use the migration utility to log in to the source and destination servers. This ensures that you have bindery connections on both file servers.

TIP

One major benefit of using MIGRATE.EXE is that you have the ability to select the information you wish to migrate. For example, you can choose to migrate all information, or just data files or bindery information. Figure 4.6 shows the individual information that can be selected for migration.

Selecting the information to migrate

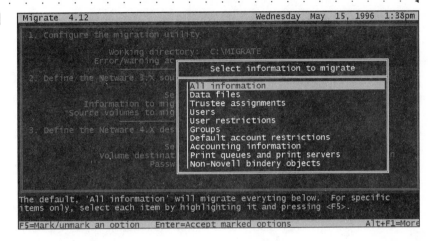

When all information to be migrated has been defined, the migration can be started by simply pressing the F10 key.

Migrating Print Services

Though Figure 4.6 shows an option to migrate print queues and print servers, it is a bit misleading. When you select this option, you are presented with the message shown in Figure 4-7.

MIGRATE.EXE migrates all bindery information except printing.

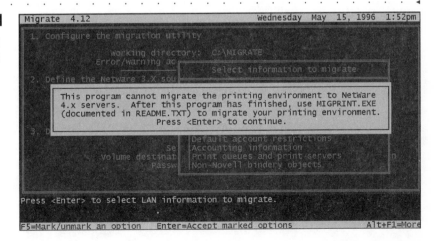

You're probably wondering, "If this program can't migrate printing, why even put the option on the menu?" Rest assured, there are some valid reasons for it. First, and probably foremost, this utility can be used to migrate many different environments: NetWare 2 to NetWare 3, NetWare 3 to NetWare 4, or even LAN Manager or LAN Server to NetWare. In most of these scenarios, printing *can* be migrated with this utility.

Another reason the printing option is on this menu is so you'll receive that ugly little message reminding you that you'll need to run MIGPRINT.EXE to complete your printing migration.

So, the next question becomes: Why isn't the MIGPRINT functionality built into MIGRATE? That one, friends, we can't answer. It could be that time ran out and the code just didn't get done in time. So, the quick fix is a command-line utility.

But, rather than wasting time speculating, accept it as is and move on. To put it another way, acknowledge and proceed. With that in mind, the details of MIGPRINT are covered next.

Migrating Printing with MIGPRINT   After MIGRATE.EXE has been run and the desired data and bindery information have been migrated, MIGPRINT can be used to migrate the NetWare 3 printing environment to NetWare 4. Well, most of it anyway. MIGPRINT migrates the following:

- ▶ Print servers

- ▶ Printers

- ▶ Print job configurations

Unfortunately, MIGPRINT does not migrate your entire NetWare 3 printing environment. What it does not migrate is the following:

- ▶ Print queues

- ▶ Print devices

- ▶ Print forms

The fact that these items are not migrated means that you may have a bit of work to do to get printing working after the migration. The amount of work depends on the size of your printing environment.

If you have a small printing environment, it may just be easier for you to re-create all of your printing objects from scratch. Creating and configuring printing with the NetWare 4 administration utilities is quick and easy (as described in Chapter 3). So, if you only have one print server and fewer than five printers, don't even bother with MIGPRINT. It is probably faster just to re-create everything.

However, if you have more than five printers and have print job configurations set up for your users, MIGPRINT is probably faster than recreating all printing objects.

Running MIGPRINT   If you experiment with MIGPRINT, you will find that it is not very intuitive or very well documented. So, to save you time, we have done the experimenting for you and have provided a list of things you need to do before running MIGPRINT. That list is as follows:

1 • Run MIGRATE.EXE.

2 • Verify the server's bindery context.

3 • Log in to the NetWare 4 file server.

4 • Log in to the NetWare 3 file server.

5 • Map a search drive to the SYS:SYSTEM\NLS directory on the NetWare 4 file server.

6 • Run MIGPRINT.

To help you understand why you need to do each step, let's go into each one in detail.

The first step is to run MIGRATE.EXE to migrate all users and groups to the NetWare 4 directory tree. This step is very important because MIGPRINT must be able to find the user and group IDs in order to migrate user and operator authorizations properly. For example, when a print server is migrated, MIGPRINT automatically assigns the same print server operators if those user accounts already exist. This is also the case if user print job configurations are being migrated. The user objects must exist in order for their print job configurations to be migrated properly.

Second, be sure that the NetWare 4 file server's bindery context is set to the same location in the directory tree that the users and groups were migrated to. Because MIGPRINT is a bindery-based utility, it places the printing objects in the file server's bindery context. As described previously, MIGPRINT must be able to find the user and group IDs in the context the printing objects are being migrated to. A file server's bindery context can be set or viewed either from the file server command line or by using the SERVMAN utility.

To view the bindery context from the file server command line, type the following:

```
SET BINDERY CONTEXT
```

A message similar to the following appears:

```
Bindery Context: OU=SLC_II.OU=AIRPORTS.O=SKYDIVE

    Maximum length:   255

        Can be set in the startup ncf file

        Description:   The NetWare Directory Services container
                       where bindery services are provided. Set
                       multiple contexts by separating contexts
                       with semicolons.
```

To change the current bindery context from the file server command line, use the SET command with the following syntax:

```
SET BINDERY CONTEXT = .OU=OrgUnitname.OU=OrgUnitname.O=Orgname
```

To set or verify the file server's bindery context using the SERVMAN utility, type the following from the file server console:

```
LOAD SERVMAN
```

SERVMAN is an NLM utility that simplifies the SET command as well as enabling you to view file server statistics. To view or modify the bindery context, select Server Parameters and then Directory Services from the SERVMAN main menu. A screen similar to the one shown in Figure 4.8 appears.

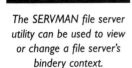

FIGURE 4.8

The SERVMAN file server utility can be used to view or change a file server's bindery context.

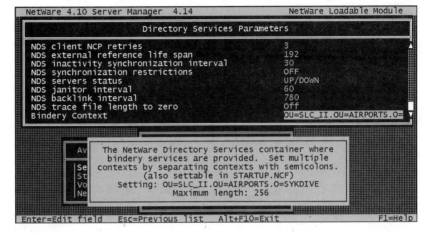

```
NetWare 4.10 Server Manager   4.14              NetWare Loadable Module
                         Directory Services Parameters
  NDS client NCP retries                         3
  NDS external reference life span               192
  NDS inactivity synchronization interval        30
  NDS synchronization restrictions               OFF
  NDS servers status                             UP/DOWN
  NDS janitor interval                           60
  NDS backlink interval                          780
  NDS trace file length to zero                  Off
  Bindery Context                                OU=SLC_II.OU=AIRPORTS.O=

   Av
          The NetWare Directory Services container where
     Se     bindery services are provided.  Set multiple
     St   contexts by separating contexts with semicolons.
     Vo             (also settable in STARTUP.NCF)
     Ne       Setting: OU=SLC_II.OU=AIRPORTS.O=SYKDIVE
                        Maximum length: 256

  Enter=Edit field    Esc=Previous list    Alt+F10=Exit            F1=Help
```

The next steps that must be completed before running MIGPRINT are to log in to the source and destination file servers. In both cases you need to be logged in as users with sufficient rights to perform the migration. On the NetWare 4 server you should be logged in as an ADMIN or equivalent user. On the NetWare 3 server you should be logged in as SUPERVISOR or an equivalent user.

Once logged in, you need to map a search drive to the SYS:SYSTEM\NLS directory. This directory contains language and message files necessary to run MIGPRINT. The following example shows the required drive mapping:

```
MAP S16:=HOME\SYS:SYSTEM\NLS
```

Using *S16*: when mapping search drives automatically maps the next available search drive.

TIP

After you complete all of the preceding steps, you are ready to run MIGPRINT. MIGPRINT.EXE can be found on the NetWare 4 CD in a directory called MIGRATE. You can run the utility directly from the CD or from a workstation subdirectory if the workstation you are using does not have a CD-ROM drive. If you plan to run it from a workstation subdirectory, you need to copy not only MIGPRINT.EXE but the necessary language and message files to your workstation. The easiest way is to simply copy the entire migrate directory to your workstation. It only takes about 1.5MB of disk space and can be deleted after the migration is complete.

Unfortunately, MIGPRINT isn't one of the most elegant utilities you will encounter. It's not GUI or even C-Worthy for that matter. It's a good ol' command-line utility. The syntax for MIGPRINT is as follows:

```
MIGPRINT /S=srcSrvr /D=dstSrvr [/VOL=queueVol] [/O=outputFile]
```

Unlike other NetWare command-line utilities, there are no shortcuts for MIGPRINT. In other words, the syntax must be entered as shown, slashes included. The /VOL and /O parameters are optional, as indicated by the brackets. Table 4.2 provides a definition for each parameter.

TABLE 4.2	PARAMETER	DEFINITION
MIGPRINT parameter definitions	/S=srcsrvr	The name of the source NetWare 3 server you are migrating printing information from.
	/D=dstSrvr	The name of the destination NetWare 4 server you are migrating printing information to.
	[/VOL=queueVol]	The name of the volume in which the print queues are created if other than the default SYS:. This parameter is optional unless no volume object exists in the bindery context.
	[/O=outputFile]	The name of the output file you wish to be created if you don't want to migrate to the default file. This parameter is optional.

Here is an example of how the MIGPRINT syntax would look:

```
MIGPRINT /S=HANGTIME /D=HOME /VOL=SYS:
```

Notice that the /VOL parameter was used. As indicated in Table 4.2, this is an optional parameter that allows you to tell MIGPRINT which volume the print queues should be created on. . . . But wait! If you were reading carefully, you will have noticed that MIGPRINT doesn't migrate print queues. What does this tell us? Well, that MIGPRINT was *supposed* to migrate print queues but doesn't. Here's the real clincher: MIGPRINT still looks for a volume and tries to create the print queues. In fact, as you run the utility the first things you see are error messages indicating that the print queues could not be created. Because MIGPRINT looks for a volume to create the queues on, if no volume exists in the bindery context you are migrating the printing objects to, you must specify a volume in the MIGPRINT syntax. (Remember, don't waste cycles trying to figure out why; acknowledge and proceed.) But, rest assured, the problems with MIGPRINT will be corrected in the next version of NetWare.

As you run MIGPRINT, a report of the migration progress is displayed on your screen. This report is saved in a file named MP000.RPT if this is the first time you've run MIGPRINT, MP001.RPT if this is the second time, and so on. Figure 4.9 shows an example of a typical MIGPRINT report.

FIGURE 4.9

A sample MIGPRINT report

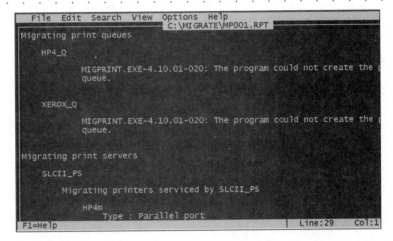

In the MIGPRINT report shown in Figure 4.9, notice the message indicating that the program could not create the print queue XEROX_Q. As indicated previously, this is normal for the version of MIGPRINT that ships with NetWare 4.1.

What to Do After the Migration   Once you've run MIGPRINT, you'll need to take some additional steps before your printing system is fully converted. These steps are as follows:

1 • Verify the migration.

2 • Re-create print queues.

3 • Assign print queues to service printers.

4 • Import print devices.

5 • Re-create print forms.

The first step is to verify that the migration was successful. The easiest way to do this is to compare the printing structure on your NetWare 3 file server to what has been migrated to NetWare 4. This is another major advantage of an across-the-wire migration: Your NetWare 3 file server remains intact and is unmodified by the migration. To do this, log in to your NetWare 3 file server as SUPERVISOR or equivalent and run PCONSOLE. Make note of the following particulars:

- ▸ Print queues (these need to be re-created later)

- ▸ Print queue users and operators

- ▸ Print servers

- ▸ Printers

- ▸ Queues serviced by printers

- ▸ Print server users and operators

While you are logged in to your NetWare 3 server, also run PCONSOLE to make note of user print job configurations defined. In addition, run PRINTDEF and make note of the print devices imported as well as print forms defined. These need to be re-created.

Now, log in to your NetWare 4 network as a user with administrative rights in the context the print objects were migrated to. Run the NWAdmin utility and verify that the items listed previously were migrated.

After you have verified that the migration was successful, you need to re-create your print queues and assign the print queues to service printers. In addition, you may need to assign print queue users and operators if the default is not sufficient for your network. The default is that all users in the container will be assigned as print queue users and ADMIN will be assigned as a print queue operator. For details on creating print queues and making assignments, refer back to Chapter 3—"NetWare 4 Print Services—Theory of Operations."

The final step in completing your print system configuration is to import any print devices you may have had in your NetWare 3 environment and re-create any print forms. Again, for details on how to do this, refer back to Chapter 3.

USING DS MIGRATE

DS MIGRATE is a migration and modeling utility developed by Novell and Preferred Systems, Inc. (PSI). DS MIGRATE is a subset of PSI's DS STANDARD utility, which is a leading NDS management product. As mentioned earlier, DS MIGRATE was added in the 4.11 release of NetWare 4 and should be used in place of MIGRATE.EXE when migrating bindery information across-the-wire to a NetWare 4.11 server.

How DS MIGRATE Works

DS MIGRATE allows NetWare 3 bindery information to be migrated across-the-wire to a new or existing NetWare 4.11 directory tree. The compelling feature of DS MIGRATE is that it allows you to model the bindery information prior to per-forming the migration. This eliminates the need to move the objects to their desired location after the migration is complete.

DS MIGRATE is run from the Tools menu of the NetWare 4.11 version of NWAdmin. When run, it converts the following bindery objects to NDS objects:

▸ Users

▸ Groups

▸ Print queues

▸ Printers

▸ Print servers

NetWare 3 file information is migrated using the File Migration utility that is also run from the Tools menu of the NetWare 4.11 version of NWAdmin.

DS MIGRATE migrates the bindery through a three-step process, as follows:

1 • The Discover step

2 • The Model step

3 • The Configure step

The Discover Step   The first phase of the DS MIGRATE process is the Discover step. During this phase, the DS MIGRATE utility "discovers" the bindery information of the NetWare 3 server that the network administrator has specified. This information is then placed in the DS MIGRATE database that is saved on the server in the BINDDISC.LOG file. This information is presented to the administrator in a graphical format that looks like an NDS tree. The administrator can then use that data to model the desired tree structure.

The Model Step   After the bindery is discovered and displayed in a graphical NDS tree-like structure, the structure is saved in a "view." The network administrator then modifies the view to create the desired tree structure. The view can be modified by adding or deleting objects, moving objects, granting or deleting rights, and so on.

The key to the Modeling step is that changes made in the view do not affect the actual NDS tree until those changes are merged to the actual tree during the Configure step.

The Configure Step   When the administrator has created a view that meets his or her needs, that view can then be merged with an existing NetWare 4.11 directory tree. This is done by logging in to the NetWare 4.11 server, opening the view that was configured previously, and then choosing the Configure option of the NWAdmin Tools/Options menu. Then, when all replicas have been updated, the new bindery information becomes part of the directory tree.

Printing Considerations when using DS MIGRATE

When you run DS MIGRATE you can see why it is the recommended way to migrate NetWare 3 binderies across-the-wire. It's easy to use and you get to determine where the migrated objects are placed in the directory tree. From the printing perspective, it is also the most complete migration utility because it doesn't require you to run additional utilities to finish the printing migration.

The only considerations that need to be made in migrating printing are in the Modeling step. Print queues will need to be modified to reflect the new NetWare 4.11 volume names where the queue directories reside and print job configurations may need to be modified to reflect any new print queue information. Once those changes are made in the Modeling phase, however, the correct information is migrated to the directory tree in the Configure phase with no clean-up work required.

Summary

As you can see, migrating your printing environment to NetWare 4 is not diffi-cult but, with the exception of 4.11's DS MIGRATE, it does take some follow-up work after the standard NetWare upgrade process. Once you've upgraded one file server, the others go quickly. However, because most companies upgrade their NetWare 3 networks to NetWare 4 one file server at a time, and it may be weeks or even months between upgrades, the following chapter provides information on coexistence. So, if you have more than one file server and happen to have some time between upgrades, move on to Chapter 5, which provides you with the details of using and administering a mixed NetWare 3 and NetWare 4 printing environment.

CHAPTER 5

Coexistence

If you are an administrator of a network with multiple file servers, you know that an upgrade of those servers generally can't take place overnight. In most cases, that upgrade won't even take place over a weekend. A real-life upgrade scenario would entail upgrading one or two file servers to NetWare 4, and letting them run a while to work out any problems before upgrading the remaining NetWare 3 servers.

Coexistence is what happens between the upgrades—some servers are running NetWare 4 and some are still running NetWare 3, coexisting on the same network. This chapter discusses the issues involved with managing and using a mixed NetWare 3 and NetWare 4 printing environment.

A mixed NetWare 3 and NetWare 4 environment presents three main printing challenges:

1 • NetWare 3 users printing to NetWare 4 printers

2 • NetWare 4 users printing to NetWare 3 printers

3 • Managing a mixed NetWare 3 and NetWare 4 printing environment

We cover each of these issues in detail in this chapter.

NetWare 3 Users Printing to NetWare 4 Printers

The goal of most administrators is to make the network as transparent to the users as possible. What this entails is enabling users to not only access files and directories on file servers other than their default, but also to print their documents without any hint of a hitch. In a NetWare 3 only environment you have two ways to enable users to share printing services across multiple file servers:

▸ Create login IDs for each user on each file server

▸ Use the predefined GUEST account

The first option is effective but very administration-intensive. In this case, the administrator must not only create and maintain multiple login IDs for each user but also multiple passwords. For users to be transparently attached to each file server through their login scripts, login IDs and passwords must be consistent across each file server. If they are not consistent, the user may be required to enter multiple login IDs and passwords during login. The benefit to this method of access to multiple file servers is that it offers greater security than using the GUEST account. The administrator has the ability to grant each user individual access rights on each file server.

When the GUEST account is used, every user that accesses a server has the same set of access rights. The benefit to using this account, however, is that the NetWare 3 CAPTURE utility is designed to automatically authenticate a user as GUEST when the /S= option is used.

For example, say user KYLE is logged in to his default NetWare 3 file server and wishes to use a printer defined on file server HANGTIME, to which he is not currently attached. He issues the following CAPTURE statement:

```
CAPTURE /S=HANGTIME /Q=HP4_Q NB NFF TI=15
```

If the GUEST account exists on server HANGTIME and has no password, KYLE is automatically attached to that file server and is captured to the queue specified. If the GUEST account does not exist—let's say it was deleted for security reasons—the user is prompted for a valid login ID and password.

So, what does all this have to do with a NetWare 3 user printing to a NetWare 4 printing environment? Well, NetWare 3 users use NetWare 4 printing services in this fashion, either by having a login ID on each file server and ATTACH statements in their login scripts, or by using the GUEST account. However, be aware of a few caveats.

First, Bindery Services must be enabled on the NetWare 4 server. Bindery Services lets a container in the NDS (Novell Directory Services) tree emulate a flat-file bindery database so that bindery utilities, such as the NetWare 3 CAPTURE command, can recognize the database structure and access the objects as if they were defined on a NetWare 3 file server. Bindery Services are enabled by using the SET BINDERY CONTEXT command at the file server console, as described in Chapter 4 (see the section on MIGPRINT). Login IDs to be used by NetWare 3 users must be created in a container defined as the file server's Bindery context.

Second, the GUEST account is not a default account under NetWare 4, so it must be manually created. This account also needs to be created in the file server's bindery context. Once created in the bindery context of a NetWare 4 server, the NetWare 3 CAPTURE command transparently authenticates to the NetWare 4 server when the /S= parameter is used, as described previously.

NetWare 4 Users Printing to NetWare 3 Printers

NetWare 4 takes a global approach to user access of network resources. Consequently, NetWare 4 enables users to print to NetWare 3 printers with much less administrative effort. In fact, NDS allows a bindery-based print queue to be created as an object in the directory tree. The result? NDS users print to NetWare 3 printers by simply sending a print job to a print queue object defined in the NDS tree. Print jobs are sent directly to the queue on the NetWare 3 file server and are printed accordingly. Authentication to the NetWare 3 file server takes place transparently through the GUEST account, if it exists. If the GUEST account has been deleted or has a password assigned, the NetWare 4 user is prompted for a login name and/or a password.

A bindery-based queue in the NDS tree can be created by using either the Windows-based NWAdmin or the DOS-based PCONSOLE utility.

CREATING A BINDERY QUEUE USING NWADMIN

To create a bindery queue using NWAdmin, log in to the NDS tree as a user with administrative rights over the container where you wish to create the print queue. Run the NWAdmin utility from your Windows 3.1 or Windows 95 desktop.

Once in NWAdmin, select the container in which you wish to create the bindery print queue and press the Insert key (or select Object and then Create from the menu bar). From the New Object menu, use the mouse or arrow keys to select Print Queue as the new type of object you wish to create. The dialog box shown in Figure 5.1 appears.

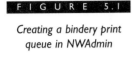

Creating a bindery print queue in NWAdmin

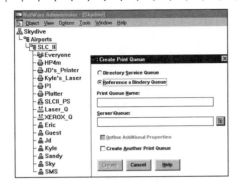

Notice the two options for the type of print queue you wish to create: Directory Service Queue or Reference a Bindery Queue. Use the mouse to click the Reference a Bindery Queue radio button.

When you create a bindery queue, you are creating an NDS object that is simply a pointer to a bindery print queue defined on a NetWare 3 or other bindery based server. So the next step is to select the NetWare 3 file server and print queue you wish to reference. To do this, select the Browse button next to the Server/Queue field. A list of the currently attached servers is displayed. If the NetWare 3 server you desire is not listed, deselect the List Only Attached Servers box. You are then prompted to log in to this server. You need to log in as SUPERVISOR or a SUPERVISOR equivalent. A list of the print queues defined on the NetWare 3 server is displayed, as shown in Figure 5.2.

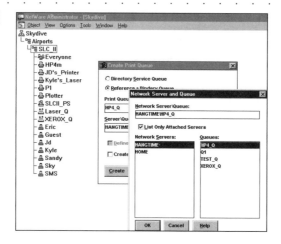

F I G U R E   5.2

Selecting the bindery print queue to reference in NWAdmin

Highlight the bindery print queue you wish to reference and click OK. The Create Print Queue dialog box is displayed again. Verify that the server and print queue selected are correct and click Create.

Once a bindery reference queue is created in the NDS tree, NetWare 4 users can send print jobs directly to the queue and the jobs are redirected to the physical queue defined on a NetWare 3 file server. The jobs are then routed by a NetWare 3 print server to the printer assigned to service the print queue.

CREATING A BINDERY QUEUE USING PCONSOLE

To create a bindery queue using PCONSOLE, log in to the NDS tree as a user with administrative rights over the container where you wish to create the print queue. Run PCONSOLE from the DOS command line. Once in PCONSOLE, verify the context shown at the top of the screen. If necessary, use the Change Context option to move to the proper context.

From the Available Options menu, select Print Queues. A list of the print queues currently created in this context is displayed, as shown in Figure 5.3.

FIGURE 5.3

Currently defined print queues in PCONSOLE

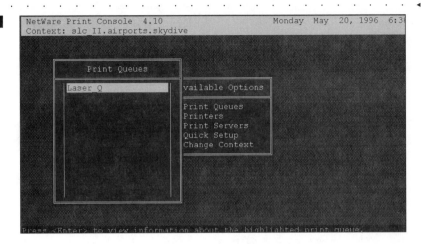

FIGURE 5.3

Currently defined print queues in PCONSOLE

Notice the options at the bottom of the screen. To create a bindery reference queue, press the F6 key. You need to select the file server where the actual print queue resides. This could be a NetWare 3 server or a NetWare 4 server in another directory tree. If you are not already attached to the server, press the Insert key to display a list of available servers. Log in to the desired server as a user with administrative rights. For example, you need to log in to a NetWare 3 server as SUPERVISOR or a SUPERVISOR equivalent. Once logged in, the server name appears on the list of available servers. Highlight the server and press Enter. A list of the bindery print queues defined on that server is displayed, as shown in Figure 5.4.

FIGURE 5.4

Creating a bindery reference print queue in NetWare 4's PCONSOLE

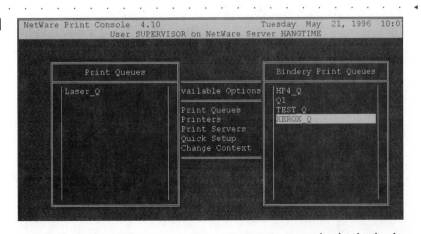

Select the desired print queue and press Enter. The bindery reference print queue is then created in the NDS context selected earlier. Once a bindery reference queue is created in the NDS tree, NetWare 4 users can send print jobs directly to the queue and the jobs are redirected to the physical queue defined on a NetWare 3 file server. The jobs are then routed by a NetWare 3 print server to the printer assigned to service the queue.

Managing a Mixed NetWare 3 and NetWare 4 Printing Environment

With each release of a NetWare operating system, Novell strives to provide complete backward compatibility. In the past, backward compatibility meant enabling users to access resources and services across all versions of NetWare. With NetWare 4, Novell has extended backward compatibility to not only enable access to resources and services but also to enable the management of resources and services. For a mixed NetWare 3 and NetWare 4 printing environment, NetWare 4 provides backward-compatible management in two ways:

▸ Bimodal printing utilities

▸ NETSYNC

BIMODAL PRINTING UTILITIES

All of NetWare 4's text-based (C-Worthy) printing utilities are bimodal. What this means is that both NetWare 3 and NetWare 4 printing services can be administered with the same utilities. The bimodal utilities included with NetWare 4 include the following:

▸ PCONSOLE

▸ PRINTCON

▸ PRINTDEF

Each of these utilities provides an F4 option at the bottom of the main menu. By pressing F4, you can switch to Bindery Mode, enabling you to administer and create printing services on bindery-based file servers such as NetWare 3. As we cover each of these bimodal utilities, you will see that the NetWare 4 versions are easier to use and in some cases provide additional functionality. As a result, Novell recommends that you use the NetWare 4 version of these utilities on all NetWare 3 servers after the first NetWare 4 server is installed on your network. In fact, the NetWare 4.1 Upgrade manual recommends that you copy the entire SYS:PUBLIC directory to any NetWare 3 or NetWare 2 file servers on your network that have not yet been upgraded to NetWare 4. If you choose to do this, refer to the Upgrade manual for specific instructions. Rather than copying the entire PUBLIC directory, you may want to just copy the printing utilities. These include the following utilities:

- CAPTURE.EXE

- NPRINT.EXE

- NPRINTER.EXE

- NPRINTER.NLM

- PCONSOLE.EXE

- PRINTCON.EXE

- PRINTDEF.EXE

- PSC.EXE

In addition to the executable files, you also need the support files for each of these utilities. These include their associated *.MSG and *.HEP files. However, before you get too "copy happy," read on. In the case of the printing utilities, there may be reason to keep the NetWare 3 versions of the utilities.

PCONSOLE

The NetWare 4 version of PCONSOLE can be used to completely manage both NetWare 3 and NetWare 4 printing services. In the case of this utility, there is no reason to keep the NetWare 3 version because the NetWare 4 version provides the same functionality and then some. Figure 5.5 shows the NetWare 3 PCONSOLE main menu.

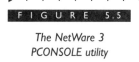

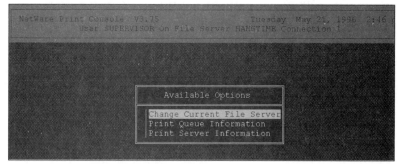

The NetWare 3 PCONSOLE utility

Figure 5.6 shows the NetWare 4 version of PCONSOLE in Bindery Mode.

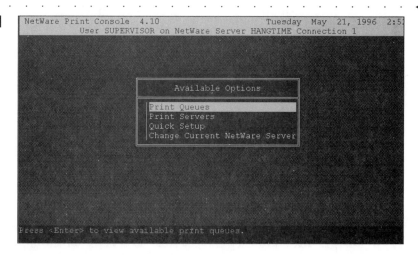

FIGURE 5.6

NetWare 4 PCONSOLE in Bindery Mode

There are two differences between the two versions of the utilities. Notice that the NetWare 4 version adds a Quick Setup option. This option extends one of the greatest enhancements of the NetWare 4 printing services to NetWare 3—the ability to create a print server, printer, and print queue all at once and have the proper assignments made automatically.

The second difference is the menu bar at the bottom of the screen that shows the available actions. Notice the F4 option to switch back to Directory Services mode. This option enables the administrator to manage a NetWare 4 printing environment with the same utility.

PRINTCON

Though PRINTCON is a bimodal utility and can be used to manage both NetWare 3 and NetWare 4 print job configurations, under certain circumstances you may still need the NetWare 3 version. The reason for this is that the NetWare 4 version of PRINTCON stores the print job configuration database differently from the NetWare 3 version. The NetWare 4 version of the utility does not recognize (and therefore cannot be used to manage) the old database format and the NetWare 3 version does not recognize the new database format. This dilemma is described in greater detail below.

In NetWare 3, print job configurations created with PRINTCON are stored as database files named PRINTCON.DAT. These files are stored in each user's SYS:MAIL subdirectory. NetWare 3 print job configurations are user-specific and can be copied between users but cannot be assigned on a global basis. NetWare 4 print job configurations can be assigned on a per-user basis or globally at the container level. The job configurations are part of the NDS database and are stored as properties of the user or container for which they are created.

When the NetWare 4 version of PRINTCON is switched to Bindery Mode by pressing the F4 key, it can be used to create and manage PRINTCON databases on NetWare 3 servers. This version of PRINTCON adds additional functionality to NetWare 3, enabling the creation of both private and global PRINTCON databases. This is shown in Figure 5.7.

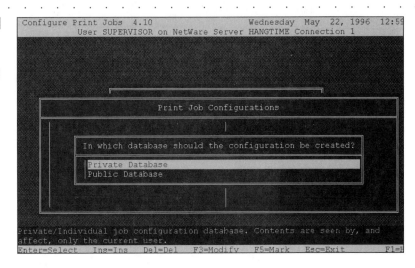

FIGURE 5.7

FIGURE 5.7

The NetWare 4 version of PRINTCON enables the creation of both private and public job configuration databases on NetWare 3 servers.

Private databases are individual user databases that are still stored in each user's SYS:MAIL subdirectory in NetWare 3 (they are properties of the user object in NetWare 4). However, to prevent confusion with the old database format, the file-name has been changed to PRINTJOB.DAT.

Public databases can be used by all users of the NetWare 3 file server. For any administrator who has spent countless hours copying print job configurations between users, the addition of global databases in NetWare 3 is a sight for sore eyes. Public databases are stored in the SYS:PUBLIC directory of the NetWare 3 server in a file also called PRINTJOB.DAT.

Old and new PRINTCON databases can coexist. If you want to maintain the old ones, however, you need to use the NetWare 3 utilities to do it. Switching to Bindery Mode in the new utilities does not maintain the old databases. Bindery Mode only enables you to maintain a bindery version of the new databases. To maintain the new databases you need to use the NetWare 4 utilities.

Although the NetWare 4 manuals say there is little reason to maintain NetWare 3 databases and recommend that you delete them, there may be circumstances where you need to keep them—for example, if you are using UNIX, any third-party utilities that use the old database format, or if you are using third-party utilities to maintain the database.

Also, there is no method to convert the old database format to the new one; consequently, any existing job configurations need to be created using the NetWare 4 version of the utility. At first glance you're probably thinking that this will be a tremendous amount of work that may not be worth the effort. However, remember that in many cases NetWare 3 users are using the same job configurations but were required to have separate databases because there was no such thing as a global PRINTCON database. These databases, like job configurations, can now be created as one public job configuration instead of numerous private job configurations.

You need to be aware of one final matter. If you are using the new database format on your NetWare 3 servers, you not only need to use the NetWare 4 version of PRINTCON to maintain the job configurations, you also need to use the NetWare 4 version of the utilities to use them. This includes CAPTURE and PCONSOLE.

PRINTDEF

The NetWare 4 version of PRINTDEF, like PCONSOLE and PRINTCON, is also a bimodal utility. By pressing the F4 key, you can switch between Bindery Mode and Directory Services Mode, enabling you to manage the PRINTDEF database on both NetWare 3 and NetWare 4 file servers.

Also, like PRINTCON, the NetWare 4 version of PRINTDEF creates a new database format. Any print devices or forms created on a NetWare 3 server with this version are stored in a database file called PRINTDEF.DAT stored in the SYS:PUBLIC directory. The NetWare 3 version of the database was stored in a file called NET$PRN.DAT, also in SYS:PUBLIC. Again, the new database format must be maintained and used with the NetWare 4 version of the utilities, and the old database format must be maintained and used with the NetWare 3 version of the utilities.

NETSYNC

In addition to the bimodal utilities, NetWare 4 provides another option for managing a mixed NetWare 3 and NetWare 4 printing environment—NETSYNC. NETSYNC is a management utility that extends the benefits of NDS, such as a central point of administration, to the NetWare 3 environment. It does this by synchronizing the Binderies of up to 12 NetWare 3 file servers to the bindery context of a single NetWare 4 file server. Initially, synchronization is bidirectional, thus any objects in the bindery context of the NetWare 4 server are copied down to the 3.x servers as well. Figure 5.8 illustrates this process.

F I G U R E   5.8

With NETSYNC, NetWare 3 Binderies are synchronized with a NetWare 4 server's Bindery context.

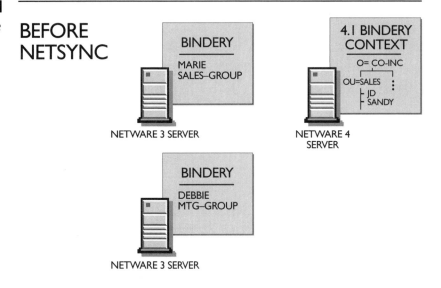

BEFORE NETSYNC

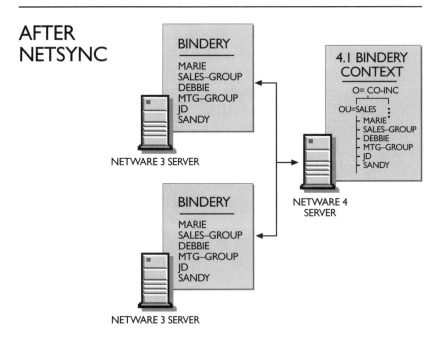

AFTER NETSYNC

NETSYNC enables the NetWare 3 file servers to be managed through NDS using the NDS administration utilities. This capability provides a central point of administration for not only NetWare 4 but also for the NetWare 3 environment.

Once a NETSYNC link has been established, any changes made in the NetWare 4 bindery context are synchronized down to the binderies of the NetWare 3 servers in the NETSYNC cluster. Although administration can take place from the NetWare 3 utilities, synchronization from the bindery to NDS does not take place automatically. Because of this circumstance, once a NETSYNC link is established it is recommended that all administration take place from NDS utilities.

NETSYNC is a series of NLMs that are loaded on both the NetWare 3 and NetWare 4 file servers. For specific information on these NLMs and how they are used, please refer to the NetWare 4 manuals. Because this is a printing book, this section covers how NETSYNC affects printing only.

How NETSYNC Affects Your Printing Environment

As just mentioned, when a NETSYNC link is established, all objects in the bindery of your NetWare 3 servers are synchronized with NDS. From the printing perspective, only print queues are synchronized. Unfortunately, managing print queues through NETSYNC doesn't quite work in the same manner as managing users or groups. When the print queues are synchronized, they are created as NDS print queues on the SYS: volume of the NetWare 4.1 server. Because the associated print server and printers from the NetWare 3 environment are not synchronized, the queues are created without print server and print queue assignments. In order for the synchronized print queues to be functional, you must assign a valid print server and printer to service the queues. Any modifications made to these print queues after the initial NETSYNC synchronization are not synchronized down to the NetWare 3 environment.

So you're probably wondering, "What good is NETSYNC for printing?" NETSYNC has another option for managing printing: moving NetWare 3.x print servers to NDS. This process enables you to merge one or more 3.x print servers into one print server on the NetWare 4 server. It also places your 3.x printers into the NetWare 4.1 Directory, where they can be managed from a single NetWare 4.1 print server. We'll cover the moving of print servers and printers later in this chapter.

Using NetWare 4 Utilities in Your NetWare 3 Environment

Another way NETSYNC affects your printing environment is that it replaces all of the NetWare 3 printing utilities with their NetWare 4 counterparts. This is an automatic process that happens when you load the NETSYNC NLMs on your NetWare 3 and NetWare 4 servers. The utilities that are copied include the following:

- ▸ CAPTURE

- ▸ NPRINT (.NLM and .EXE)

- ▸ NPRINTER

- ▸ PCONSOLE

- ▸ PRINTCON

- ▸ PRINTDEF

- ▸ PSC

In addition to these utilities, all of the support files needed to run them are copied. As mentioned earlier in this chapter, you may at times require the older versions of PRINTCON and PRINTDEF (see the section on bimodal printing utilities earlier in this chapter). If you need to maintain the NetWare 3 versions of the PRINTCON and PRINTDEF databases, rename PRINTCON.EXE and PRINT-DEF.EXE to .SAV files before establishing your NETSYNC link. Doing this enables you to rename those files back to .EXE files when you need to maintain the old databases.

If you have remote printers attached to workstations running RPRINTER, you need to load NPRINTER on these workstations. Doing so ensures compatibility with all utilities and provides better printing performance.

Upgrading of Databases

When the initial NETSYNC synchronization takes place, all PRINTCON and PRINTDEF databases on the NetWare 3 server are synchronized with the NetWare 4 server. PRINTDEF databases are then copied back to all the NetWare 3 servers in the NETSYNC cluster. PRINTCON databases, however, are not synchronized back to the NetWare 3 servers.

When the databases are copied to the NetWare 4 server, they are updated to the NetWare 4.1 format and duplicated in the NetWare 4.1 database. After the synchronization is completed, you need to make any changes to these databases on the NetWare 4.1 server using the NetWare 4.1 utilities.

Moving Print Servers with **NETSYNC**

If you want to truly manage your NetWare 3 printing environment with NET-SYNC, you need to move the NetWare 3 print servers to NetWare 4. When you move a NetWare 3 print server, all properties and associated printer configurations are also moved. You have the option of moving multiple NetWare 3 print servers to multiple NetWare 4 print servers or merging multiple NetWare 3 print servers into one NetWare 4 print server. This is illustrated in Figure 5.9.

▶ · ◀

F I G U R E   5.9

Merging multiple NetWare 3 print servers into one NetWare 4 print server

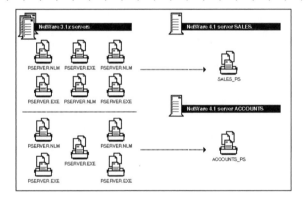

When you merge print servers, the first print server moved retains all of its previous configuration information. This includes printer numbers and all other properties. Subsequent print servers merged will have their printer numbers adjusted accordingly. For example, as shown in Figure 5.10, NetWare 3 print servers PSERV_1 and PSERV_2 are merged into a single NetWare 4 print server called SALES_PS. Both NetWare 3 print servers had printers 0 and 1 defined as P0 and P1, respectively. When the print servers are moved to NetWare 4, the printer numbers are reassigned. If PSERV_1 is the first moved, its printer numbers remain P0 and P1. When PSERVER_2 is moved, its printer numbers are renamed P2 and

P3. To resolve the duplicate printer names, NETSYNC adds a prefix of -001 to differentiate the printers.

NETWARE 3 PRINT SERVERS   **NETWARE 4 PRINT SERVER**

When multiple NetWare 3 print servers are merged into one NetWare 4 print server, duplicate printer numbers and names are changed to prevent overwriting an existing name or number.

PRINTER CONFIGURATION
PRINTER 0–P0
PRINTER 1–P1

PSERV–1

PRINTER CONFIGURATION
PRINTER 0–P0
PRINTER 1–P1

PSERV–2

PRINTER CONFIGURATION
PRINTER 0–P0
PRINTER 1–P1
PRINTER 2–P0-001
PRINTER 3–P1-001

SALES–PS

Printers configured as "local" printers on the NetWare 3 print server are configured as "manual load" (remote) printers when the print servers are moved to NetWare 4. To use these printers attached to a NetWare 3 file server, you need to load NPRINTER.NLM at those file servers. PSERVER.NLM is no longer required on the NetWare 3 server because the printers are now managed by a NetWare 4 print server. If the "local" printers were attached to a dedicated workstation NetWare 3 print server running PSERVER.EXE, you need to load NPRINTER.EXE in place of PSERVER.EXE. Once you do this, the print server is no longer a dedicated device and can be used as a regular network workstation.

You need to be aware of a few security issues when moving print servers. First, if you had passwords on your NetWare 3 print servers, those passwords are deleted when the print servers are moved to NetWare 4. To prevent unauthorized users from loading the print server, you should assign a new password to the NetWare 4 print server when the merge is complete.

Another security issue that you need to be aware of is print server operators. If you are moving multiple NetWare 3 print servers to one NetWare 4 print server, all of the users designated as operators of the NetWare 3 print servers automatically become operators of the NetWare 4 print server. If you do not wish to have multiple operators, be sure to change the operator assignments after the merge is complete.

Reference Print Servers

When you move a NetWare 3 print server to NetWare 4, a bindery object is created on the NetWare 3 server called a *reference print server*. This object is used by the NetWare 4.1 print server to attach to in order to service the print queues on the NetWare 3 file server. This can be viewed in PCONSOLE. In doing so, however, you will find that the reference print server has no assigned properties or configured printers. This print server also does not need to be loaded; it is created and used by NETSYNC only and requires no administrative action whatsoever. One thing to be aware of, though: This object should not be deleted. If it is, the NetWare 4 print server will not be able to service the print queues defined on the NetWare 3 file server. If you inadvertently delete this print server, it can be re-created using PCONSOLE.

Bindery Reference Queues

When you move a NetWare 3 print server to NetWare 4, print queues are created to represent the NetWare 3 print queues. These print queues are created as *bindery reference queues*. Bindery reference queues are simply pointers to the actual NetWare 3 print queues.

When the Bindery reference queues are created, they are assigned names that are enclosed in braces. For example, if print queue LASER_Q on the NetWare 3 file server HANGTIME was moved to a NetWare 4 print server, the name of the Bindery reference queue created in NDS would be {HANGTIME_LASER_Q}.

All users and operators of print queues remain the same when print queues are moved to NetWare 4 print servers.

How to Move NetWare 3 Print Servers to NetWare 4

Moving NetWare 3 print servers to NetWare 4 is a very simple process. Once the NETSYNC NLMs have been loaded on both the NetWare 3 and NetWare 4 file servers, a NETSYNC3 Options menu is displayed at the NetWare 3 file server console. To move a print server, select the Move a Print Server option. A list of the print servers currently defined on the NetWare 3 server is displayed. Select the name of the print server you wish to move. You are then prompted for the name of the NetWare 4 print server you wish to merge this print server with. At this point you can either enter the name of an existing print server or enter a new print server name. If the print server doesn't already exist, it is created at this time. If it does already exist, the printer names and numbers are merged as described previously. Repeat this process for any additional print servers you wish to move to NetWare 4.

Summary

With the release of NetWare 4, Novell was very aware of the fact that companies would not be upgrading their networks overnight. This is quite evident in the backward compatibility provided with the NetWare 4 utilities. And, for once, printing gets the attention it deserves and is not treated like the ugly step child. As we saw in this chapter many of the NetWare 4 printing utilities provide the ability to manage not only a NetWare 4 printing environment, but also NetWare 3.

CHAPTER 6

Managing NetWare 3 Print Services

Network managers are the unsung heroes of most companies today. Their efforts keep the network up and running so users can remain productive. Unfortunately, as any network manager would agree, it's a thankless job. Users expect the network to be up and running at all times, and they become quite unreasonable when it's not. Every company has at least one user that is, shall we say, "highly sensitive." You know the guy—let's just call him Fred—he's late for a meeting and his report won't print. He comes into your office with a red face, flaring nostrils, and a vein bulging on his forehead that's so large you think it might explode. He wants his print job and he wants it *now!*

Printing problems tend to be at the top of everyone's hate list, so a good knowledge of the NetWare print system can be a valuable asset for any network manager. Users like Fred don't have the patience for trial-and-error network management. This chapter takes an in-depth look at the utilities available to manage NetWare 3 print services. This chapter should give you the tools you need to get your job done—before Fred has you for lunch!

PCONSOLE

In Chapter 2, we took a good look at using PCONSOLE to set up a NetWare 3 printing system. But there is a lot more to PCONSOLE than just creating printers, print queues, and print servers. PCONSOLE is also the main tool used for managing an existing NetWare 3 printing system.

Because PCONSOLE.EXE is located in the SYS:PUBLIC directory, it is a utility that can be accessed by all users. However, a user's access to the information found in PCONSOLE is limited to his or her security authorization. For example, a user logged in as SUPERVISOR or a SUPERVISOR equivalent has complete access to all information found in PCONSOLE. This includes the ability to manage all existing printing objects and create new printing objects such as print queues and print servers. On the other hand, regular network users are limited to managing only print jobs they have submitted and to viewing information about existing printing objects.

Access to the information found in PCONSOLE is controlled through three user designations:

▸   SUPERVISOR (or SUPERVISOR equivalent)

▸   Printing Operators

▸   Printing Users

As indicated previously, any user logged in as SUPERVISOR or a user account made equivalent to the user SUPERVISOR has complete access to all information found in PCONSOLE. Any user that does not have SUPERVISOR privileges can be designated as a printing operator, user, or both.

PRINTING OPERATORS

Let's face it, a network manager is often one of the busiest people in a company. To make the job a little easier, NetWare provides network managers with the ability to delegate certain network administration tasks to other users without giving them full SUPERVISOR security access. Printing-administration tasks can be delegated to special user types called *print queue operators* and *print server operators*. A user designated as a print queue operator can manage an existing print queue. A user designated as a print server operator can manage an existing print server. These users do not, however, have the ability to create new printing objects.

Assigning Print Queue Operators

To designate an existing user as a print queue operator, you must first be logged in as a SUPERVISOR or a SUPERVISOR equivalent. Run PCONSOLE from the DOS command line and choose Print Queue Information from the main menu. A list of the currently defined print queues is displayed. Choose the print queue you want to assign an operator for and select Queue Operators from the Print Queue Information menu as shown in Figure 6.1.

F I G U R E   6.1

The Print Queue
Information menu in
PCONSOLE enables you to
assign print queue
operators.

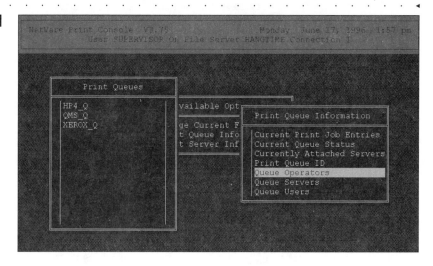

When you choose Print Queue Operators, a list of the current operators is displayed. To add a new operator, press the Insert key and select the user, users, or groups you want to manage this print queue. Figure 6.2 shows a list of print queue operator candidates.

F I G U R E   6.2

Assigning print queue
operators in PCONSOLE

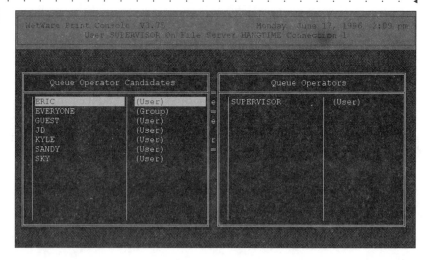

TIP

The F5 key can be used to tag multiple users, making it easy to assign multiple operators. Functions like the F5 key are standard across all Novell DOS-based utilities. Pressing the F1 key twice provides a list of all the available function key assignments.

To remove a user from the operator list, use the arrow keys to select the user in the Queue Operators list and press Delete.

Assigning Print Server Operators

Designating a user as a print server operator is similar to assigning a print queue operator. The only difference is that from the PCONSOLE main menu (logged in as SUPERVISOR or a SUPERVISOR equivalent), select Print Server Information. A list of the currently defined print servers is shown. Select the print server you want to assign an operator for and choose Print Server Operators, as shown in Figure 6.3.

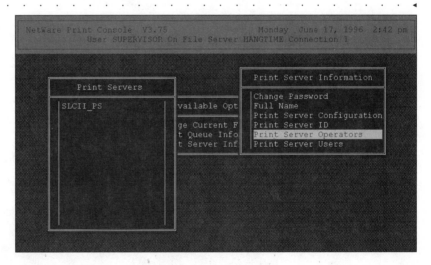

The Print Server Information menu in PCONSOLE enables you to assign print server operators.

A list of the currently defined operators appears. To add a new operator, press the Insert key and a list of print server operator candidates appears. Select a single operator by using the arrow keys and pressing Enter or use the F5 key to tag multiple users or groups.

To remove a user from the operator list, use the arrow keys to select the user in the Print Server Operators list and press Delete.

PRINT QUEUE USERS AND PRINT SERVER USERS

To authorize users to submit print jobs to a queue, a user type called *print queue user* was created. By default, the group EVERYONE is added to the print queue user list of all print queues. This automatically gives all users the ability to send print jobs to all queues. Print queues can be restricted for use by specific users by deleting the group EVERYONE from the print queue user list and adding the specific users or groups. In addition, the group EVERYONE is added to the print server user list of all print servers by default. This authorizes all users' print jobs to be serviced by all print servers.

Assigning Print Queue Users

If the default assignment of EVERYONE as a print queue user does not meet your needs for a particular print queue, you must remove the group from the print queue user list and add the users or groups you do want. This can be done in PCONSOLE by a user logged in as SUPERVISOR, a user designated as a SUPERVISOR equivalent, or a user designated as a print queue operator.

To assign print queue users, select Print Queue Information from the PCONSOLE main menu. A list of the currently defined print queues is displayed. Use the arrow keys to select the print queue you want to assign users to and press Enter. From the Print Queue Information screen, select Print Queue Users, as shown in Figure 6.4.

▶ · ◀

Selecting Queue Users from the Print Queue Information menu in PCONSOLE enables you to authorize users to submit jobs to a print queue.

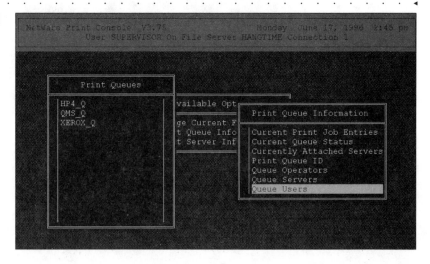

Once Queue Users has been selected from the Print Queue Information menu, a list of the current users or groups authorized to submit jobs to this print queue appears. To delete a user or group from this list, use the arrow keys to select the user or group and press the Delete key. To add queue users to the list, press the Insert key. A list is displayed of queue user candidates, as shown in Figure 6.5.

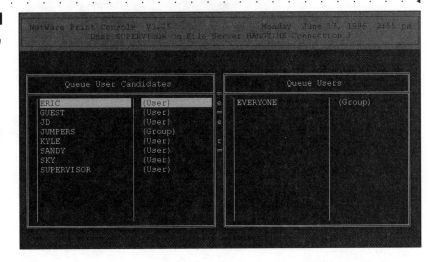

F I G U R E   6.5

Pressing the Insert key from the Queue Users menu produces a list of queue user candidates.

To add a new print queue user, use the arrow keys to select the user or group and press Enter. To add multiple users or groups at once, use the F5 key to tag each item.

Assigning Print Server Users

As with assigning operators, the process of assigning print server users is similar to the process of assigning print queue users.

Again, if the default assignment of the group EVERYONE (as a print server user) does not meet your needs for a particular print server, remove the group from the print server user list and add the users or groups you do want. This can be done in PCONSOLE by a user logged in as SUPERVISOR, a user designated as a SUPERVISOR equivalent, or a user designated as a print server operator.

To assign print server users, select Print Server Information from the PCONSOLE main menu. A list of the currently defined print servers is displayed. Use the arrow keys to select the print server you want to assign users to and press Enter. From the Print Server Information screen, select Print Server Users, as shown in Figure 6.6.

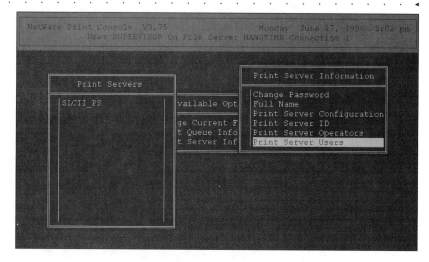

Selecting Print Server Users from the Print Server Information menu in PCONSOLE enables you to authorize users to have their print jobs serviced by this print server.

Once the Print Server Users option has been selected from the Print Server Information menu, a list of the current users or groups authorized to have their print jobs serviced by this print server will be shown. To delete a user or group from this list, use the arrow keys to select it and press the Delete key. To add users or groups to the list, press the Insert key. A list of print server user candidates will be displayed, as shown in Figure 6.7.

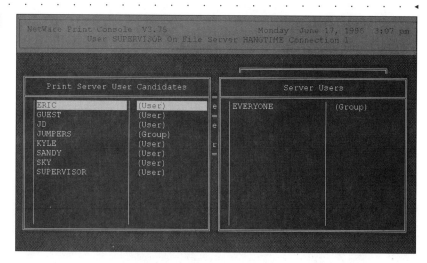

Pressing the Insert key from the Print Server Users menu provides a list of print server user candidates.

To add a new print server user, use the arrow keys to select the user or group and press Enter. To add multiple users or groups at once, use the F5 key to tag each item.

Printing User and Operator Tasks

Now that you know how to assign printing operators and users, you are probably wondering exactly what tasks each can perform in a NetWare 3 printing environment. We have created Table 6.1 to provide you with a quick summary of the printing tasks that can be performed by printing operators and users.

MANAGING YOUR PRINTING ENVIRONMENT WITH PCONSOLE

Now that you understand who can manage what in a NetWare 3 printing environment, let's take a look at how to actually perform those management tasks. In a NetWare 3 printing environment there are four basic management tasks:

- ▸ Managing print jobs

- ▸ Managing print queues

- ▸ Managing print servers

- ▸ Controlling printers

Each task is covered in detail in the following sections.

MANAGING PRINT JOBS

Every print job printed on a NetWare network passes through a print queue while it waits to be serviced by a print server. While print jobs are waiting in the queue, they can be managed in a number of ways, including:

- ▸ Viewing print job status

- ▸ Adding print jobs to the queue

- ▸ Deleting jobs from the queue

Printing tasks that can be performed by users and operators.

TASK	SUPERVISOR OR EQUIVALENT	PRINT QUEUE OPERATOR	PRINT SERVER OPERATOR	PRINT QUEUE USER	PRINT SERVER USER
Create print queues	X				
Submit jobs to print queues	X			X	
Reorder jobs in the queue	X	X		Job owners can reorder their own jobs	
Delete jobs from the queue	X	X		Job owners can delete their own jobs	
Change print job entry information	X	X		Job owners can change the job entry information of their own jobs	
Assign print queue operators	X				
Assign print queue users	X	X			
View print queue information	X	X		X	
Create print servers	X				
Have jobs serviced by print server	X				X
Change print server password	X	X			
Change print server configuration	X		X		
Assign print server operators	X				
Assign print server users	X		X		
Down an active print server through PCONSOLE	X		X		

▸ Placing jobs on hold/Deferring printing

▸ Changing the order of jobs

▸ Modifying CAPTURE parameters

Once the print server begins servicing a print job, you can no longer manage it. Figure 6.8 shows an example of a print job being serviced by a print server. Notice the single box around the Print Queue Entry Information screen. This indicates that the information displayed here cannot be modified.

F I G U R E   6.8

A print job being serviced by a print server cannot be managed, as indicated by the single box around the screen.

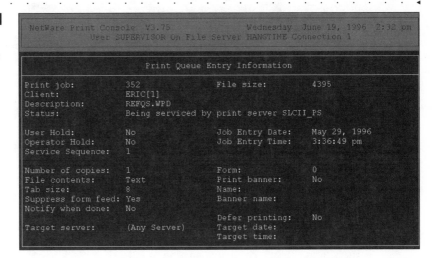

Now look at Figure 6.9: This figure shows a print job that is waiting to be serviced by the print server. Notice that the box around the Print Queue Entry Information screen for this print job has a *double* line. This double line indicates that the displayed information, such as the number of copies, can be modified.

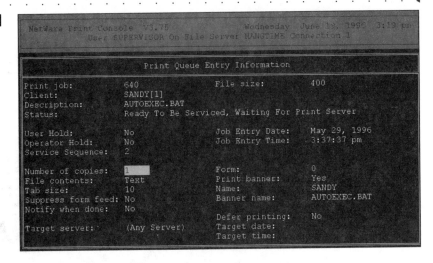

FIGURE 6.9

While a print job is waiting to be serviced by the print server, the Print Queue Entry information can be modified.

> **TIP**
>
> **When using any of the Novell DOS-based utilities (not just PCON-SOLE), a double box around a menu option indicates that the displayed information can be modified. A single box indicates that the information cannot be changed.**

Viewing Print Job Status

Viewing the status of print jobs in the queue is something that can be useful to both users and administrators. From the user perspective, it's nice to be able to see the status of your print job and be able to delete the job if, for example, you sent it to the wrong printer. On the administrative side, viewing the status of print jobs in a queue is one of the first steps in troubleshooting printing problems.

To view the status of print jobs in a print queue, run PCONSOLE from the DOS command line. From the PCONSOLE main menu, select Print Queue Information. A list of the currently defined print queues is displayed. Select the queue you want to view the print job status for and select Current Print Job Entries. A screen similar to the one shown in Figure 6.10 is displayed.

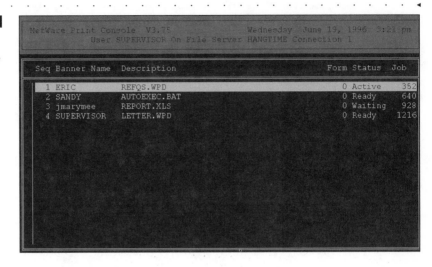

FIGURE 6.10

Viewing the current print job entries of a print queue

This screen provides five useful pieces of information. The first is the column labeled "Seq." This column indicates the sequence number of each print job, which is also the order in which the print jobs will be serviced.

The second column shows the "Banner Name." This is the name specified with the N= parameter of CAPTURE. If a banner name is not specified when the CAPTURE command is entered, the default banner name will be the job owner's name.

The next column of the Print Job Entries screen is a description of the jobs in the queue. This description is generally the filename of the print job.

Following the "Description" column is "Form." The Form column indicates the PRINTDEF form number requested with the CAPTURE parameters of each print job. This option is useful in troubleshooting if, for example, the print queue is being blocked by a print job requesting a form number other than the one currently mounted for the printer servicing this queue. Depending on the queue's Form Service Mode, it is possible that none of the jobs in the queue will be serviced until the requested form is mounted. We'll cover this scenario in greater depth later in this chapter.

The next column is the "Status" column. A print job's status will be one of the following:

▸ **Active.** Print job is being serviced by the print server.

▸ **Ready.** Print job is ready and waiting to be serviced by the print server.

▸ **Held.** A user or operator hold has been placed on the print job.

▸ **Adding.** The print job is currently being added to the queue.

▸ **Waiting.** Printing has been deferred and the system is waiting for the target date and time before releasing the print job.

The final column in the Current Print Job Entries screen is "Job." This column indicates the job number assigned to each print job. As you can see in Figure 6.10, there doesn't seem to be any logic behind the job numbers shown. Well, there isn't. This number is arbitrarily assigned to each job by the system and has no practical purpose.

Adding Print Jobs to the Queue

Print jobs can be added directly to the queue from PCONSOLE. This is most useful when you don't want to print a text file from the DOS command line or use a text editor.

Let's say, for example, you would like to print a hard copy of your AUTOEXEC.NCF file using PCONSOLE. In the Current Print Job Entries screen under Print Queue Information, simply press the Insert key. A screen similar to the one shown in Figure 6.11 will appear.

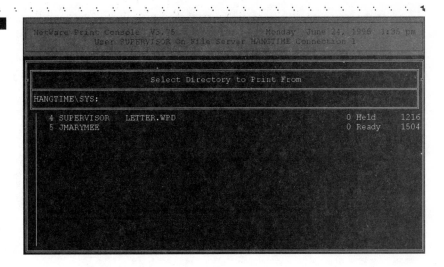

Selecting a directory to print from in the PCONSOLE utility

At this point you have one of two choices: You can type the path and filename that you want to print from. Or, you can use the Insert key again to browse the network drives or local drives until you find the file you want to print. While browsing, pressing Enter on a directory or subdirectory moves you deeper in the directory structure. Pressing Enter on the two dots (. .) moves you up the directory structure to the parent directory. If you continue to press Enter on the two dots, you eventually move all the way to the top of the structure, which shows all the available network file servers and local drives.

When you find the desired directory you want to print from, highlight it and then press Enter. Press Escape once to return to the directory selection window and then press Enter. A list of the files in the selected directory will appear, as shown in Figure 6.12.

FIGURE 6.12

Selecting a file to print using PCONSOLE

NetWare Print Console V3.75 Monday June 24, 1996 1:51 pm
User SUPERVISOR On File Server HANGTIME Connection 1
Select Directory to Print From
HANGTIME/SYS:SYSTEM
4 SUPERVISOR LETTER.WPD
5 JMARYMEE
Available Files
0 Held 1216
0 Ready 1504
AIODGMEM.NLM
AIODGXI.NLM
AIOESP.NLM
AIOWNIM.NLM
ATOTAL.EXE
AUTOEXEC.NCF
BINDFIX.EXE
BINDREST.EXE
BREBUILD.NLM
BROUTER.NLM

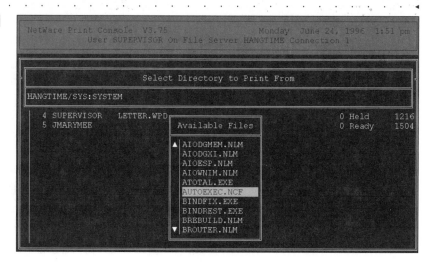

Highlight the file you want to print and press Enter. A list of available print job configurations will appear if they have been created in PRINTCON. Select the job configuration that you want to use with this print job, or if no job configurations exist, select the PCONSOLE defaults option. A screen similar to the one shown in Figure 6.13 will appear.

FIGURE 6.13

Defining the parameters of a print job being sent to the queue through PCONSOLE

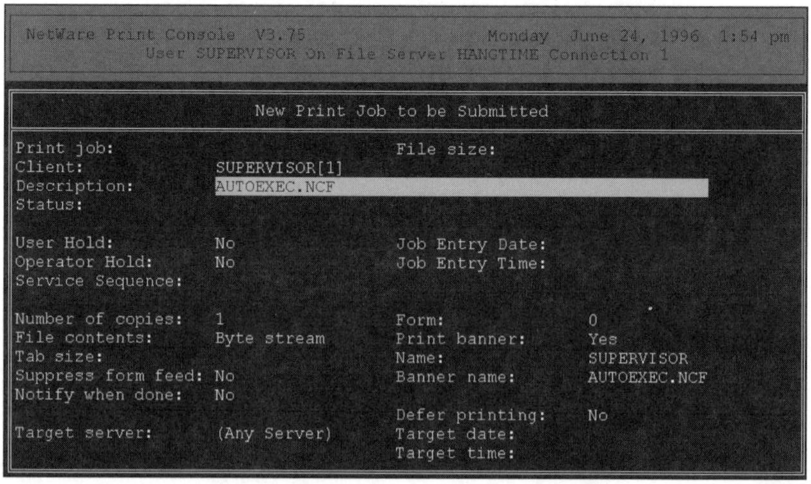

NetWare Print Console V3.75 Monday June 24, 1996 1:54 pm
User SUPERVISOR On File Server HANGTIME Connection 1
New Print Job to be Submitted
Print job:
File size:
Client: SUPERVISOR[1]
Description: AUTOEXEC.NCF
Status:
User Hold: No
Job Entry Date:
Operator Hold: No
Job Entry Time:
Service Sequence:
Number of copies: 1
Form: 0
File contents: Byte stream
Print banner: Yes
Tab size:
Name: SUPERVISOR
Suppress form feed: No
Banner name: AUTOEXEC.NCF
Notify when done: No
Defer printing: No
Target server: (Any Server)
Target date:
Target time:

This screen displays the printing parameters for this print job. If you look closely you will notice that these parameters are the CAPTURE parameters. And, because this print job is being sent directly to the queue from PCONSOLE (as opposed to being redirected by CAPTURE), the CAPTURE defaults are used. To change any of these parameters, simply use the arrow key to highlight the option and enter the desired value. When you have finished modifying the print job parameters, press Escape and then Enter to save the changes. The job will then be placed in the queue in the order submitted.

Deleting Print Jobs from the Queue

We've all done it once or twice, inadvertently sent a PostScript print job to a printer that only supports PCL printer codes. The result? Pages and pages of "garbage" and a whole bunch of wasted paper. Most users (and some administrators) think nothing can be done once the job is sent to the network for printing. They just cringe when they realize their mistake, grab the wasted paper, and run for the nearest recycling bin. This is a perfect example of when you may want to use PCONSOLE to delete a print job from the queue.

Deleting print jobs from the queue is simple. From the PCONSOLE main menu, select Print Queue Information and then choose the queue you want to delete the job from. From the Print Queue Information menu, select Current Print Job Entries. A list of jobs currently in the queue will appear (see Figure 6.10). Use the arrow keys to highlight the job you want to delete from the queue and press the Delete key.

If the job has already begun printing, there is a chance that it can still be deleted (especially if the printer is receiving invalid printer codes). If the job is still displayed in the Current Print Job Entries screen, highlight it and press Delete. You will receive a message like the one shown in Figure 6.14.

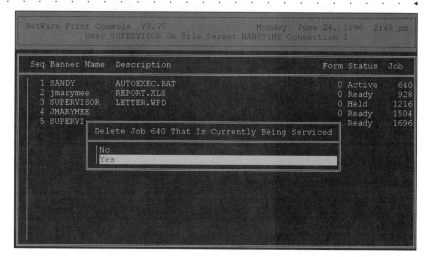

Once you have verified that you are deleting the correct job, answer Yes and the job will be deleted from the queue. Keep in mind that printing may not stop immediately, because most printers can store a significant amount of printing data in memory. In general, you can clear a printer's memory by turning it off.

Placing Print Jobs on Hold

In some printing scenarios you may not want a print job to print immediately. Let's say, for example, you have a very large report that will take 30 minutes to print and it needs to be sent to a printer that is used frequently by other network users. If you want to keep your reputation as a considerate person, you may want to think about printing that job after-hours or during the lunch hour when nobody needs the printer. Deferred printing can be done three different ways:

▸ Using the NoAutoendcap option of CAPTURE

▸ Placing a user or operator hold on the job

▸ Deferring printing with PCONSOLE

NoAutoendcap   Earlier, when we discussed the CAPTURE command, we mentioned that a print job redirected to the network by CAPTURE will wait in the print queue until an ENDCAP is issued.

If you don't recall how CAPTURE works, you may want to review the CAPTURE sections of earlier chapters.

NOTE

By default, an automatic ENDCAP or *Autoendcap* will be issued if a *TImeout* (TI=xx) value is defined. Once the Autoendcap is issued, the print job's status switches to "ready" and it is printed in the order in which it was submitted to the queue.

If you do not want a print job to print immediately, you can use the *NoAutoendcap* (NA) option when CAPTURE is issued, as shown in the following example:

```
CAPTURE Q=HP4_Q L=2 NB NFF NA
```

In this example, we have specified that we want all print jobs directed to LPT2 to be redirected to the HP4_Q on our default file server. We are also indicating that we do not want a banner page or a form feed to print and that all jobs should be held in the queue until an ENDCAP is issued. While the jobs are being held in the queue, they will have a status of "adding."

When we are ready for the print jobs to be released from the queue, we will need to type the following from the DOS command line:

```
ENDCAP L=2
```

This will end the capturing of LPT2 and release the job (or jobs) for printing. When the ENDCAP is issued, the job status will switch to "ready" and the print jobs will be serviced in the order received.

There are two disadvantages to this method of placing print jobs on hold. The first is that you have to be present to manually enter the ENDCAP. This may not be convenient if you want the job to print after-hours. Second, all print jobs sent to the LPT port captured (LPT2 in our example) will wait in the queue until the ENDCAP is issued. This may be overkill if you want to place a hold on only one print job.

User or Operator Hold   Another way to prevent a job from printing immediately is to place a user or operator hold on the job. This can be done using PCONSOLE, through the Print Job Entries option under Print Queue Information. The

Print Job Entries screen will show a list of print jobs currently in the print queue. Use the arrow keys to highlight the print job you want to place on hold and press Enter. You will then be presented with the Print Queue Entry Information screen, shown in Figure 6.15.

FIGURE 6.15

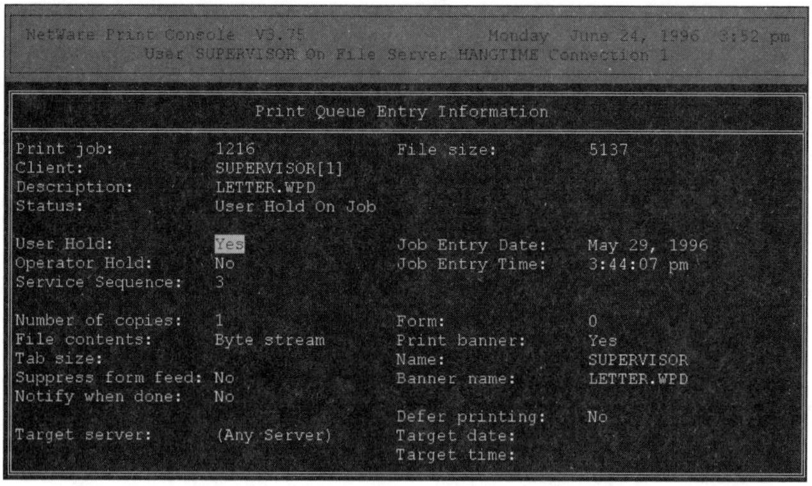

The Print Queue Entry Information screen can be used to place a user or operator hold on a print job.

```
NetWare Print Console  V3.75                 Monday  June 24, 1996  3:52 pm
              User SUPERVISOR On File Server HANGTIME Connection 1

                        Print Queue Entry Information

Print job:          1216            File size:        5137
Client:             SUPERVISOR[1]
Description:        LETTER.WPD
Status:             User Hold On Job

User Hold:          Yes             Job Entry Date:   May 29, 1996
Operator Hold:      No              Job Entry Time:   3:44:07 pm
Service Sequence:   3

Number of copies:   1               Form:             0
File contents:      Byte stream     Print banner:     Yes
Tab size:                           Name:             SUPERVISOR
Suppress form feed: No              Banner name:      LETTER.WPD
Notify when done:   No
                                    Defer printing:   No
Target server:      (Any Server)    Target date:
                                    Target time:
```

From this screen, you can use the arrow keys to place a user hold on the print job (if you are the job owner) or an operator hold on the job (if you are a print queue operator.) Once a hold has been placed, the print job status appears as "held." The hold can be released by returning to this screen and removing the hold.

As with the NoAutoendcap option, the disadvantage of this hold method is that you must be present to release the hold, which may not be convenient in some situations.

Deferring Printing with PCONSOLE   The most convenient method of placing print jobs on hold may be to actually *defer* the printing in PCONSOLE. This option enables you to set the date and time when you want the print job to begin printing. This means that you do not have to be present to release the hold on the job as you do with the other methods.

To defer printing in PCONSOLE, select Print Queue Information from the main menu. Next, choose the queue that the print job is in and select Current Print Job Entries. A list of the jobs currently in the queue appears. Choose the job you want to place on hold and press Enter. From the Print Queue Entry Information screen, shown in Figure 6.16, use the arrow keys to move to the Defer Printing field in the lower right portion of the screen. When the Defer Printing option is changed to Yes, you will have the ability to set the target date and time.

▶ · ◀

```
NetWare Print Console  V3.75                    Tuesday  June 25, 1996  11:33 am
                  User SUPERVISOR On File Server HANGTIME Connection 1

                          Print Queue Entry Information

  Print job:          1504              File size:          2052
  Client:             SUPERVISOR[1]
  Description:
  Status:             Waiting for Target Execution Date and Time

  User Hold:          No                Job Entry Date:     June 19, 1996
  Operator Hold:      No                Job Entry Time:     3:38:29 pm
  Service Sequence:   4

  Number of copies:   1                 Form:               0
  File contents:      Text              Print banner:       No
  Tab size:           8                 Name:
  Suppress form feed: Yes               Banner name:
  Notify when done:   No
                                        Defer printing:     Yes
  Target server:      (Any Server)      Target date:        June 26, 1996
                                        Target time:        2:00:00 am
```

Deferred print jobs in the queue will have a status of "waiting." When the target date and time is reached, the status will switch to "ready" and the job will be serviced in the order in which it was received.

WARNING

If the printer, file server, or print server is turned off when the target date and time is reached, the print job will not print. For best results, be sure these devices are on by the target date and time. Otherwise, the job will not print until they are turned on again.

Deferring printing with PCONSOLE is the best way to put print jobs on hold, because you don't have to be present to release the job when you are ready for it to print. The only disadvantage to this method is that the printer, print server, and file server must all be up and running when the target date and time is reached.

Preventing Jobs from Printing Before You Can Put Them on Hold   At this point you may be wondering how you can prevent a job from going to the printer before you have a chance to place it on hold. This is a very common problem when you send a job to a queue that is not very busy or one that is being serviced efficiently by the printer. Sending a print job from an application and then quickly jumping into PCONSOLE to put it on hold (before the print server begins servicing it) can be quite tricky. But, not to worry, because there is a way: Use NoAutoendcap with the other hold options.

TIP

To ensure you have enough time to put a print job on hold before the print server begins servicing it, issue a NoAutoendcap with CAPTURE. This will ensure that the job stays in the queue while you go into PCONSOLE and either defer printing or set the user or operator hold.

To use NoAutoendcap with the other hold options and prevent a print job from printing immediately, take the following steps:

1 • Issue CAPTURE with the NoAutoendcap flag. For example:

```
CAPTURE L=2 Q=HP4_Q NB NFF NA
```

2 • In your application, send the print job to the LPT port you just captured.

3 • Run PCONSOLE.

4 • Select the appropriate print queue in Print Queue Information.

5 • Choose Current Print Job Entries and the job you want to place on hold.

6 • Press Enter on the desired job. Either set a user or operator hold on the job or say Yes to Defer printing and set the target date and time.

7 • Exit PCONSOLE and issue an ENDCAP. For example:

```
ENDCAP L=2
```

This is probably the best way to place a print job on hold, because it guarantees that the job won't start printing before you have a chance to defer it.

Changing the Order of Print Jobs in the Queue

Let's assume for a moment that it's just another day in your life as a network administrator. Everything seems to be running smoothly until your phone rings. It's the CEO's secretary. The conversation goes something like this: "Hello, this is Mr. Frankenburg's secretary. Bob has sent a very important document to a printer in your area, yet it seems that everyone else's jobs are printing before his. He needs this document immediately and doesn't have time to wait." You tell his secretary not to worry, you're on the case. You spring into action.

Your first step is to find Mr. Frankenburg's print job. You quickly go into PCONSOLE and begin checking the print job entries of all print queues assigned to be serviced by printers in your area. You find the job in a queue that is being serviced by a color laser printer normally used to print color graphics. It seems that Bob is trying to print a color presentation, but his job is waiting behind two other jobs that could take quite some time to print. To save your reputation (and your job!) you will need to reorder the jobs in the queue so Bob's job will print as soon as possible.

First you check the status of the print jobs, as shown in Figure 6.17. You see that the service sequence of Bob's print job is 3. You also notice that the file GRAPHS.SHW has an "Active" status, indicating that the print server is currently servicing this job. Once the print server begins servicing a job, you cannot move another job ahead of it.

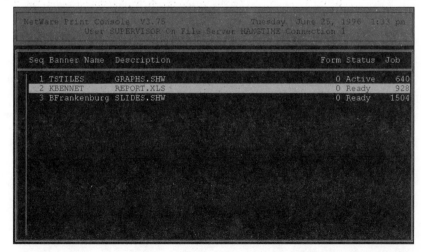

FIGURE 6.17

When changing the order of print jobs in the queue, you cannot move a job in front of another job with an "Active" status.

After you have verified the status of the jobs in the queue, you can select Mr. Frankenburg's job by highlighting it with the arrow keys and pressing Enter. The Print Queue Entry Information screen will appear, as shown in Figure 6.18. Use the arrow keys to select the service sequence field and change the job's service sequence from 3 to 2. The desired print job will then be serviced immediately after the active job.

▶ • ◀

FIGURE 6.18

Changing the service sequence of a print job reorders the jobs currently in the queue.

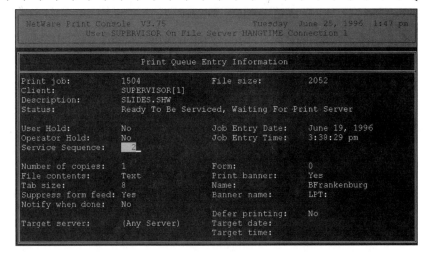

Changing the service sequence of print jobs can also be useful if you would like to move jobs back in the queue—for example, if you have a very large print job you would like printed last.

The service sequence of print jobs in the queue can only be changed by SUPERVISORs or SUPERVISOR equivalents, or by a user that has been authorized as a print queue operator. While regular users can change most of the Print Queue Entry Information of jobs they have submitted, they cannot change the service sequence.

Modifying CAPTURE Parameters

After a print job has been sent to the queue, you may want to modify some of the CAPTURE parameters associated with it. The following CAPTURE parameters can be modified once a job is in the queue:

▶ Number of copies

▶ File contents—Tabs/No Tabs

▶ Form Feed/No Form Feed

▶ Notify/No Notify

▶ Form number

▶ Banner information

All of these options can be changed from the Print Queue Entry Information screen in PCONSOLE. (An example of this screen was shown in Figure 6.18.)

MANAGING PRINT QUEUES

Although regular users can manage print jobs, they have no authority to manage print queues. Managing all print queues in PCONSOLE can only be done by SUPERVISOR or a SUPERVISOR equivalent. Users designated as print queue operators have the ability to manage only the queues that have been assigned to them.

Print queue management in PCONSOLE consists of the following:

▶ Viewing or modifying a print queue's status

▶ Viewing attached print servers

▶ Viewing a print queue's bindery ID number

▶ Viewing or assigning print queue servers

Assigning print queue users and operators is another aspect of print queue management, as discussed earlier in this chapter. Management of print queues is done primarily from the Print Queue Information menu, as shown in Figure 6.19.

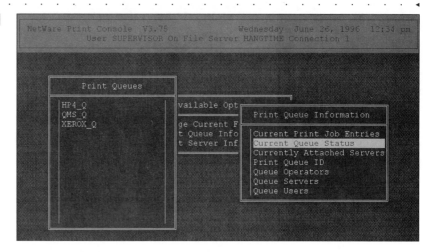

F I G U R E   6.19

The Print Queue Information menu in PCONSOLE is used to manage existing print queues.

This menu is accessed by selecting Print Queue Information from the PCON-SOLE main menu and then selecting the print queue you want to manage.

Viewing or Modifying a Print Queue's Status

If you want to view a print queue's status or set operator flags (indicating whether new jobs can be placed in the queue or whether new servers can attach to the queue, for example) select the Current Queue Status option of the Print Queue Information menu. This menu is shown in Figure 6.20.

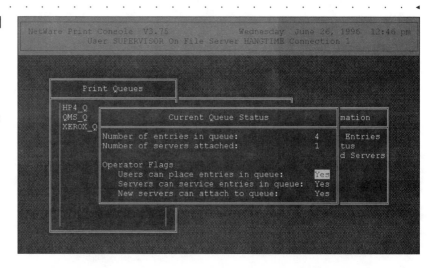

F I G U R E   6.20

The Current Queue Status option of PCONSOLE enables the network administrator or print queue operator to view a print queue's status and set operator flags.

The first two options on this screen are for information only. They show the queue's current status, including the number of print jobs currently waiting in the queue (four in this case) and the number of print servers attached to this queue. The latter option can be useful in verifying a print queue's configuration. If no print servers have been configured to service this print queue, or if the print server is not running, this option will show 0 servers attached.

The bottom half of the screen gives you the option to place operator flags on the print queue. All of these options default to Yes, enabling jobs to be sent to the print queue and assigned print servers to attach to the queue. You may want to use these flags if, for example, you will be performing maintenance (either on the printer or print queue) and you do not want users to use the queue or printer.

Users Can Place Entries in Queue   If you set the first option to No, users will not be able to send jobs to the queue. If they do, they will receive the following message from the system:

```
Print queue has been halted. No job may be submitted at
this time.
```

This option is useful if you will be changing the configuration of the queue (assigning a new printer to service it, for example) and you do not want additional jobs to be placed in the queue.

Servers Can Service Entries in Queue   The second option is useful if you want users to be able to place print jobs in the queue, but you do not want the jobs to print yet. Setting this option to No enables users' jobs to accumulate in the queue but does not enable the assigned print server or print servers to service the jobs. Essentially, this option places a hold on the entire queue. To release the hold and print the jobs that have accumulated in the queue, set this option back to Yes.

New Servers Can Attach to Queue   This option controls whether new print servers can attach to the print queue. When a print server comes up, it automatically attaches to the print queues it was assigned to service. If you want to bring a print server up, but you do not want it to attach to a particular queue (if the printer is out of order, for example) set this flag to No.

Viewing the Print Servers Currently Attached to a Print Queue

If you would like to view the print servers currently servicing a particular print queue, select Currently Attached Servers from the Print Queue Information menu for that print queue. When you select this option, a screen similar to the one shown in Figure 6.21 will appear.

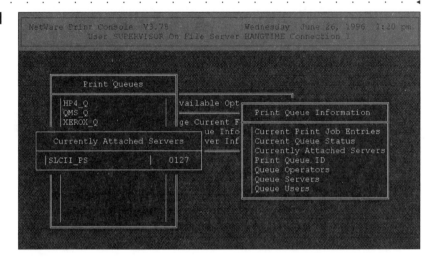

The Currently Attached Servers option of PCONSOLE displays the print servers assigned to service the print queues that are currently running.

Notice the single box around this screen. The single line indicates that this option is for information only and you cannot make changes within the screen.

NOTE

While this example shows only one print server, it is possible that more than one print server is assigned to service a single queue. However, this option will only show print servers that are running. If only one print server is assigned to service a queue and that print server is down, this box will be empty.

Viewing a Print Queue's Bindery ID Number

As mentioned earlier in this book, a print queue is a physical subdirectory that, in the case of NetWare 3, is located in the SYS:SYSTEM directory. The subdirectory name is the print queue's hexadecimal bindery ID number. To view the bindery ID number for a particular print queue, select Print Queue ID from that queue's Print Queue Information menu in PCONSOLE. A screen similar to the one shown in Figure 6.22 will appear.

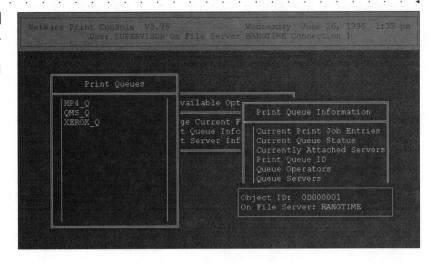

F I G U R E   6.22

The Print Queue ID number is the name of the subdirectory in SYS:SYSTEM where the print queue physically resides.

All print queue subdirectories have a *.QDR extension. Therefore, the actual name of the subdirectory for the print queue in Figure 6.22 is:

```
SYS:SYSTEM\0D000001.QDR
```

Viewing or Assigning Print Queue Servers

The Queue Servers option of a Print Queue Information menu shows the print servers currently assigned to service this queue. The difference between the information displayed in the Queue Servers option and the information shown in the Currently Attached Servers option is that the former shows *all* print servers assigned to service this queue. The Currently Attached Servers option shows just those print servers that are *attached* or running.

The Queue Servers option also enables you to add a print server to the list of queue servers. Simply press the Insert key and choose a print server from the list, as shown in Figure 6.23.

WARNING

Although a print server can be added to the list of queue servers using this menu option, additional steps are necessary for the print server to actually service this queue. Specifically, you must assign a printer to service the queue. (Refer to Chapter 2 for detailed information on how to assign printers to print queues.)

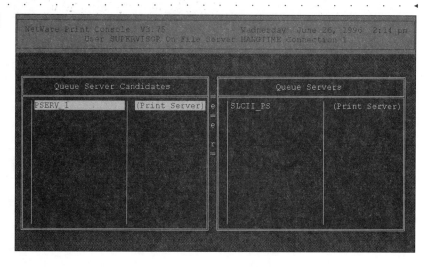

FIGURE 6.23

A print server may be added to the list of queue servers through a Print Queue Information menu. However, this does not configure the print server to service the queue.

When a printer is assigned to service a print queue through the Print Server Information/Print Server Configuration menu, the print server that the printer is configured on is automatically added to the list of queue servers.

We do not recommend using the Queue Servers option (of the Print Queue Information menu) to add a print server to the list of queue servers, because this method does not complete the configuration. You are required to assign a printer to service the queue anyway, so why add the server to the list here when it will be done automatically when you make the printer assignment?

Although there has to be a logical reason why this option enables print servers to be added to the queue server list, we have yet to find it.

MANAGING PRINT SERVERS

Managing print servers on your network is probably the least time consuming of all print management tasks, mostly because once a print server is configured, there really isn't much to manage except for bringing it up or taking it down. Most of the print server management tasks modify the initial print server configuration. This chapter covers print server management tasks only. (The creation and configuration of NetWare print servers was covered in depth in Chapter 2.)

Management of all print servers in PCONSOLE can be done by SUPERVISORs or SUPERVISOR equivalents. Management of specific print servers can be done by users designated as print server operators. Regular users can view specific information about print servers in PCONSOLE but do not have any management authority.

Most print server management tasks are done in PCONSOLE by selecting Print Server Information from the main menu and then selecting the print server you want to manage. The Print Server Information menu will then appear, as shown in Figure 6.24.

F I G U R E   6.24

Most print server management tasks are accomplished using the Print Server Information menu in PCONSOLE.

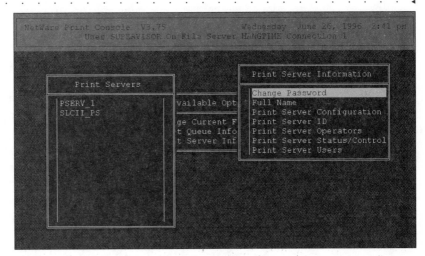

This PCONSOLE menu can be used to manage a print server in the following ways:

- ▶ Assigning a print server password

- ▶ Providing a description of the print server

- ▶ Modifying a print server's configuration

- ▶ Viewing a print server's bindery ID number

- ▶ Viewing the status of and controlling a print server that is currently running

The Print Server Information menu can also be used to assign print server users and operators, as described in the beginning of this chapter.

Assigning a Print Server Password

It is very important that you assign a password to all print servers. There are two reason for this: First, any users that know the name of a print server can attempt to bring it up at a workstation, or if they have access to it, at a file server. If the print server has been assigned a password, a password prompt will appear and the print server will not load until the proper password has been provided. If no password exists, the print server will load automatically.

The second, and probably most important reason to assign a password to print servers, is to avoid a security breach.

WARNING

An individual who has an in-depth knowledge of the internal NetWare processes and knowledge of programming could use a print server that lacks a password to break into a NetWare 3.12 file server. For this reason, we strongly recommend that you assign a password to all print servers.

To assign a print server password, select Print Server Information from the PCONSOLE main menu and then choose a print server. From the Print Server Information screen, choose the Change Password option. You will be prompted to enter the password and then re-enter it to verify that the password is correct.

Providing a Description of the Print Server

When you create a new print server, it may be helpful to you or others to provide a description of that print server for future reference. For example, if the print server services the Marketing department in Building F, you may want to include that information in the Full Name field of the Print Server Information menu. This option enables you to provide a description of the print server up to 62 characters in length.

Modifying a Print Server's Configuration

The Print Server Configuration option of a Print Server Information menu may be used to change the existing configuration of the print server. This includes modifying or configuring new printers to be serviced by this print server or changing or adding the printer's queue assignments. The Print Server Configuration menu is shown in Figure 6.25.

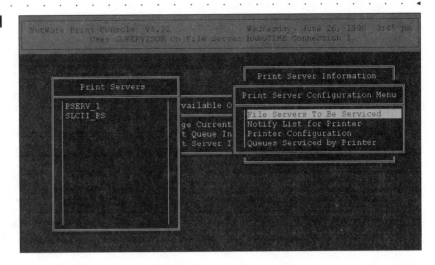

FIGURE 6.25

*A print server's
configuration can be
changed using the Print
Server Configuration menu
of PCONSOLE.*

In Chapter 2, we covered in depth the menu options for configuring printers and assigning queues to be serviced. If you would like more information on configuring NetWare 3 print servers, refer back to that chapter. In the following section, we cover the remaining two menu options.

File Servers to Be Serviced   In Chapter 2, we discussed configuring a print server to service up to eight different file servers. Part of that configuration process is assigning the print server to handle those file servers. This can be done using the File Servers to be Serviced option of the Print Server Configuration menu.

When you select this option, a screen similar to the one shown in Figure 6.26 will appear. By default, this list will show the file server where the print server is defined. To authorize this print server to service additional file servers, press the Insert key and select the servers from the list.

▶ · ◀

FIGURE 6.26

The File Servers to be Serviced option of PCONSOLE enables you to define up to eight file servers for this print server to handle.

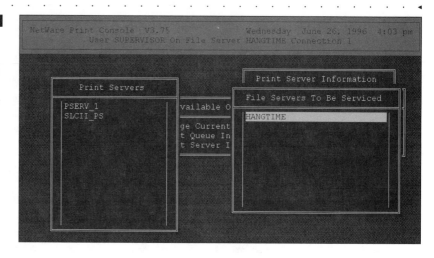

NOTE

Adding servers to the File Servers to be Serviced list is only one step in configuring a print server to handle multiple file servers. Refer to Chapter 2 for details on the complete process.

Notify List for Printer   Nothing is more aggravating than going to the printer to retrieve your print job and finding the printer out of paper before your job has even started. NetWare provides the option to identify a person to be notified when a printer needs attention. A message pops up on the designated person's screen, notifying him or her of a printer mishap. While this method can be annoying, it keeps printer problems from holding up everyone else's print jobs.

To set up someone to be notified about problems with a specific printer, select Notify List for Printer from the Print Server Configuration menu. Then select the printer you want to set notification for and press the Insert key. A list of users that are candidates for notification will appear, as shown in Figure 6.27.

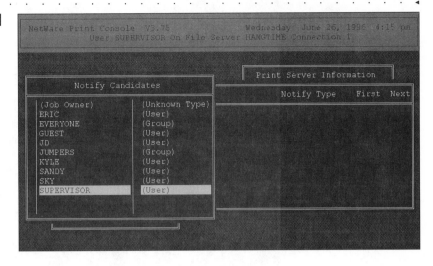

The Notify List for Printer option enables a user to be notified when the printer needs attention.

As you look at the Notify Candidates screen, you can see that a specific user can be set up to be notified or the job owner can be notified. You can even have an entire group notified. When you select a user or group to be notified, you will be prompted to define the notification intervals. "First" is the number of seconds after the printer needs attention before the first notice is sent. "Next" is the number of seconds between subsequent notices.

Viewing a Print Server's Bindery ID Number

Like print queues, print servers are objects in the NetWare 3 bindery. If you want to view a print server's bindery ID number, choose Print Server ID from the Print Server Information menu, shown in Figure 6.24. In general, the only reason (other than general curiosity) you might need to view this number is for troubleshooting problems with the bindery. If you receive a bindery error message, a bindery object number may be displayed. Use this option to trace that number back to a print server.

Viewing the Status of and Controlling a Print Server

Have you ever experienced a situation in which you go to a place where you swear you saw something earlier and it isn't there? Most of the time you either think you're going crazy or somebody's playing a trick on you.

PCONSOLE has a neat little peculiarity that might make you think you're losing your marbles. That feature is a disappearing menu option. Look at the Print Server Information menus in Figures 6.28 and 6.29. Notice that one has a Print Server Status/Control option and the other doesn't.

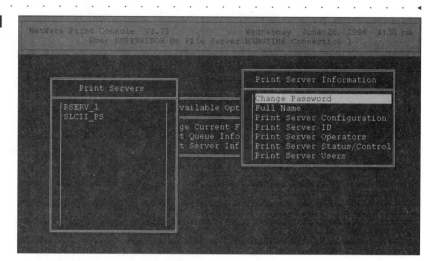

FIGURE 6.28

PCONSOLE Print Server Information menu showing the Print Server Status/Control option

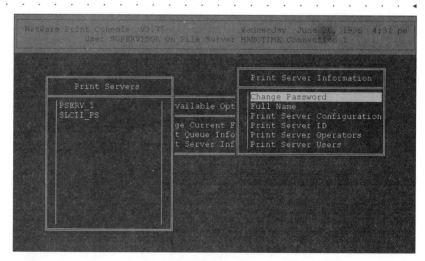

FIGURE 6.29

PCONSOLE Print Server Information menu without the Print Server Status/Control option

The first figure shows the Print Server Information menu for the print server SLCII_PS. The second figure shows it for the print server PSERV_1. Why the difference? Because SLCII_PS is running and PSERV_1 is not. It's a pretty simple explanation once you know the answer, but it would have you spinning in circles for a while if you didn't know that the option only shows up when a print server is loaded. Especially if you *think* that the print server is up, but it's really not.

So, with that bit of trivia out of the way, let's take a look at the Print Server Status and Control menu. This menu is shown in Figure 6.30.

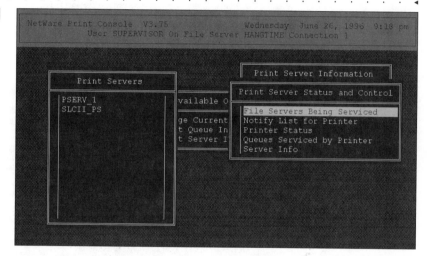

| FIGURE | 6.30 |

The Print Server Status and Control menu enables you to manage a print server that is currently running. If the print server is not up, this menu option will not show on the Print Server Information menu.

Defining Temporary Print Server Configurations   As you look closely at this menu, you will notice that three of the options—File Servers Being Serviced, Notify List for Printer, and Queues Serviced by Printer—are the same as the options we looked at in the Print Server Configuration menu. Though they appear to be the same, there is a difference: When changes are made to these three options in the Print Server Status and Control menu, the changes are *temporary*. When these options are modified in the Print Server Configuration menu, the changes are permanent.

So, what does temporary mean? Temporary, in this case, means during this print server session or while the print server is loaded. The next time the print server is taken down and reloaded, these options will be set back to what is defined in the Print Server Configuration menu.

Because these options were previously covered in depth, we won't bore you by covering them again. If you have a short memory or are picking up in the middle of this chapter, refer back to the "Managing Print Queues" section above for details on these three options.

Viewing a Print Server's Status   If you want to view information about a print server that is running, such as the print server version or the number of printers it is servicing, select the Server Info option from the Print Server Status and Control menu. When you choose this option, a screen similar to the one in Figure 6.31 will appear.

FIGURE 6.31

The Print Server Info/Status screen of PCONSOLE enables you to view information about the print server and to change a print server's status.

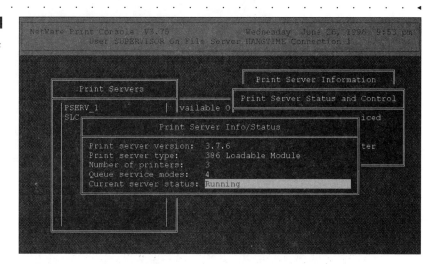

The options shown on this screen are briefly described below:

- ▸ **Print server version.** This option shows the version of print server software currently running. Novell will periodically release new versions of the print server software; this option is useful in determining if you are running the most current version. New releases can be obtained by accessing Novell's World Wide Web home page at http://www.novell.com or from Novell's NetWire bulletin board, accessible through CompuServe.

▸ **Print server type.** This option shows whether the print server is running as an NLM (as in Figure 6.31) or as a dedicated workstation print server using PSERVER.EXE.

▸ **Number of printers.** This option shows the number of printers being serviced by this print server.

▸ **Queue service modes.** This option shows the number of queue service modes available for this print server. Queue service modes determine how a print server services print jobs requesting multiple PRINTDEF form types. Queue service modes are set when a print queue is created.

▸ **Current server status.** This option shows the current status of the print server. A print server's status will be either Running, Going down after current jobs, or Down.

Downing a Print Server   If a print server is loaded as an NLM at a file server, there are two ways to take it down:

1 • Unload the NLM by typing:

UNLOAD PSERVER

2 • Use the Print Server Info/Status option of PCONSOLE.

If PSERVER.EXE has been loaded at a dedicated workstation, the print server must be taken down using PCONSOLE.

To down a print server using PCONSOLE, go to the print server's Print Server Information menu and select Print Server Status/Control. (Remember, if the print server is not running, this menu option will not appear.) Then select the Server Info option. A screen similar to the one shown in Figure 6.31 will appear. With the cursor on Current server status, press Enter. A menu appears, as shown in Figure 6.32.

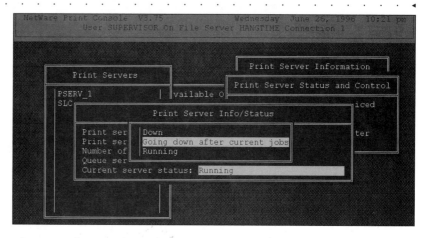

FIGURE 6.32

Taking a print server down in PCONSOLE

This menu gives you three options:

▸ **Down.** This option takes the print server down immediately, regardless of any print jobs that may be in the print queue. If jobs are in the queue when the print server is taken down, they will be saved and printed when the print server is brought back online.

▸ **Going down after current jobs.** This option enables all print jobs in the queue to finish printing before the print server is taken down.

▸ **Running.** This option indicates that the print server is up and running. If you have selected Going down after current jobs, you can switch the print server's status back to running if you decide you do not want it to go down.

CONTROLLING PRINTERS

Nothing is more frustrating and time-consuming for administrators than constantly walking over to the printer just to press the little form feed button. Likewise, the trial-and-error process of lining up forms or invoices to print is enough to make administrators pull their hair out.

PCONSOLE provides some hope for those of you who can relate to this. The Printer Status option of the Print Server Status and Control menu enables the administrator to control printers without leaving his or her desk. This option is shown in Figure 6.33.

F I G U R E   6.33

The Printer Status option of PCONSOLE enables the administrator to remotely control a printer.

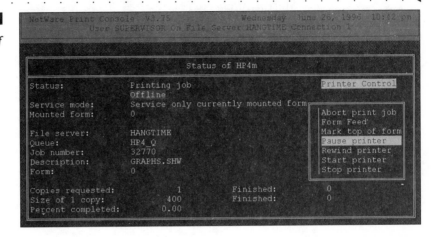

To access the Printer Control menu in the Printer Status option, use the arrow keys to highlight Printer Control on the right-hand side of the screen and press Enter.

NOTE

Each of the options shown on the Printer Control menu are described below:

- ▶ **Abort print job.** This option causes the printer to abandon the current print job. The job will be deleted from the queue.

- ▶ **Form Feed.** This option causes the printer to issue a form feed.

- ▶ **Mark top of form.** This option is useful when trying to align forms. When selected, it prints a line of asterisks (*) across the page.

- ▶ **Pause printer.** This option places the current job on hold. While the job is on hold, no additional printing takes place until a Start command is given.

▸ **Rewind printer.** This option enables you to reprint specific pages of a print job without having to resubmit the job. This is useful in the case of paper jams at the printer. This option also enables you to position the paper forward to skip pages of a print job.

▸ **Start printer.** This option will restart the printer after a Pause or Stop command has been issued.

▸ **Stop printer.** This option stops the printer and returns the current job to the queue. The printer will not print any additional jobs until the Start command has been issued.

Most of the other items on this screen are for information only. However, there are two additional menu options that can be modified—Service mode and Mounted form. The Service mode option enables you to change the print queue's service mode, as described earlier in this chapter. However, any changes made here to the Service mode field are only temporary. When the print server is taken down and restarted, the queue service mode will return to the default configured in the Print Server Configuration menu in Print Server Information.

Changing Currently Mounted Form

If you are using multiple paper types on a single printer and have defined PRINTDEF forms, the Mounted form field shown in Figure 6.33 may be used to view the form currently mounted on the printer. You can inform the print server that you have mounted a different form by changing it here.

Summary

While managing printing seems to occupy much of a network manager's time, understanding how the NetWare printing system works and being familiar with the tools available to manage that system can make the task faster and easier. In this chapter we took an in-depth look at managing a NetWare 3 printing system with PCONSOLE. If you are managing a mixed NetWare 3 and NetWare 4 printing environment, or if you plan to upgrade to NetWare 4, move on to the next chapter. If you would like detailed step-by-step instructions on managing NetWare 3 printing, refer to Part II of this book.

CHAPTER 7

Managing NetWare 4 Print Services

Now let's assume that your printing system is up and running. More than likely, you've just been hired on and you're *inheriting* a system set up previously! Regardless of how the system was created (by yourself or someone else) you now need to manage the system and all its daily hiccups. We'll assume that the system is printing now, but you just wish to make changes to the way it operates, or perhaps add access to new users and such.

In this chapter, we'll discuss these matters as well as the use of a tool provided free of charge to users of NetWare 4 and Novel Directory Services (NDS) called NetWare Application Launcher (NAL). Through it, you can automate how applications use printing in a much simpler way than the traditional methods of scripting. To obtain the NAL software, download it from Novell's Web site at www. novell.com. Or, if you have NetWare 4.11, it is included on the NetWare 4.11 CD.

Some of the day-to-day items covered in this chapter include the following common management tasks:

- Finding/Inventorying print devices

- Setting up scripting for automated user access

- Resequencing jobs in queue

- Checking job detail information

- Placing holds on jobs or deleting them

- Stopping and starting printer servicing

You can also refer to the Swift Track Guide in the second half of this book once you're familiar with how to work with these services.

Required Rights for Administration

As you may recall from earlier chapters, a user needs very little access in order to print to the system. If a user has at least *user* access to a queue, he or she can print to the printing system (see Figure 7.1). Even user access to print servers is not necessary unless you want users to check print server status on their own. If the users rely on you, or print administrators, then user access to the print server is not necessary.

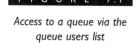

Access to a queue via the
queue users list

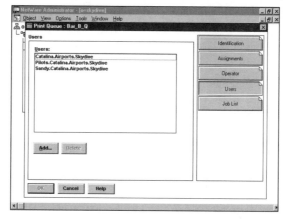

Container, Group, or Specific Access

Users can be given access to printing services in several ways. In some cases, more than one assignment may be necessary to give a person access to manage the print system or part of it. Here are the three possible access rights that can be given to a user:

I • **Container Access**. This aspect uses the Directory Service to control printing rights. If access is given to a container instead of a person or a group, then anyone in that container will have that access. For example, if you put the container Catalina.Airports.Skydive into the Queue Operators detail page, any users that exist in the Catalina.Airports. Skydive container will be able to exercise operator privileges to that queue (see Figure 7.2). Any user that gets moved *out* of Catalina. Airports.Skydive automatically loses that privilege (see Figure 7.3).

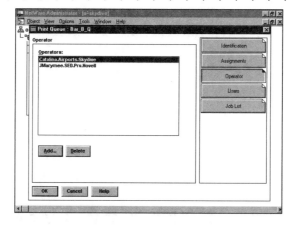

F I G U R E   7.2

*Operator access given
to a container*

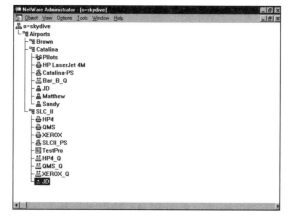

F I G U R E   7.3

*Drag-and-drop
administration*

The preceding makes enormous sense when resources such as printers are treated as local items. For example, a user in San Diego will
not need access to a printer in Salt Lake City. If the person gets *moved*
to Salt Lake City, though, the user should lose rights to the San Diego
printer (because he or she no longer needs it) and gain access to the
Salt Lake City one. NDS enables you to model your network this way
if you choose, creating a "management by exception" environment.
You only need to change specific rights access if the user falls outside
of the norm. Otherwise, user moves will adhere to the rules you've
embedded in the NDS tree.

Another aspect of dealing with containers is the creation of new printing system objects. To have the ability to create new queues, printers, and print servers, you must have Create privileges to the container. This right can be assigned in NWAdmin by right-mouse clicking on the container and adding trustee access to the selected user or under NETADMIN (the DOS version of NWAdmin) (see Figure 7.4). Lastly, to enable a user to add *other* users as operators or normal users of queues and print servers, the user must have Write privileges to the container's properties (see Figure 7.5). This access is set up from the same area as Object Creation. You can also choose a print queue object and do the same thing at the object level. The benefit of doing it this way is that it enables a user to add other objects as members of the Users or Operators detail pages, but does not enable the user to add information to other objects within the container (see Figures 7.6 and 7.7).

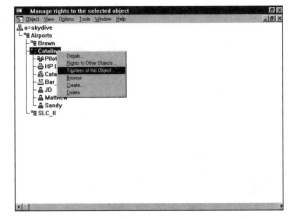

FIGURE 7.4

Selecting trustee assignments via NWAdmin

FIGURE 7.5

Object creation and property rights to whole container

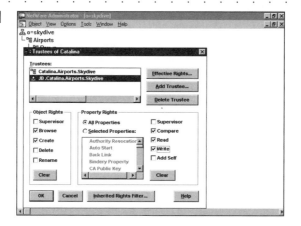

FIGURE 7.6

Trustee rights to a particular object (print queue)

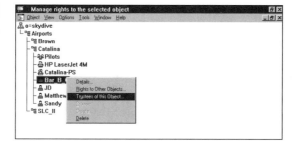

FIGURE 7.7

The property access right write ability to grant access only to this object

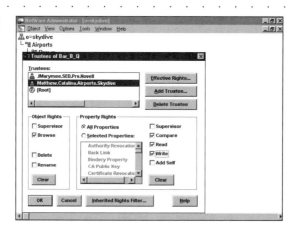

2 • **Group Access**. Group access to print objects works just like other group access in NetWare. You can create a group and make that group a queue operator, print server operator, print server, or queue user, and so on. The biggest difference is that when a user is moved (dragged and dropped) into a new container, his or her group membership follows, which also maintains his or her ability to exercise these rights, such as Create, Delete, Add, and so on.

3 • **Specific Access**. Just for clarity's sake. This is the ability to allow a particular user to manage a part of the system, be it as a print server operator, queue operator, user, and so on (see Figure 7.8).

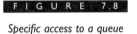

FIGURE 7.8

Specific access to a queue

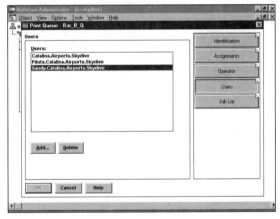

Table 7.1 summarizes the basic management access types.

TABLE 7.1

Basic management access types

PRINTING TASK	SECURITY ACCESS REQUIRED
Print to the print system	Container access (lost if user object is moved) *or* Object (such as a user) added to the Print Queue Users detail page.
Delete print jobs	Member of the queue's operator list. This can be given at a container, group, or user level.
Resequence jobs	

(continued)

	PRINTING TASK	SECURITY ACCESS REQUIRED
TABLE 7.1 *Basic management access types (continued)*	Place holds on jobs	
	Delete jobs	
	Change other job-related information	
	Abort print jobs	Member of the print server's operators list. This can be done via container, group, or specific access the same way as for queue operators.
	Stop jobs	
	Rewind jobs	
	Mount new forms	
	Add new users, groups, or containers to the operators or users lists of queues and print servers	You *must* have either write capabilities to the container object where the print objects reside *or* write access specifically to the object to which you want to add users, groups, or containers.
	Add new printing components, such as printers, print servers, and queues	You must have Create privileges to the container where you want to create additional components. Note that Create enables you to create other objects (such as other users, servers, and so on) other than just printing objects. With this capability, you can create users, groups, other subcontainers, and any other objects the system supports.

▶ · ◀

Management Tasks Under the Printing System

Once we now know what kind of access we need, we can then start to manage the system based on those rights. If in doubt about your access, you might want to check first before getting frustrated because you can't do something. A word to the wise: Even administrators can be blocked from doing some actions under printing. For example, if, as an administrator, you cannot delete a job in the queue, it could be because you are not a queue operator! But because you *are* an administrator, you can add yourself as a queue operator. The printing system is very strict in controlling its access. If you're used to dealing with the file system, administrator privilege means you can do anything. Not true with printing.

Print Services Inventorying and Searching

Whether you've installed the system or inherited it, a time comes when you will want to get a list of all printing resources that have currently been set up. This could be to check for old setups that are no longer used or just to make an inventory of what you've got.

NetWare 4 provides the capability to do this from a Windows or DOS environment. It's easier to do so under Windows than DOS, but the DOS version can be piped out to a file and used to document the system if you wish. The Windows version prints records as well, but in a graphical format rather than straight ASCII text.

Inventory Under NWAdmin

To inventory under NWAdmin, choose Search from the Object menu. If you are using NetWare 4.11 you can also use the new toolbar provided with that version of NWAdmin. To search for an object, simply click the Search button.

Whichever method you use to initiate the search, when the dialog box comes up, you can choose where to start the search, and whether you wish to search all areas below the starting context. Under Search For select Printer. Then choose OK (see Figure 7.9). You will be presented with a browser screen such as the one shown in Figure 7.10. At this point, you can double-click on any of the presented objects to manage them. If you wish to print the list, choose Print from the Object menu.

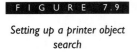

F I G U R E   7.9

Setting up a printer object search

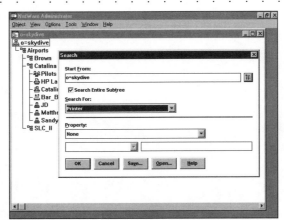

Printer inventory list

Inventory Under DOS

Under DOS, you can do inventory either under NETADMIN or using the command-line utility. NLIST enables you to output the results of the search by piping the output to a file for documentation purposes, while using NETADMIN is mostly just to view the search results. You can neither view print object details nor output the search results to a file. Consequently, for serious searching or inventorying, you're better off using NWAdmin or NLIST.

To Inventory/Search under NETADMIN, choose Search from the main menu. Then choose the parameters of the search. To do a whole tree search, choose [root] as the starting point. Then choose printer under the class option. When those choices are complete, press F10 to begin the search (Figure 7.11). As in NWAdmin, a window is presented with the results of the search. See figure 7.12 for details.

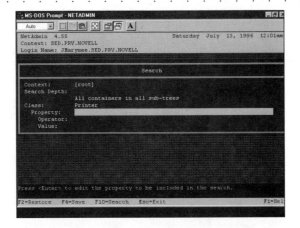

F I G U R E   7.11

Searching for printer objects using NETADMIN

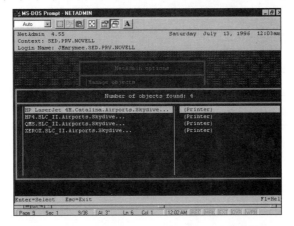

F I G U R E   7.12

Results of search

Under DOS, the utility to use is NLIST. NLIST provides a very straightforward way to search/inventory items. To do a simple query similar to the last two examples, type in the following command at the prompt:

```
C:> NLIST Printer /r /c /s
```

What you'll see is the listing of all printers in your tree and where they are contained (Figure 7.13). To pipe this to a file, type in:

```
C:> NLIST Printer /r /c /s > file.txt
```

You can then use the file to augment your system documentation.

F I G U R E   7.13

NLIST list of all searched printer objects

Searching Under NetWare 4 and NDS

For searching to be effective, you must add enough data to the directory to make a meaningful search. For example, if you include descriptions in NDS when you create a printer/print server/queue, you can use that information during a search. One of the options for a printer is to add information on any cartridges that the printer supports—for example, tax cartridges. If you put "Tax" into that property of the printer, you could then do a search of the entire system (or just a partial search) to look for that particular printer based on what cartridge it supported. See Figures 7.14 and 7.15.

F I G U R E   7.14

Searching for objects based on object criteria

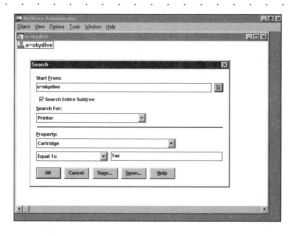

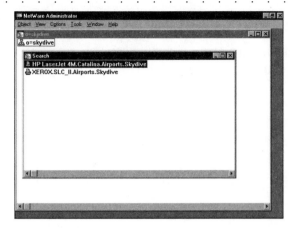

FIGURE 7.15

Result from specific feature search

This option can be extremely useful for administrators or users when looking for a printer that supports a particular service such as PostScript. You can also search and find what access a particular user has to queues on the network. Set the search parameters to look for all queues with the property User equal to username (see Figure 7.16). The searching mechanism is very flexible and enables searching of nonprint objects as well.

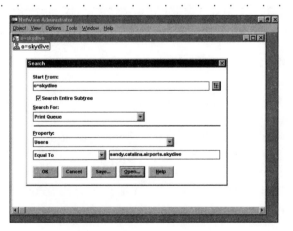

FIGURE 7.16

Searching for user access to queues

Managing the Printers

As you recall, three primary components make up the print system: the printer, the queue, and the printer server. We'll first talk about the printer.

Printer Tasks

Printers are the end reason why the printing system is set up. Day-to-day tasks include keeping the printers running and servicing user needs. NetWare provides several management tools to enable you to remotely manage printers.

NOTE

You must have been given access to the print server as an operator or a user under the print server object. If not, you will not see the Printer Status detail page under NWAdmin, and the Printer Status option under PCONSOLE will indicate UNAVAILABLE.

The main tasks you might do when managing the printer include the following:

▸ **Starting/stopping the printer.** This could be due to a paper jam, to reload paper, or for other reasons. If you use forms, you may need to remount a form in the printer remotely. You can also do this from the server, if necessary.

▸ **Marking forms.** If you use preprinted forms, you may need to set the form in the printer and be able to position it properly. Using the Mark Form option prints a row of asterisks at the beginning part of the form enabling you to gauge how far into the printer the form must be fed. This usually applies to dot matrix form-feed types of printers rather than laser printers.

▸ **Setting up notification.** You may wish to modify who gets notified in case of printer problems.

To accomplish these primary printer management tasks, you'll need to run either NWAdmin or PCONSOLE. We'll start first with NWAdmin.

Printer Management with NWAdmin

Printer management is straightforward with NWAdmin. The following are the three primary printing tasks as accomplished with NWAdmin.

Starting and stopping printers   You start and stop a printer when paper jams occur, when the paper supply gets low, or in any situation where you might need to stop the printer temporarily to make a quick adjustment. The steps are simple:

1 • Find the object you wish to manage and open it by double-clicking. Or, if you are using NetWare 4.11, you can click the View or Modify Object Properties from the toolbar.

2 • From the Details page, choose Printer Status.

3 • Choose Pause to stop the printer or Start to restart it (see Figure 7.17).

F I G U R E   7.17

Printer options

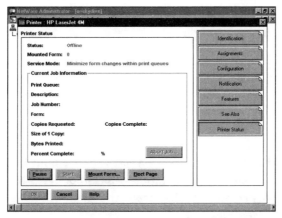

Mark/eject page   This option can be used to eject a sheet of paper in the printer. The ability to select Mark Form is not available in NWAdmin, only PCON-SOLE. First find the object you wish to manage and open it by double-clicking. Or, if you are using NetWare 4.11, you can click the View or Modify Object Properties from the toolbar. Highlight Printer Status and choose Eject Page.

Change notification   This option differs from the capture flag notification. In capture, the system can notify the user when the job is complete. Notification in

. . . . . .
227

this setting only applies when problems occur. By default, the person who sub-mitted the job will be notified. Others can be added, if desired. All you have to do, with printer information open, is select the Notification detail page.

Note that Job Owner is the default. By choosing Add you can add a container, group, or user, or a combination of all three. You can also determine how often a notification is sent when a problem arises (see Figure 7.18).

F I G U R E   7.18

Setting the NOTIFY option

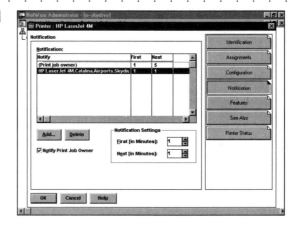

Printer Management with PCONSOLE

Printer management is also straightforward with PCONSOLE. To manage your printer under DOS, run PCONSOLE, choose Printers from the main menu and select the printer desired.

NOTE

PCONSOLE in NetWare 4 has support built in to "see" printing components as either bindery-based or NDS-based. To toggle this option, press the F4 key from the main menu as soon as PCONSOLE starts (see Figure 7.19).

F I G U R E   7.19

Toggling bindery or NDS view under PCONSOLE

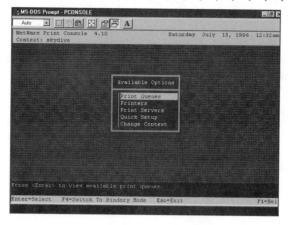

NOTE

Because some configuration changes cannot take hold until the printer server has been restarted, PCONSOLE has some notations to show what is [A]ctive and what is [C]onfigured. If you see [AC] **following an assignment, it means the current configuration for this parameter is also the one that's active (see Figure 7.20).**

F I G U R E   7.20

Active/Configured options under NETADMIN

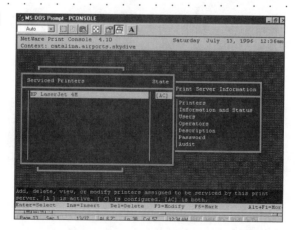

The following are the three primary printing tasks as accomplished with PCONSOLE.

Starting and stopping printers   Under PCONSOLE, the Stop command and the Pause command are identical if no jobs are in the queue. If a job is currently being serviced, Pause stops the job in mid-stream and makes it wait for a restart. Stop, on the other hand, stops printing and returns the job to the queue. In effect, it fully rewinds the job to the beginning and awaits a restart of the printer. Here are the steps:

1 •   In PCONSOLE, Choose Printer Status.

2 •   Choose Printer Control.

3 •   Select Pause or Stop to stop the printer, and Start to continue (see Figure 7.21).

F I G U R E   7.21

PCONSOLE printer options

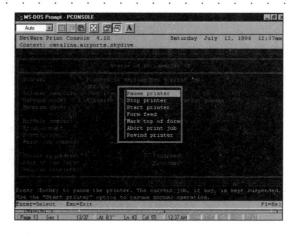

Mark/eject page   From the same menu as described previously, choose Mark Top of Form. Although the names are slightly different in NWAdmin and PCONSOLE, the functionality is the same.

Change notification   After you select the desired printer (after you select Printers from the main menu in PCONSOLE), choose Notification from the bottom of the list. You can then add another object to get notification by pressing the Insert key. Delete removes a user (see Figure 7.22).

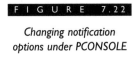

F I G U R E   7.22

Changing notification options under PCONSOLE

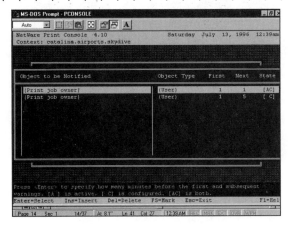

Managing Queues

The queue is the center of the whole printing system. Regardless of any third-party items that you add, you will need a queue most of the time. As a result, management can take place in several areas. Bear in mind that you need Operator status as a user to complete any of these tasks, with one exception: manipulation of your own submitted print jobs.

NOTE

If you have submitted a print job, you can act upon it in several ways without being a print queue operator. You can place a user hold upon the job (which holds it indefinitely in the queue), change form types, print a banner or description, or do anything else that does not affect other user print jobs. This includes deleting your print job if you so choose.

The main tasks that you can accomplish are as follows:

▶ **Controlling access to the queue.** This is not so much access by user as access by the rest of the system. You can prevent a print server from servicing your print queue temporarily, you can prevent any new print servers from attaching to the queue, and you can disable acceptance of new print jobs. This could be useful in a system where a queue is being used for a specific purpose. For example, you could have one queue that serves as the payroll queue and one that acts as the invoice queue. By disabling one or the other and connecting the printer or form that it needs in order to print, you can prevent a print job from being printed on the wrong paper or form (see Figure 7.23).

F I G U R E   7.23

Queue service options

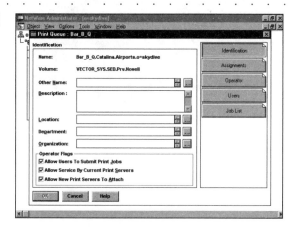

▸ **Viewing details of print jobs.** This option comes in handy when a job refuses to print. You can view stats about the job to diagnose what the problem might be. One example of a problem is a job that requires a different form type than what's being serviced at the printer.

▸ **Resequencing jobs.** At times certain jobs need to be reordered ahead of others. These could be payroll checks, the boss's letter, the latest stock quote, or anything that needs to be bumped up in the queue. Remember, you must be a print queue operator to do this! (See Figures 7.24 and 7.25.)

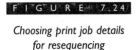

F I G U R E   7.24

Choosing print job details for resequencing

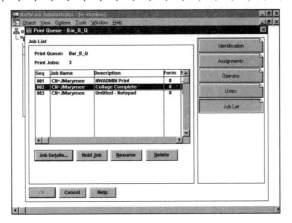

F I G U R E   7.25

Setting the resequence number

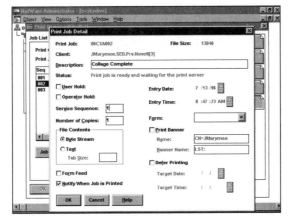

Managing Queues via NWAdmin

To manage queues with NWAdmin, first select the queue you wish to manage and double-click on it to open the Detail pages. Or, if you are using NetWare 4.11, you can click the View or Modify Object Properties from the toolbar.

Controlling Queue Service

The first detail page is Information. At the bottom of the page, you can select one or more of the three options, as follows:

▶ **Allow users to submit print jobs.**

▸ **Allow service by current print servers.** This means one or more print servers may have attached to the queue as configured. You can keep the queue from servicing jobs temporarily.

▸ **Allow new print servers to attach.** Because a queue can be serviced by more than one print server, this option makes sense. You may wish to restrict this queue only to the currently attached print servers in order to limit traffic.

Viewing Details of Jobs

To view details of jobs, perform the following steps:

1 • With the dialog detail pages open, select Job List.

2 • Click on the job you wish to view or change.

3 • Click on Job Details. You can now view or change information about the job. Note that if you are just a queue user, you can place a hold on your own job as well as change aspects of the job that do not affect other users.

Resequencing Print Jobs

In the Details view, locate the Service Sequence field. By changing the number and exiting, you can see that the job changes positions in the queue.

Managing Queues with PCONSOLE

Print queues can also be managed using the DOS-based utility PCONSOLE. Logged in as ADMIN or an equivalent user, run PCONSOLE from the DOS command line.

NOTE

When using PCONSOLE, note the context displayed at the top of the screen. This is the context where you will be managing print queues. If the queue you wish to manage is not in the context shown, use the Change Context option from the PCONSOLE main menu to set the desired context.

Controlling Queue Service

From the PCONSOLE main menu, select Print Queues and then the queue you want to control the queue service of. From the Print Queue Information screen, choose Status. You will then be presented with three options for controlling the servicing of the queue, as follows:

▸ **Enable users to submit print jobs.** When set to No, users cannot send print jobs to this queue. The default is Yes. This option is useful when performing printer maintenance or when a new printer is being installed.

▸ **Enable service by current print server.** When set to No, the print server can service jobs in this queue. The default is Yes. This option enables print jobs to go to the queue but does not enable the print server to service them. This is useful when the printer will be temporarily unavailable.

▸ **Enable new print servers to attach.** If you set this flag to No, no servers can attach to the print queue. The default is Yes. Because more than one print server can service a queue, this option is useful in preventing print servers other than the one currently attached from servicing the queue.

Viewing Print Job Details

To view the details of a print job through PCONSOLE, select Print Queues from the main menu and then the print queue that contains the job you want to view. Then do the following steps:

1 • Choose Print Jobs from the Print Queue Information menu.

2 • Highlight the job you want to view or change the job status of and then press Enter.

3 • Change the parameters of the print job by using the arrow keys to move through the fields.

If you are a print queue user (nonoperator) you can place a hold on your own job as well as change the job parameters. You cannot, however, change the jobs of other users.

Resequencing Print Jobs

To change the service order of print jobs in the queue (resequencing), from the PCONSOLE main menu, select Print Queues and then select the print queue that contains the jobs you want to resequence. Then perform the following steps:

1 • Choose Print Jobs from the Print Queue Information menu.

2 • Highlight the job you want to change the sequence of and then press Enter.

3 • Use the arrow keys to move to the Service Sequence field and change the service sequence as desired.

Only print queue operators can move one user's job ahead of another user's job. Print queue users can only resequence their own jobs.

Print Server Management

Typically, very little is needed to manage the print server itself. The main thing you may want to do is unload the print server after a change has been made so the changes take effect. One major redeeming option under NWAdmin is the ability to get a bird's eye view of the system and status of each component.

Remember, users need access as print server users only to check the status of a job *once it is being serviced by the print server.* Up until that time, they can check the queue and see when the job will most likely be serviced by the print server. If a user is *not* a print server user or operator, the Printer Status detail page will not be visible under NWAdmin (see Figure 7.26).

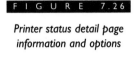

F I G U R E   7.26

*Printer status detail page
information and options*

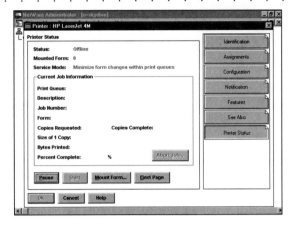

Print Server Management with NWAdmin

To manage a print server with NWAdmin, select it under NWAdmin and double-click to open the Detail pages. Or, if you are using NetWare 4.11, you can click the View or Modify Object Properties from the toolbar.

Unload running Print Server

You can unload a running print server from a workstation, but to reload it you must run RCONSOLE or restart the print server from the server itself.

If you have operator access to the print server, you will see the Unload option in the Identification detail page. After you have selected it, you can choose whether to unload immediately (regardless of any jobs being serviced) or unload after any current print jobs have been serviced. The latter is the more polite way of downing a print server (see Figures 7.27 and 7.28).

F I G U R E   7.27

Unload option with print server operator status

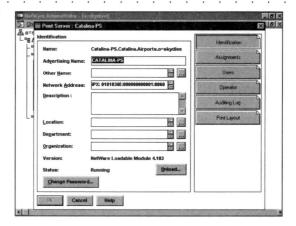

F I G U R E   7.28

Unload options

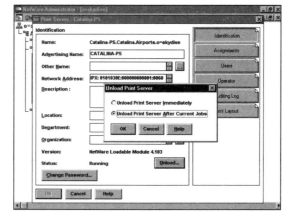

Viewing the Printing System Layout and Status

This option is handy for taking a quick look at potential problems. If any component of the system has a problem, an exclamation point appears next to the object. You have several options when viewing the printing system layout and status, as follows:

▸ Select Print Layout from the detail pages list to see the printing layout (see Figure 7.29).

Printing layout by print server

▶ Double-click on any component to have the view collapse.

▶ If you select an object and choose Status, you can get a dialog box of status information. You can also click on an object and right-click with the mouse to view the same information! (See Figure 7.30.)

Status info under Print Layout

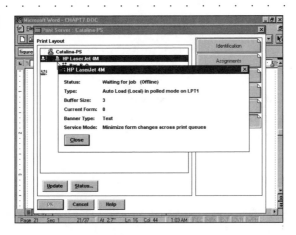

▶ Click on Update to update the display in case a problem has resolved itself or a new one has come up.

When Changes Take Effect

Most changes to the system take effect immediately. If they can't, they take effect when the print server is reloaded.

Print Server Management under PCONSOLE

To manage a print server through PCONSOLE, you must be logged in as a print server operator. Then run PCONSOLE from the DOS command line.

Unload a Running Print Server

To unload a print server that is up and running, choose Print Servers from the PCONSOLE main menu. Then do the following steps:

1 • From the Print Server Information menu, choose Information and Status.

2 • Use the arrow keys to move to the Current Server Status field.

3 • Press Enter and select Going Down After Current Jobs to have the print server finish any print jobs currently in progress before going down.

4 • Or, select Down to have the print server go down immediately. The current print jobs are returned to their print queues.

NOTE
 The Information and Status option of the Print Server Information menu is only displayed if the user is logged in as a print server operator.

Making Life Easier for You and the Users

You have several ways to automate printer capture under the printing system. Regardless of which method you choose, users will still want to change printer settings occasionally. Ideally, the administrator has made some provision for automating usage of the printing system for users.

A few ways to automate the system include the following:

▸ Create Login scripts that define printer mappings that will guarantee the user at least *one* printer capture in case the application does not support automatic network captures. Scripts can be created per container, profile, or user.

▸ Set up automatic capture under Windows 95. When defining a new printer under Windows 95, you can have that definition automatically occur every time you log in. The same can be done under Windows 3.1x using a NetWare tool called NWUSER that comes with the VLM client.

▸ Use Network Application Launcher. This free NetWare utility uses NDS to launch applications stored on the network. The beauty of this launcher is that the printer capture doesn't get executed until the application is launched. And the capture is removed when the application terminates.

Using Scripts with Captures

When you use scripting under NetWare 4, you have several ways to deploy printing commands. This book is not designed to answer all questions regarding scripts, but a small primer will be helpful in understanding what's involved.

The three major types of scripts are container, profile, and personal. The three types of scripts have the following functions:

▸ **Container script.** This script executes for a user whenever he or she logs in if the user exists within that container. Other users in other containers may or may not have their own scripts. A container script executes first upon login.

▸ **Profile script.** A profile script is actually a separate object within the directory services tree (see Figure 7.31). It can be given a login script of its own. Then the profile can be attached to one or more users. Because it is attached to the user directly, the script still executes for him or her, even when the user is moved. In a container script, if the user gets moved, the new container may or may not have a script. Consequently, use profile scripts when a printer capture must follow the user.

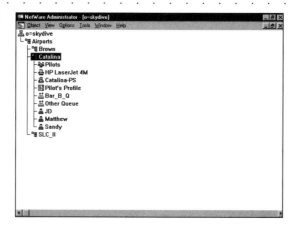

Profile script object in directory services

▶ **Personal script.** A personal script is just that: personal. If anything needs to be custom-tailored to a user, use a personal script. The difference between a personal script and a profile script is that once the profile script is written and assigned to one or more users, a change to the profile script automatically applies to all assigned users with no further intervention. If it were a personal script, you would have to modify every user.

Login Script Philosophy—Locale-Based Printers

Typically, most print capture assignments are applied at the container level in the container login script. Most users receive queue privileges *because* they exist within the container where the queue exists, so it makes sense to have the container script automatically capture the user to the queue. If they get moved *out* of the container, they'll no longer need the same printer capture to execute when they log in (see Figure 7.32). In fact, if the script still executed you would get an error because you would no longer have access to the queue.

F I G U R E 7.32

Locale-based print system access and login scripts

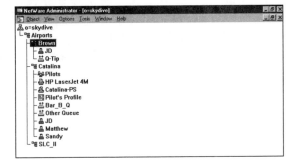

Login Script Philosophy—User-Based Printers

If a user or a group of users needs access to a queue/printer, the best method is to grant the group/user direct access to the queue. Then either create a profile script and assign it to *all* members of the group or create a personal script for each of the users that specifies capture to that queue/printer.

NOTE

Profile script objects can *only* be applied to users, not to groups or containers (see Figure 7.33). As a result, if you assign capture via profile scripts, you'll have to manually assign it to each user that's a member of the group.

F I G U R E 7.33

Assigning profile scripts to users

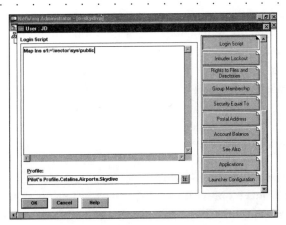

NOTE The printer and queue objects are interchangeable here because you can capture to either. If you capture to a printer object the user will ultimately be sending data to a queue assigned to the printer.

When assigning a capture under a login script, it's always a good idea to use the full name of the object. If a queue/printer called HPLaser existed under Catalina.Airports.Skydive and the user did as well, you *could* use just the name HPLaser as follows:

```
Capture q=HPLaser
```

However, if the printer/queue were in another container, you would have a capture statement similar to this:

```
Capture q=.HPLaser.Catalina.Airports.Skydive
```

It's always a good practice to use full names when capturing to the print system. This habit avoids the potential issue of referring to the wrong printer. In addition, if the user gets moved, the full naming still works. A partial name will not.

Users of Windows 95

Under Windows 95, you can also create a printer under the Start menu (choose Start, then Settings, and then Printers). When you create a new printer, you have the option of making it a local or network printer. In addition, you can choose to make that printer the default when you use Windows applications. This automatically becomes available when a user logs in to Windows 95. Although this can simplify things for the user (the same as login scripts) if still means the administrator has to configure each workstation to support one or more printers. This task can be automated in a large environment using setup files. See the Windows 95 Resource Kit for details on how to do this.

NOTE For applications to print under Windows 95, you must set up at least one printer object under Windows. Whether that printer prints to a network queue (such as \\server\queuename) *or* to a local LPT device (LPT1, LPT2, LPT3) does not matter. The NetWare client can be configured to handle either implementation (see Figure 7.34).

F I G U R E   7.34

Capturing under Windows 95

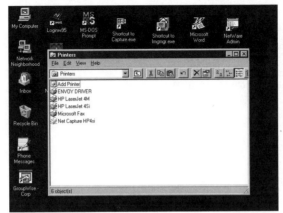

Using NetWare Application Launcher with Network Printing

NetWareApplication Launcher (also called NAL or AppLauncher) is a utility that comes with the Novell Client32 kit and with NetWare 4.11. Using it under Windows 3.x and 95 and NT environments, you can deploy applications down to the desktop without scripting or manually changing a user's workstation. This includes printing parameters, as described next.

Typical Printing Support

Usually you must set a printing environment for users so that when they log in, printing will be active for them. In some cases, that printing setup may need to be changed as the user works, as in the following sequence of events:

1 • The user's application needs a form feed after printing, whereas most of the other applications don't.

2 • One application must print to the HPLaser queue while another should go to the Payroll queue.

3 • The user accidentally stops capturing to the network. What will happen when he/she starts to print?

Administrators can deal with these issues in several different ways, as follows:

1 • Have batch files created that execute when an application is launched. This could be a PIF file, for example.

2 • Set the lowest common denominator parameters, such as extra form feeds for all applications. This option, unfortunately, wastes paper.

3 • Use network-aware applications that store such parameters locally.

Using NDS as an Application Configuration Store

The NetWare Application Launcher takes a different approach than typical printing support. Realizing that every single application can have potentially different print settings, AppLauncher (as it's often called) enables each application object to have different settings. Then, when the user launches the AppObject (as it's also often called), the settings automatically take hold and proper printing takes place. Custom drive mappings and command-line parameters can be preset as well.

Application Launcher Configuration

The AppLauncher consists of the user utility (or window) and the NWAdmin snap-in. The NWAdmin snap-in is an extension to NWAdmin that enables the administrator to create and manage application objects.

NOTE

If you don't have NetWare 4.11, you may obtain the NetWare Application Launcher free of charge by downloading Client32 for Windows 95 or Client32 for DOS/Windows 3.x from Novell's Web site at www.novell.com.

To customize an application, you'll need to perform the following four steps:

1 • Create a new application object.

2 • Specify drives/ports.

3 • Choose the users who will be able to launch the application.

4 • Run AppLauncher (NALW95.EXE or NALW31.EXE) and launch the application.

Each of the preceding steps consists of several further steps, discussed in detail next.

Create a new application object When creating an object, you must have already installed the application somewhere. This installation could be local (not recommended but possible) or on the network. You can point to it by using either UNCs (such as \\Server\Volume\Path\file) or a drive letter. You can also use the Directory Map Object under NDS.

When creating the application object for this example, create it in a container where the desired user object exists. For example, if it exists under SLC_II. Airports.Skydive as Stevens, create the new application object under SLC_II. Airports.Skydive as well. To create the application object, perform the following steps:

1 • Under NWAdmin, choose Create a New Object from the File menu. Or, if you are using the NetWare 4.11 version of NWAdmin, click the Create Object button from the toolbar.

2 • Choose Application for either Windows 95 or Windows 3.x depending on what operating system you're using (see Figure 7.35).

F I G U R E   7.35

Creating a new application object

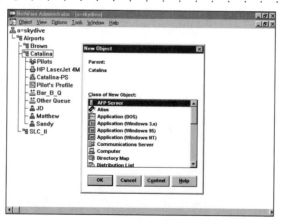

3 • Give the new object a meaningful name and platform type (Windows 3.x, Windows 95, and so on).

4 • Specify where the application is installed (such as C:\WINDOWS\ CALC.EXE).

5 • Click on Define Additional Properties.

6 • Click on Create.

Specify drives/ports

Here's where you can customize drives and printer port settings. When specifying a queue name, ensure you use a full name to avoid any ambiguities (for example, .Bar_B_Q.sales.Acme).

I • Click on Drives/Ports (see Figure 7.36).

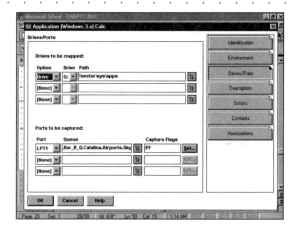

Setting drive/ports options

2 • Click on Port and choose LPT1.

3 • Enter a queue name. Using the browser is easiest. Use full names.

4 • Set capture flags. Click on Form Feed and Override Workstation Settings.

Choose the users who will be able to launch the application   This is where you specify the users who can launch the application. Note that each user still needs file access to the location where the application resides. For example, if DOOM2.EXE resides on SYS:GAMES, the user will need access rights (such as Read and File Scan) in order to launch the application, even if he or she has been given the rights to launch the application here. To choose the users who will be able to launch this application, perform the following steps:

1 • Click on Associations.

2 • Choose Add (see Figure 7.37).

FIGURE 7.37

Adding application object access

3 • Choose the container, group, or user that will be permitted to launch this application. You can add more than one.

4 • When you are done adding, click on OK to save changes.

Run AppLauncher and launch the application Once in AppLauncher, you should see the application object you just created. By choosing Properties you can see the information you placed in the object. Note that it is not editable from the launcher itself—only from NWAdmin with the proper rights! After terminating the application, note that AppLauncher cleans up all the resources that were allocated when the application was launched. Here are the steps to launch an application from the Application Launcher:

1 • Run AppLauncher (NALW95.EXE or NALW31.EXE, depending on your operating system). Note that the application object you created is available for launch.

2 • Click on Properties to view application information.

3 • Go to a DOS box and note capture settings (CAPTURE SH).

4 • Return to the AppLauncher window and double-click on the object to launch it.

5 • Go to the DOS box again and note capturing in effect.

6 • Terminate the application and look at the DOS box again.

Creating and managing objects can only be done through NWAdmin. NETADMIN does not have the extensions that enable the creation of custom NDS objects.

NOTE

This is just a small example of what NDS can do for you in the printing world. With AppLauncher and tools similar to AppLauncher, you can do much more centralized administration than ever before.

Using Print Job Configurations

Another way to simplify printing management is to create print job configurations. Print job configurations enable the administrator to create *printing templates* that specify multiple items related to printing. Put simply, configurations can be set up once to do all the dirty work and then be applied on a larger scale. You can deploy print job configurations in two different ways:

▸ **As a container setting.** Each container can have multiple configurations with one possibly designated as a default. Once established, the configurations will then be available to all users within the container. If you set one as a default, then all users within that container will have that configuration as their default.

▶   **As a user setting.** Each user can also have multiple configurations with one potentially chosen as the default. If one has not been chosen as a default, the container's default will apply if one has been selected.

The primary reason for using configurations is not to ease the capturing of printers. It *does* make capture easier for a user because the user can just execute the CAPTURE command (such as in a login script) and the proper settings will take place. But because most users have their default settings precaptured within a login script, why bother? Aside from simplifying the administrator role somewhat, one other good reason is the use of print devices.

Print Devices Under NetWare

Usually, you only need a device if you have a printer or printing device that needs to be preconfigured through NetWare. In other words, you may not have a driver or be able to set up the device properly through the application or Windows. This is seldom the case, but it may happen.

When you use devices, you are basically creating a driver for your device under NetWare. Once instituted, the only way to invoke this new driver (under NetWare) is via a print job configuration. When you create a configuration, you can specify some very common settings that may need to be set when printing. These settings include the following (asterisks indicate settings that can also be defined using the CAPTURE command or Windows capture):

▶   Form name*

▶   Content type* (usually Byte Stream)

▶   Form feed*

▶   Queue name to use*

▶   Printer device and mode

▶   Timeouts and print banners*

Creating Print Devices, Forms, and Job Configurations with NWAdmin

To set up a simple configuration and device, first launch NWAdmin. Then select the container you wish to affect (one with users) and open it. Then follow the steps given for each of the following options.

Importing a device   This option imports one of the pre-existing device files distributed with NetWare. These files can be modified to fit a particular need if necessary. You can also export them to a file and enable other systems to import them. Here's how to import a device:

1 • Open Details on the container using the right mouse button (see Figure 7.38). Or, if you are using the NetWare 4.11 version of NWAdmin, click the View or Modify Object Properties button on the toolbar.

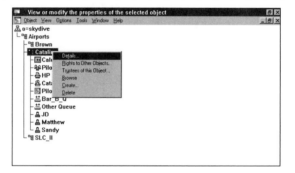

F I G U R E   7.38

Editing container details

2 • Choose Print Devices.

3 • Choose Import.

4 • Specify SYS:PUBLIC.

5 • Choose a device file name such as HP2.PDF.

Create a new device   In addition to importing devices, you can also create new devices. Devices are comprised of functions and modes. Functions you get from your printer manual. Once you've created a list of functions for your device, you can build modes. Modes are simply a list of one or more functions to be sent to the printer if your device is used in a job configuration. Note that Re-Initialize is a default mode, but has no functions unless you give it some. Note also that you have the option of ordering the functions. This ensures that functions are sent to the printer in the proper order. You would not want to send a Re-Init right after you put the printer into Landscape mode, for example. Here are the steps for creating a new device:

I • Under the Print Devices option of the container's Details page, Choose Create.

2 • Give the new device a name (Mega-Jet) and click on OK (see Figure 7.39).

F I G U R E   7 . 3 9

Creating a new print device

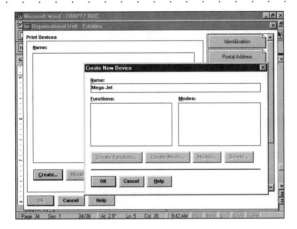

3 • Choose Modify and then Create Function (see Figure 7.40).

F I G U R E   7 . 4 0

Creating a new function

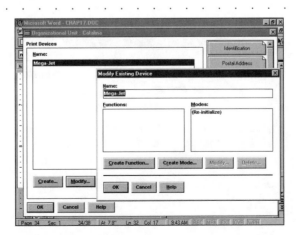

4 • Give the new function a name (such as Reset).

5 • Provide the escape code needed for the new function and click on OK (see Figure 7.41).

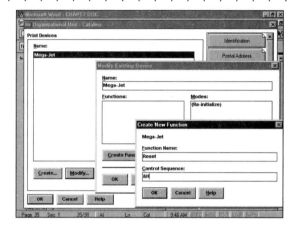

F I G U R E   7.41

Setting the function escape code

6 • Select the Re-Initialize mode and choose Modify.

7 • Click on the function you just created (Reset) and choose Add Below or Add Above and choose OK (see Figure 7.42).

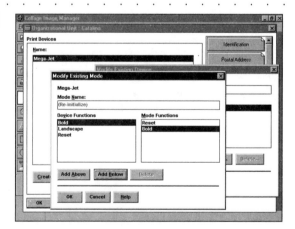

F I G U R E   7.42

Adding functions to the mode

8 • Choose OK again.

Create two forms   This option is only used if you use preprinted forms on a single printer. It lets the printer know when you need to switch from invoices to payroll checks, for example. By default, the starting form for a newly created printer is 0. The first form name is 0 as well. Make sure that the most common paper that you use matches the starting form on the printer. Otherwise, the minute the print server comes up for the day, you'll have to mount a new form at the printer. Here's how to create two forms:

1 •   With the container's Details page open, choose Printer Forms.

2 •   Choose Create.

3 •   Give the form a name (such as `white`, `green bar`, or whatever).

4 •   Ensure the form has a unique number; otherwise, it will not be created. (Note that length and width are not used.)

Create a print job configuration—container level   Now we tie everything together with the print job configuration. Remember that any users existing in the container will be able to see and use the configurations created at the container. When completed, you can select one as the default, or have none as the default. The benefit is that the user can just type in the CAPTURE command and all the configuration parameters will be used.

NOTE

In NWAdmin, if you do not select a queue within the same container, you will not see forms and devices for that container.

The steps for creating a print job configuration are as follows:

1 •   With the container's Details page open, choose Print Job Configuration.

2 •   Choose New.

3 •   Give it a name, such as `Main`.

4 •   Select a queue at the bottom. Choose a queue within the same container (see Figure 7.43).

Creating a print job
configuration

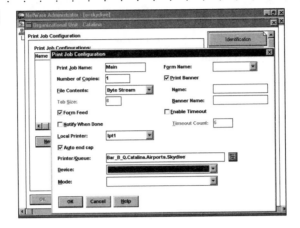

5 • Choose a form (upper right). Note that it is the one just created.

6 • Choose a device (lower left) and a mode for it (Re-Initialize).

7 • Change anything else you wish to and click on OK.

8 • To make this the default configuration, select it and click on Default.
You'll see a little printer icon next to the configuration you just set as
the default. The Default button is a toggle, so you can deselect it if
you wish. (See Figure 7.44.)

Setting a default print job
configuration

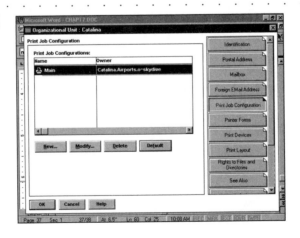

Create a print job configuration for a user

This option enables the supervisor or user to create additional user-specific configurations. This may be handy if the user uses a variety of printers and services. Note that any default configuration you designate for the user will override the default set at the container. Here's how to create a print job configuration for a user:

1 • From NWAdmin, choose a user within the container you've been working with and open the Details page by double-clicking the object. Or, if you are using the NetWare 4.11 version of NWAdmin, click on the View or Modify Object Properties button from the toolbar.

2 • Choose Print Job Configuration.

3 • You should see the configuration created at the container (see Figure 7.45). If you made it the default, it will be the default for this user.

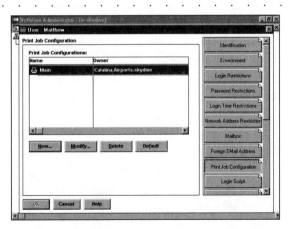

F I G U R E   7.45

Container print job configuration is available to the user (Matthew)

4 • Create a new configuration the same way you did for the container.

Creating Print Devices, Forms, and Job Configurations from DOS Utilities

To create a print job configuration and use a NetWare-defined print device, you must use two separate utilities, PRINTDEF and PRINTCON (the same task using Windows requires only one utility, NWAdmin). Print devices defined in PRINT-

DEF can only be used through a print job configuration. Print job configurations are created in PRINTCON. The following sections describe the processes of importing and creating new print devices, creating printer forms, and then using those forms in a print job configuration created in PRINTCON.

Importing Print Devices under PRINTDEF   To use one of the print devices provided with NetWare 4, log in as ADMIN or an equivalent user and run PRINTDEF from the DOS command line. Then perform the following steps:

1 •   From the PRINTDEF main menu, select Print Devices.

2 •   Choose Import Print Device.

3 •   At the Source Directory prompt, enter SYS:\PUBLIC and press Enter.

4 •   Use the arrow keys to select the print device for your printer and press Enter.

NOTE   **If the print device for your printer is not on the list, it is possible that the printer you are using emulates another printer type. Check your printer manual for details.**

Creating a new print device in PRINTDEF   As described in the NWAdmin section previously, print devices are comprised of functions and modes. Various printer functions are specific to individual printer types and can generally be found in the printer's manual. Once you've created a list of functions for your device, you can build modes. Modes are simply lists of one or more functions that are sent to the printer if your device is used in a job configuration. In creating a print MODE with PRINTDEF, you must assign the functions in a specific order (unlike with NWAdmin, which enables you to change the order once created). This step ensures that the functions are sent to the printer in the proper order.

To create a new print device, log in as ADMIN or an equivalent user and run the PRINTDEF utility from the DOS command line. Then go through the following steps:

1 •   From the PRINTDEF main menu, choose Edit Print Devices.

2 •   From the Defined Print Devices menu, press the Insert key to add a new device and then give it a name.

3 • Select the device from the Defined Print Devices menu and press Enter.

4 • Choose Device Functions and use the Insert key to create a new function.

5 • Enter the function name and control sequence.

6 • Continue to create the Device Functions for the mode of printing you want to define.

7 • From the Device Options menu, select Device Modes.

8 • To add a new mode, press the Insert key and give it a name.

9 • Select the mode from the Modes for Device list and press Insert to add the functions for this mode in the proper order (as defined by your printer manual).

10 • When you finish defining this Device Mode, press Esc to save the changes.

Creating print forms with PRINTDEF   Print forms are used if you use preprinted forms on a single printer. They let the printer know when you need to switch from invoices to payroll checks, for example. By default, the starting form for a newly created printer is 0. The first form name is 0 as well. Make sure that the most common paper that you use matches the starting form on the printer. Otherwise, as soon as the print server comes up for the day, you will have to mount a new form at the printer.

To create a new form with PRINTDEF, log in as ADMIN or an equivalent user and run PRINTDEF from the DOS command line. The next steps are as follows:

1 • From the PRINTDEF main menu, choose Printer Forms.

2 • To create a new form, press the Insert key.

3 • Enter the form name, number, length, and width.

The length and width parameters in the form's definition are for information only and have no effect on the formatting of a print job.

NOTE

4 • When you finish defining the form, press Esc and save the changes.

Creating container-level print job configurations with PRINTCON As mentioned earlier, print devices must be used through print job configurations. When a print job configuration is created at a container level, any users in that container will be able to see and use those configurations. You can also choose one configuration to be the default. As a result, when the user types CAPTURE at the DOS command line, the parameters defined in the default job configuration will be used.

To create a container-level job configuration, log in as ADMIN or an equivalent user and run PRINTCON from the DOS command line. Then run through the following steps:

1 • From the PRINTCON main menu, select Change Current Object.

2 • Use the Insert key to browse the directory tree for the container you want to define the job configuration for. When you have found it, highlight it and press F10.

3 • From the PRINTCON main menu, select Edit Print Job Configurations.

4 • Press the Insert key to add a new job configuration and give it a name.

5 • Select the job configuration from the list and press Enter.

6 • Use the arrow keys to move to the Device field and press Enter.

7 • Select the desired device from the list.

8 • Use the arrow keys to move to the Mode field and press Enter.

9 • Choose the desired mode of printing.

10 • Move to the Form Name field and press Enter.

11 • Choose the desired form from the list.

12 • Change other fields as desired and when you finish, press Esc to save the changes.

Create a user-level print job configuration   User-level print job configurations are useful if the user uses a variety of printers that may not be defined at the container level. The default job configuration set at the user level overrides the default set at the container level.

To create a print job configuration for a user, log in as the user or as ADMIN or equivalent and run PRINTCON from the DOS command line. Then carry out the following steps:

1 • Verify the current object displayed at the top of the screen. If necessary, use the Change Current Object option to select the user you want to create a job configuration for.

2 • From the PRINTCON main menu, select Edit Print Job Configurations.

3 • Press the Insert key to add a new job configuration and give it a name.

4 • Select the job configuration from the list and press Enter.

5 • Use the arrow keys to move to the Device field and press Enter.

6 • Select the desired device from the list.

7 • Use the arrow keys to move to the Mode field and press Enter.

8 • Choose the desired mode of printing.

9 • Move to the Form Name field and press Enter.

10 • Choose the desired form from the list.

11 • Change other fields as desired and when you finish, press Esc to save the changes.

Summary

Managing a network printing system tends to be a relatively easy task, provided you know where to find the information you need. If you add on management systems such as ManageWise from Novell or third-party add-ons (such as JetDirect cards, discussed in Chapter 8), you can enhance systems management, but you will still manage the system essentially the same way. As Novell enhances the printing system with NDPS (Novell Distributed Print Services), management becomes more detailed, but the main aspects remain the same.

Ideally, the printing system can be set up so that management should be minimal. Only in extreme cases is intervention necessary. Some of the more advanced printers can automatically solve minor problems to minimize administrative interaction. Your system reliability will vary, depending on how you have deployed printing services.

CHAPTER 8

Integrating Third-Party
Solutions

Now we come to the fun part: interacting with hardware and software beyond the NetWare sphere of influence. Although this chapter indicates we'll be talking about third-party devices (and we will), we won't cover all components that may interoperate with NetWare. Because all of these devices come with hardware instructions, we won't go into that topic either (hopefully you've saved the manuals!). Instead, we'll look at a few of the most common printer additions that are designed to work with NetWare and how integration is accomplished.

As the network industry evolves, especially with new technologies such as Novell's NDPS (Novell Distributed Print Services), no doubt new hardware and software will emerge to take advantage of it.

Why Use Third-Party Printing Solutions?

NetWare has a variety of printing solutions that come with NetWare 3.x and 4.x. So why add on third-party devices? What sort of enhancements do they bring to the tangle of cables lurking in your office walls? Many NetWare printing environments operate without any additional products. And although this is the case, additional printing support products offer a number of advantages worth leveraging. Here are what most third-party solutions offer NetWare printing systems:

- **Improved manageability.** Several of the add-ons available today use SNMP (Simple Network Management Protocol) to manage the printer. Management software is usually included with the printer as well. A major benefit to using SNMP, though, is that other SNMP managers (such as Novell's ManageWise or HP Openview) can manage the device as well. In a mixed system, where all of the components need to interact, this flexibility enables the network to run much more smoothly. In a small network, it means useful knowledge—knowing when a part of the system is failing or about to fail.

- **Easier network use.** Because most embedded devices are connected via a standard network connection, such devices have no serial printer cables to use or worry about. Printers can be placed closer to where the users actually work. Specifically, this means the printer is no longer attached to the server via a serial or parallel cable (see

Figure 8.1). Because these cables typically restrict you in range (usually 8 to 10 feet), enabling the printer to be a node on the network allows for a greater range when setting up printers.

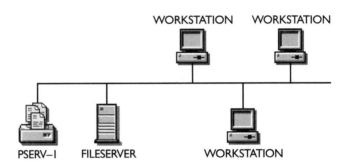

NETWORK-ATTACHED PRINTER

FIGURE 8.1

Network-attached connections vs. server-attached connections

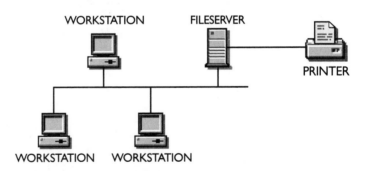

SERVER-ATTACHED PRINTER (PARALLEL)

▶ **Increased throughput performance.** Typically, one of the most apparent bottlenecks when it comes to printing is the connection from the print server to the printer. A network-attached printer does not connect via a serial or parallel connection. Rather, it is connected via a twisted-pair or coax network cable just like any other node. Provided the network isn't already overloaded, you may find a noticeable performance increase.

▶ **Automatic multiprotocol support.** You may only have just one backbone protocol in your network. You may have two or more, such as TCP/IP and IPX. How can you support them both? Although several network-attached printers available today can support only one given protocol at a time, some printers (such as from HP, QMS, and Lexmark) dynamically swap protocols in the printer, based on whatever protocol is desired. In effect, it means not having to deploy multiple printers in order to support multiple protocol types required by multiple people. (See Figure 8.2.)

F I G U R E   8.2

*Multiprotocol printer
support*

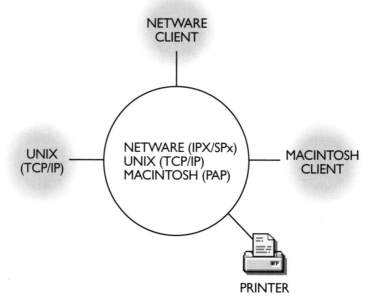

NETWARE
CLIENT

UNIX
(TCP/IP)

NETWARE (IPX/SPx)
UNIX (TCP/IP)
MACINTOSH (PAP)

MACINTOSH
CLIENT

PRINTER

▶ **Direct printing.** As you recall from earlier chapters, the printing job always goes to a queue on a server somewhere. The print server then routes the job to an appropriate printer. In the default printing system, the print job *never* goes directly to the printer. Using an add-on, it becomes possible to bypass the queuing mechanism and talk directly to the printer. This will be an option with Novell's NDPS when it is released, but can be done today via third-party support.

PRINTER EVOLUTION

If you look at how printing has evolved over the last decade, you can observe that most printers have been typically unintelligent devices. The host system (be it PC or mainframe) sent information to it to be printed and only wanted to know if something went awry. In that case, the printer could indicate a fault condition. This system of printing provides only the most basic services for printing systems. As a matter of fact, printers were one of the original reasons LANs came into existence. Nobody wanted to purchase multiple printers (they were usually dot matrix) to support an office. Instead, expensive printers could be shared less expensively through a LAN. Usually the administrator hardly cared about features. If the printer could be shared, that was usually enough.

Today, many devices (printers and otherwise) carry some sort of embedded intelligence that can be exploited in the network. Vendors such as IBM, HP, Lexmark, QMS, and others have an actual CPU on the printer itself capable of handling some of the more mundane chores of printing. Through a combination of hardware and software, the printer can even take care of a majority of the services that are typically provided by the network operating system.

BUILDING ON A FOUNDATION

When deploying a printing system, NetWare provides software that enables the greatest flexibility and control, provided you are using generic devices. A vendor can add specific enhancements to its own hardware (such as HP and Lexmark hardware) while providing complete support for the NetWare components. Effectively, embedded software and hardware at the printer augments rather than replaces existing printing services.

What Third-Party Print Solutions Can Do For You

As added features, vendor-enhanced printing may support one or all of the following features:

- ▶ **Plug and print support.** Before the network can support printing, the components usually must be configured and installed. This means the printer, queues, print servers, and such must be set up through an administration utility before services can be rendered. But what if you merely had to plug the printer into the network and the system automatically discovered the printer? This would mean significantly less time to get printing running.

▸ **Enhanced management.** NetWare enables a great amount of management through NWAdmin (the graphical administration tool) and PCONSOLE. But what if you wanted to download new font support to the printer? Download new firmware revisions? Run printer diagnostics? These sort of tasks require specific knowledge about the device, something the vendor can readily provide.

▸ **NDS awareness.** Traditional unintelligent printers have no concept of a LAN. It seems to the printer that it's locally attached. A network-attached printer has a better concept of what's going on. In addition, an intelligent printer can be aware of NDS, enabling easier integration using technologies such as plug and print. Devices can have the same name but be registered in a different part of the directory to guarantee uniqueness. Users can then see the printers as a real department resource.

▸ **Directly addressable printers.** Because the printer is usually another "client" on the network (like a network-attached device), it is directly addressable by the network operating system. This results in direct communication as opposed to communicating via a parallel or serial cable interface. That, in turn, means a more manageable printer available over the LAN instead of one dependent on the printer server remaining up. It also means that a management protocol on top of the printer (such as SNMP) can be readily implemented.

NETWARE PRINTING FUTURES

Novell has announced a new printing system to be available within the timeframe of the NetWare 4.11 release. The new system, called NDPS, builds in extensive support for third-party, intelligent devices while retaining support for older, unintelligent devices. Novell's partners in this technology are Xerox and HP. Through NDPS, you'll be able to support the following features:

- **Plug and print.** Just plug the printer into the network and users can immediately use the new printer. This totally eliminates initial intervention from the administrator in order to provide printing services from a new device. The administrator can customize print options and security after the fact.

- **Automatic driver download.** This feature enables the system to provide the correct printer driver when a user wants to print something. The administrator has to add the driver to the system only once. After that, when a user wants to print, the new driver is pulled from Novell Directory Services and installed on the workstation. This process can potentially eliminate support calls stemming from improperly installed or nonexistent drivers.

- **Full graphical administration.** NDPS enables the administrator to completely see and manage the printer by using a graphical representation of the device. A printer is viewed as a separate object. To configure options on the printer, the administrator only has to point and click on the graphical representation of that printer.

- **Novell Embedded Systems Technology.** NDPS relies on the Novell Embedded Systems Technology, known as NEST. NEST enables NetWare end-node intelligence to be native to a printer. This means the printer is another client to the NetWare operating system. As a result, it becomes a service provider on the network, brokering print server and printing services. Embedded technology is also the key to providing more extensive management, because more information is provided to the administrator via the client software embedded in the printer.

Note that although standard NetWare printing offers some major new additions, add-ons do exist—in abundance. The basic printing system described in this book will remain largely the same, even after NDPS becomes available.

THIRD-PARTY DEVICES—JETDIRECT/QMS/LEXMARK/INTEL NETPORT

Today, many different third-party offerings enhance NetWare's printing system. Enhancement can actually be embedded software/hardware in the printer (as described already) or a network-attached device that provides close to the same functionality as a network-attached printer. The benefit to using the latter is that existing printers can be supported, even though the printer itself may not support network attachments. (See Figure 8.3.)

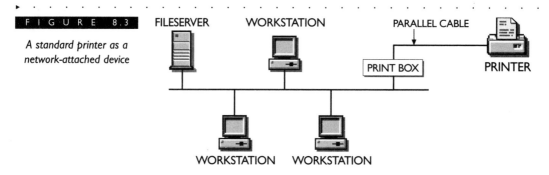

FIGURE 8.3		
A standard printer as a network-attached device	FILESERVER WORKSTATION PARALLEL CABLE	
	PRINT BOX PRINTER	
	WORKSTATION WORKSTATION	

Table 8.1 lists printing services and their chief characteristics.

TABLE 8.1 *Printing services*	PRINTING SERVICE	CHARACTERISTICS
	HP JetDirect	Can be embedded in the printer or purchased and added later.
		Uses SNMP for management.
		HP provides management software (JetAdmin).
		Supports protocol switching on the fly.
		Works only with HP printers of certain models.
	Lexmark Printers	Use SNMP for management.
		Provide stand-alone management software as well as a Novell ManageWise snap-in (common console).
		Can act as print servers as well as remote printers.
		Work only with Lexmark printers.

TABLE 8.1	PRINTING SERVICE	CHARACTERISTICS
Printing services	QMS Printers	Use SNMP management.
		Can be embedded print servers.
		Can support direct printing to the printer, bypassing the NetWare queue.
		Work only with QMS printers.
	Intel NetPort	Network-attached box.
		Remote management software provided.
		Can support any parallel-attached printer.

Now let's dive into more specific detail on working with these solutions. Actual hardware installation is not covered here. Consult your manual on specific settings for your chosen solution. We *do* cover how to properly set up these devices with your NetWare system.

HP JetDirect Solution

Hewlett-Packard has been in the printer business a long time. As a result, its offerings are complete and work well within NetWare. HP provides two major types of solutions in the NetWare environment (regardless of NetWare 3.x or NetWare 4.x), as follows:

- **HP's JetDirect card.** Plugs into an existing HP printer that supports it. Even the older HP LaserJet IIs had a JetDirect port, but they do not work with the newer printers such as the LaserJet 5 and 4Sv.

- **JetDirect EX.** This option enables the same functionality as an Intel NetPort; namely, you can place this external box somewhere in your building and plug a network cable into it. You can then attach a standard parallel cable from it to the printer. This enables some management while also providing a way to place printers anywhere where a network cable runs.

HP JETDIRECT CARDS

Several components make up the JetDirect implementation. They include the following:

- ▸ **JetDirect card.** This plugs into an existing printer, using a special HP-designed slot in the back of the printer. As part of the newer cards equipped with a *Flash SIMM*, they can even update the onboard software remotely from a workstation. Cards that do not have the SIMM or are not capable of supporting a SIMM add-on usually are upgraded by purchasing new hardware.

- ▸ **JetAdmin software.** This administration software is provided as an additional utility to manage JetDirect-equipped printers. We'll talk in more detail on this later on, but aspects of JetAdmin features include doing diagnostics, checking and changing the printer name, specifying *how* the printer will print (as a remote printer or a print server), and so on. The JetAdmin software communicates directly to the JetDirect port, via IPX or TCP/IP. As a result, it has no dependency on the server being up in order to manage it.

- ▸ **Remote Update software.** This utility works in conjunction with the JetAdmin software. It enables remote downloading of new firmware to JetDirect cards equipped with Flash SIMM, as just mentioned. You may or may not need this utility.

JetDirect software (especially in the newest versions) can support either NetWare 3.x or 4.x with full directory support. If you have an older card, you can still work with JetDirect. You will notice, however, that a bindery object is created in the context of the tree where bindery emulation has been turned on (Figure 8.4). Fear not! You can still print to the standard NetWare queues as you would under an all-NetWare system. From an administration viewpoint, though, you *must* ensure that the 4.x server you are supporting has bindery emulation enabled and set to the context where the bindery object resides.

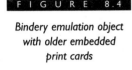

F I G U R E   8 . 4

Bindery emulation object with older embedded print cards

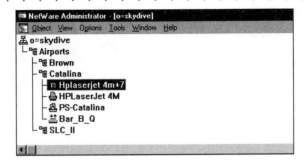

If you are running NetWare 4, the NDS queue or remote printer object can be placed anywhere in the tree and referenced via JetAdmin when the JetDirect card is being configured.

To set up a JetDirect card, you need first make a simple decision: Should the printer act as a stand-alone print server (instead of running PSERVER.NLM at the server) or should it run as a remote printer? Choosing remote printer would be the equivalent of using RPRINTER/NPRINTER at a remote workstation (described earlier).

If you're running JetDirect as a remote printer, use the following steps as a guideline:

1 • Install the JetDirect card into your desired HP printer.

2 • Run NWAdmin if you're running NetWare 4 or PCONSOLE if you're running NetWare 3.x.

3 • Create a print server, print queue, and a printer.

4 • When you create the printer, ensure that it is configured as Remote (see Figure 8.5).

*Choosing remote printer
instead of local*

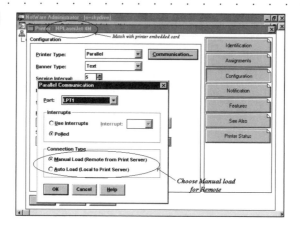

 **Make sure the name you give the remote printer is *exactly* the same
as the name you will choose for JetDirect via JetAdmin. If they do
not match, printing will not work!**

WARNING

5 • Run JetAdmin.

6 • Select the name you will use for the printer. Remember that it *must*
match the NetWare printer name created previously (see Figure 8.6).

Choosing the printer name

7 • Select which mode you'll use for JetDirect (print server or remote printer—in this case remote; see Figure 8.7).

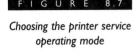

F I G U R E   8.7

Choosing the printer service operating mode

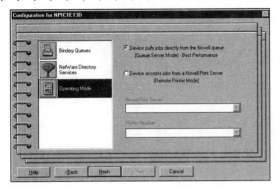

8 • Save the settings. You now should be able to print to a queue (created earlier) and have the output appear on the HP printer.

If you're running JetDirect as a print server, use the following steps as a guideline:

1 • Run NWAdmin and create a queue that you want to service. You do not need to create a print server or a printer object.

2 • Run JetAdmin.

3 • Select a name for your printer on the network. When JetAdmin creates the print server in NDS, this is the name that appears.

4 • Select Print Server Mode instead of Remote Printer.

5 • Select a tree where the print server will be created. JetAdmin supports NDS by selecting a tree name and context first (see Figure 8.8) and then the server name and queue (see Figure 8.9).

6 • Save settings and start to print!

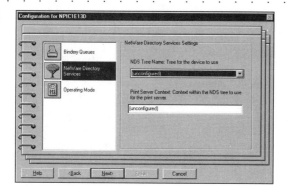

FIGURE 8.8

Selecting tree name and context with JetAdmin and NDS

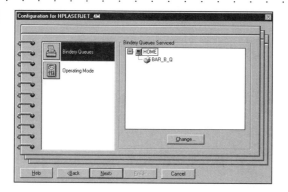

FIGURE 8.9

Selecting the queue to be serviced under JetAdmin and NDS

MANAGING WITH THE JETDIRECT CARD AND JETADMIN

You will still use PCONSOLE or NWAdmin to manage your printers and print servers day to day, even with JetDirect. The printer appears as a managed object under NDS or PCONSOLE. When JetDirect is acting as a print server, JetAdmin will have created a print server object under NDS. If the JetDirect card does not support NDS, it will appear in NDS as a bindery object that is not manageable under NWAdmin.

Usually, the management tasks that you can only do with JetAdmin are seldom required. Chores such as renaming a printer, doing diagnostic "pings," or reassigning a printer to a particular queue are not usually required on a regular basis. When you *do* need to do these jobs, JetAdmin is the only tool you can use to do them.

Another management task where you need JetAdmin and the Remote Download utility is upgrading the Flash SIMM in the printer. If the JetDirect card has been equipped with a Flash SIMM module, you can remotely download updated versions of the firmware directly to the JetDirect card. This enables any new patches or features to be added without your purchasing another JetDirect card.

NOTE **Not all JetDirect cards come with a Flash-upgradeable SIMM. If yours does not, you may need to replace the card in order to support new features.**

Lexmark Printer Support

Another very popular printing solution that augments NetWare is the Lexmark line of printers and printer boxes. Lexmark makes two types of devices:

▶ Print service embedded printers

▶ Printer boxes for standard parallel-attached printers

Using either one of the preceding devices provides the two basic printing solutions as part of the HP solution (described previously). Again, the administrator has a choice of supporting printers (Lexmark) with embedded software or attaching standard parallel-attached printers to a network node printer box.

LEXMARK SUPPORT OF NETWARE

Lexmark does an excellent job of providing choice to the printing administrator. Lexmark has full support for bindery and NDS (NetWare 4) systems and provides an extensive system of management. Much like the HP solutions, a Lexmark printer can be attached and can service jobs in two ways:

▸ **As a remote printer.** This alternative (as described before) requires the creation of a NetWare print server, queue, and printer in order to service print jobs.

▸ **As a print server.** Only a queue must be created on the NetWare server in order to service jobs.

Lexmark also furnishes the utilities to remotely download new drivers, manage printer/print server setup, and monitor the state of the printer. One item that stands out, however, is the complete support Lexmark provides for network management.

LEXMARK'S INDUSTRY-STANDARD MANAGEMENT

Most of the vendors supplying print services offer support for remote management to some degree or another. This includes HP and QMS. Lexmark supports SNMP (Simple Network Management Protocol) at a fairly detailed level. This means administrators can do more extensive management than they can with other printing systems. Lexmark provides a stand-alone console to manage the Lexmark printing system known as MarkVision (Figure 8.10). Through it, you can get vital information about how the system is operating as well as be alerted when a potential problem occurs. This is all accomplished using SNMP.

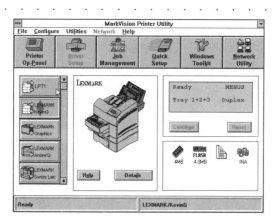

F I G U R E   8.10

MarkVision from Lexmark

The NetWare Tie-In

MarkVision was also engineered to "snap-in" to Novell's management solution known as ManageWise. Because ManageWise provides a complete all-in-one desktop for managing and monitoring the system, no other console, should be needed. All alarms and query information can be compiled into the ManageWise console, providing full printer management while retaining the ManageWise look and feel. Using MarkVision or MarkVision with ManageWise, the administrator actually gains a fuller management capacity than when using the NetWare printing system by itself.

Network Views

Using the ManageWise snap-in, administrators can see all network printers (Lexmark) as peer network resources (see Figure 8.11). Expanded view enables you to open a particular printer and manage aspects of it (see Figure 8.12). Options such as start and stop, change forms, set parameters, and even the ability to lock the printer's local console are possible.

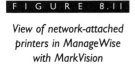

FIGURE 8.11

View of network-attached printers in ManageWise with MarkVision

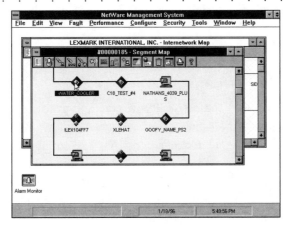

FIGURE 8.12

MarkVision management of Lexmark printers under ManageWise

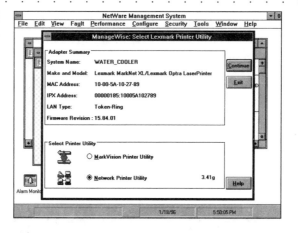

NOTE

As is the case with the other systems, when supporting NetWare printing as a remote node, you must ensure that the printer name (configured with Lexmark's utility) and the NetWare-defined printer name are the same. If they do not match, printing will not be available.

QMS Printers

QMS also provides the capability to integrate printing into a NetWare system both as a remote printer and a print server. As with the other printing systems, QMS provides a remote management tool for configuring the printer from a Windows desktop.

If you're working in a NetWare 3.x environment, the QMS approach is well-supported. Most of the printer line has a provision for adding a network card to enable the printer to be network-connected. If you're running NetWare 4, the only support is through bindery emulation. This method does work, although you'll see a custom NDS object within the area of the tree where the bindery context is set. If the bindery context is changed, the QMS printer can no longer see the objects it needs to communicate with, and you won't be able to print.

NOTE

Bindery emulation enables older software programs to communicate with NetWare using bindery calls. Through bindery calls, the software can create and use NDS objects without being NDS-aware. Because the bindery is a flat naming system, in order for this to work NetWare 4 can set a *bindery context*. In essence, this is a pointer to an area of NDS that the older program can call into. If the context is changed, the pointer no longer points to the right area in the NDS tree. NetWare 4.1 helps to eliminate this problem by providing the capability to point into multiple areas of the tree at once.

Intel NetPort

Intel's NetPort has also been around for a while and provides network attachment of standard printers. Intel makes neither printers nor interfaces that connect to printers. Instead, Intel provides a box that can be configured either as a printer server or a remote printer in the network. Once that task is done, you can attach a standard parallel printer to it and away you go!

REMOTE MANAGEMENT

As with the other print boxes, you manage normally within the NetWare system. If you need to change the printer box's name or do a reset, you can use a remote utility, similar to the other implementations we've discussed, and change basic information. Intel offers two implementation types, as follows:

- ▸ **Embedded printer card/software.** Hardware and software are embedded in the printer for better management and more printer control. Examples of embedded printer cards with software include HP (JetDirect), Lexmark, and QMS.

- ▸ **Network-attached printer box.** This is a "black box" that has a network connector and a parallel port. The box is attached to the network normally and the printer attaches to the parallel port. Management of the printer is limited to what the printer supports via the parallel port. Examples include HP JetDirect EX and Intel NetPort.

Summary

Whichever system you decide to use with NetWare, third-party services can help you enhance your system greatly and make the system easier to maintain and deploy. Because add-ons are basically an extension to the NetWare system, management and deployment do not change significantly. This means that, with an existing system, you can add on services without having to re-engineer the system and trigger downtime. Users typically should not even see the difference except to discover that printing will be faster (via network-attached printers), more reliable (using auto-driver download), and more proximal (network-attached) than before.

PART II

NetWare Printing Swift Track Guide

About this Guide

This Swift Track Guide provides a quick reference for network administrators, printing operators, and users who need a quick reference for the basic steps involved in setting up and administering network printing. Some tasks outlined in this guide must be performed by a user with administrative rights (SUPERVISOR or equivalent for NetWare 3, ADMIN or equivalent for NetWare 4), others can be performed by Print Queue or Print Server Operators, and a small handful can be performed by users. At the top of each Swift Track, you will find an Access Key that indicates who can perform the task outlined.

Abbreviations

The following table provides a legend of the Access Key used at the top of each Swift Track:

TABLE 1	ACCESS KEY	USER
Access keys	S	SUPERVISOR or SUPERVISOR equivalent (NetWare 3 tasks)
	A	ADMIN or ADMIN equivalent (NetWare 4 tasks)
	PQO	Print queue operator
	PSO	Print server operator
	U	Regular network user

Instruction Types

Each Swift Track includes two types of instructions:

- **Quick Reference**. A quick reference that shows the menu options only. For example, to create a print queue, the Quick Reference instructions would be:

```
PCONSOLE/Print Queue Information
```

- **Swift Track**. Detailed step-by-step instructions that guide you through every keystroke involved in completing the task.

We've included both types of instructions, because we realize that at times you will just need a quick reminder of where to go to perform a task (Quick Reference), and other times you will want to be guided through each step (Swift Track).

Assumptions

This guide makes the following assumptions:

▶ Your NetWare file server has been installed and is functional.

▶ You are logged in as a user with the necessary rights to perform the task at hand. Refer to the notation at the top of each Swift Track before beginning.

▶ You are using a DOS version 5.0 or higher or Windows version 3.1 or higher network workstation.

Function Keys for DOS Utilities

The following tables provide lists of the keys that allow you to use and navigate DOS-based printing utilities provided with NetWare. These include PCONSOLE, PRINTDEF, and PRINTCON. Most functions are valid for both the NetWare 3 and NetWare 4 versions of these utilities, except where indicated.

TABLE 2	PRESS THIS KEY:	TO DO THIS:
Using PCONSOLE	Esc	Back up to the previous menu or exit from the utility from the main menu.
	Alt F10	Exit the utility.
	Backspace	Delete a character.
	Ins	Add an item.
	Del	Delete an item.
	Enter	Accept or select an item.
	F1	Get online help.
	F1 F1	View available function keys (NetWare 3 only).

(continued)

	PRESS THIS KEY:	TO DO THIS:
TABLE 2	F3	Rename, modify, or edit an item.
Using PCONSOLE *(continued)*	F4	Change modes from NDS to Bindery/Bindery to NDS (NetWare 4 only).
	F5	Mark multiple items.
	F6	Add a Bindery Reference Queue (NetWare 4 only).
	F7	Cancel markings or changes.
	F10	Save.

	PRESS THIS KEY:	TO DO THIS:
TABLE 3	Tab	Cycle through fields.
Navigating the PCONSOLE menus	Up arrow	Move up one line.
	Down arrow	Move down one line.
	Left arrow	Move left one position.
	Right arrow	Move right one position.
	Ctrl PgUp	Move to the beginning.
	Ctrl PgDn	Move to the end.
	Home	Move to the beginning of the line.
	End	Move to the end of the line.
	PgUp	Move up one page.
	PgDn	Move down one page.
	Ctrl Left arrow	Move left one field or word.
	Ctrl Right arrow	Move right one field or word.

Where to Go for More Information

If you require more details on the printing tasks provided in this Swift Track Guide, refer to the appropriate section in Part I of this book. Other sources of information on NetWare print services include the online help of each printing utility and the online documentation provided with NetWare 3 and NetWare 4.

Creating a Basic NetWare 3 Print System

SWIFT
TRACK

Creating a Print Queue

Access Key: S

PCONSOLE/Print Queue Information

1 • Run the PCONSOLE utility from the DOS command line by typing:

PCONSOLE

2 • Use the arrow keys to select Print Queue Information and press Enter.

3 • From the print queue list, press the Insert key to add a new print queue.

4 • Assign a descriptive name for the queue from 1 to 45 characters and press Enter.

5 • Press Escape to return to the PCONSOLE main menu or Alt-F10 to exit PCONSOLE entirely.

NOTE

For this print queue to be functional, you must assign a print server and printer to service this queue and the print server must be running.

Creating a Print Server

SWIFT TRACK

> Access Key: S
> PCONSOLE/Print Server Information

I • Run the PCONSOLE utility from the DOS command line by typing:

PCONSOLE

2 • Use the arrow keys to select Print Server Information and press Enter.

3 • From the print server list, press the Insert key to add a new print server.

4 • Assign a descriptive name for the print server from 1 to 47 characters and press Enter.

5 • Press Escape to return to the PCONSOLE main menu or Alt-F10 to exit PCONSOLE entirely.

NOTE

For this print server to be functional, you must configure at least one printer and assign a queue to be serviced and the print server must be running.

SWIFT
TRACK

Creating Printers

> Access Key: S, PSO
> PCONSOLE/Print Server Information/Print Server Configuration/
> Printer Configuration

I • Run the PCONSOLE utility from the DOS command line by typing:

```
PCONSOLE
```

2 • Use the arrow keys to select Print Server Information and press Enter.

3 • From the print server list, use the arrow keys to select a print server you wish to create a printer on and press Enter.

4 • Select Print Server Configuration and press Enter.

5 • Select Printer Configuration and press Enter.

6 • Use the arrow keys to select the printer number you wish to install (0–15) and press Enter.

7 • Assign a descriptive name for the print server up to 47 characters and press Enter.

8 • Use the arrow keys to select Type and press Enter.

9 • Select the printer type using the following table as a guide:

TABLE I

IF THE PRINTER WILL BE ATTACHED TO	THEN SELECT
The print server's LPTx port	Parallel, LPTx (Replace x with the LPT port the printer is attached to)
The print server's COMx port	Serial, COMx (replace x with the COM port the printer is attached to)
A workstation's LPTx port	Remote, Parallel LPTx (replace x with the LPT port the printer is attached to)
A workstation's COMx	Remote, COMx (Replace x with the COM port the printer is attached to)
On a network other than the default (see Part I, Chapter 2 for details)	Defined elsewhere

10 • Define the remaining printer configuration. (See Part I, Chapter 2 for details.)

11 • When the printer's configuration is complete, press Escape and Yes to save the changes.

12 • Press Escape four times to return to the PCONSOLE main menu or Alt-F10 to exit PCONSOLE entirely.

NOTE

For this printer to be functional, you must assign it to service at least one print queue and the print server must be running. If a remote printer was defined, RPRINTER.EXE must be loaded at the workstation with the printer attached.

SWIFT TRACK

Assigning Queues to be Serviced by Printer

> Access Key: S, PSO
> PCONSOLE/Print Server Information/Print Server Configuration/
> Queues Serviced by Printer

1 • Run the PCONSOLE utility from the DOS command line by typing:

PCONSOLE

2 • Use the arrow keys to select Print Server Information and press Enter.

3 • From the print server list, use the arrow keys to select the print server the printer is defined on that you wish to make a queue assignment for and press Enter.

4 • Select Queues Serviced by Printer and press Enter.

5 • Use the arrow keys to select the printer you wish to make the queue assignment for and press Enter.

6 • Press the Insert key for a list of the available print queues.

7 • Use the arrow keys to select the queue you would like this printer to service and press Enter.

8 • Enter a queue priority from 1 through 10 (1 being the highest) and press Enter.

9 • Optional. Repeat steps 6–8 for each additional print queue you would like this printer to service.

10 • When you have finished selecting print queues, press Escape five times to return to the PCONSOLE main menu or press Alt-F10 to exit PCONSOLE entirely.

For the printer and print queue to be functional, the print server must be running.

NOTE

Starting the Print Server—PSERVER.NLM

> Access Key: S, PSO, U
>
> At the server console type: LOAD PSERVER Print Server Name

1 • Go to the console of the file server you wish to load the print server on or establish an RCONSOLE session from a workstation by running RCONSOLE.EXE and choosing the server you wish to load the print server on.

2 • From the server console prompt, type:

```
LOAD PSERVER Print Server Name
```

For example:

```
LOAD PSERVER SLCII_PS
```

3 • Enter the print server's password (if one has been assigned) and press Enter.

 To establish an RCONSOLE session with a file server, you must first load REMOTE.NLM and RSPX.NLM at the server's console.

NOTE

 For remote printers to attach to the print server, you must load RPRINTER.EXE at the workstations with the printers attached.

NOTE

 Because a regular user can load a print server, it is important that all print servers be assigned a password to prevent an unauthorized user from loading it.

WARNING

**SWIFT
TRACK**

Starting the Print Server—PSERVER.EXE

> Access Key: S, PSO, U
>
> From a DOS workstation type: PSERVER Print Server Name

1 • Verify that the workstation's NET.CFG file contains the following line:

```
SPX CONNECTIONS = 60
```

If necessary, use a text editor to add this line.

2 • Load the NetWare Client software at the workstation to attach to the server where the print server is defined.

3 • Verify that the workstation has access to the following files:

```
IBM$RUN.OVL

PSERVER.EXE

SYS$ERR.DAT

SYS$HELP.DAT

SYS$MSG.DAT
```

These files are located in the SYS:PUBLIC directory of the NetWare server, so they can be accessed by logging in to the server or they can be copied to a local directory on the print server station.

4 • Load the print server software by typing:

```
PSERVER Print Server Name
```

For example:

```
PSERVER SLCII_PS
```

5 • Enter the print server's password (if one has been assigned) and press Enter.

NOTE

For remote printers to attach to the print server, you must load **RPRINTER.EXE** at the workstations with the printers attached.

WARNING

Because a regular user can load a print server, it is important that all print servers be assigned a password to prevent an unauthorized user from loading it.

SWIFT TRACK

Starting Remote Printers

> Access Key: S, PSO, U
>
> From the workstation with the printer attached type: RPRINTER PrintServerName PrinterNumber

I • Verify that the workstation's NET.CFG file contains the following line:

```
SPX CONNECTIONS = 60
```

If necessary, use a text editor to add this line.

2 • Load the NetWare Client software at the workstation to attach to the server where the printer is defined.

3 • Verify that the workstation has access to the following files:

```
IBMRUN.OVL
RPRINTER.EXE
RPRINTER.HLP
SYS$HELP.DAT
SYS$MSG.DAT
SYS$ERR.DAT
```

These files are located in the SYS:PUBLIC directory of the NetWare server so they can be accessed by logging in to the server or they can be copied to a local directory on the workstation.

4 • Load the remote printer software by typing the following from the DOS command line:

```
RPRINTER PrintServerName PrinterNumber
```

For example:

```
RPRINTER SLCII_PS 2
```

For a printer to attach to a print server, the print server must be running before RPRINTER is loaded.

NOTE

Creating Print Job Configurations

SWIFT TRACK

> Access Key: S, U
>
> PRINTCON/Edit Print Job Configurations

1 • Run the PRINTCON utility from the DOS command line by typing:

PRINTCON

2 • Use the arrow keys to select Edit Print Job Configurations and press Enter.

3 • Press Insert to add a new print job configuration for the user you are currently logged in as.

4 • Enter a unique descriptive name for this job configuration and press Enter.

5 • Edit the print job configuration's parameters by using the arrow keys to move through the fields.

6 • Press Escape and answer Yes to save changes.

7 • Press Escape once to return to the main menu or press Alt-F10 to exit PRINTCON entirely.

Setting a Default Print Job Configuration

SWIFT TRACK

Access Key: S, U

PRINTCON/Select Default Print Job Configuration

I • Run the PRINTCON utility from the DOS command line by typing:

```
PRINTCON
```

2 • Use the arrow keys to select Select Default Print Job Configurations and press Enter.

3 • Highlight the job configuration you wish to make the default and press Enter.

4 • Press Escape once to return to the main menu or press Alt-F10 to exit PRINTCON entirely.

Copying Print Job Configurations Between Users

SWIFT
TRACK

Access Key: S
PRINTCON/Copy Print Job Configurations

1 • Run the PRINTCON utility from the DOS command line by typing:

   PRINTCON

2 • Use the arrow keys to select Copy Print Job Configurations and press Enter.

3 • Enter the name of the user that you wish to copy the job configurations from.

4 • Enter the name of the user you are copying the job configurations to.

5 • If you wish to delete the target user's existing print job configurations, answer Yes and the new print job configurations will be copied. If you do not wish to overwrite the existing job configurations, answer No.

To avoid overwriting job configurations, copy job configurations from other users before defining specific configurations for the user.

TIP

SWIFT TRACK

Importing Print Devices (*.PDFs)

> Access Key: S
> PRINTDEF/Print Devices/Import Print Devices

1 • Run the PRINTDEF utility from the DOS command line by typing:

```
PRINTDEF
```

2 • Use the arrow keys to select Print Devices and press Enter.

3 • Use the arrow keys to select Import Print Devices and press Enter.

4 • Enter the source directory by typing:

```
SYS:PUBLIC <Enter>
```

Or, if the PDF file you wish to import is in another location, press the Insert key and browse through the directory structure until you find the desired directory and press Enter.

5 • Use the arrow keys to select the appropriate PDF file for your printer and press Enter.

6 • Press Escape once to return to the main menu or press Alt-F10 to exit PRINTDEF entirely.

Creating a Print Device

SWIFT
TRACK

Access Key: S
PRINTDEF/Print Devices/Edit Print Devices

1 • Run the PRINTDEF utility from the DOS command line by typing:

   PRINTDEF

2 • Use the arrow keys to select Print Devices and press Enter.

3 • Use the arrow keys to select Edit Print Devices and press Enter.

4 • To add a new print device, press Insert.

5 • Enter the new device name.

6 • Select the new device by pressing Enter.

7 • Define the device functions and modes for your printer.

8 • When you have finished defining device functions and modes, press Escape three times to return to the main menu or press Alt-F10 to exit PRINTDEF entirely.

Always check the PDF files provided with NetWare to see if there is one for your printer before defining a new print device. If no PDF file exists, see if your printer emulates another printer that a PDF file is provided for. This could save you hours of work.

TIP

Most printer manuals include the printer codes recognized by that particular printer. If your printer manual does not include these codes and there is no NetWare provided PDF file, contact the manufacturer.

NOTE

SWIFT TRACK

Creating Device Functions

Access Key: S
PRINTDEF/Print Devices/Edit Print Devices/Device Functions

1 • Run the PRINTDEF utility from the DOS command line by typing:

    PRINTDEF

2 • Use the arrow keys to select Print Devices and press Enter.

3 • Use the arrow keys to select Edit Print Devices and press Enter.

4 • Use the arrow keys to select the print device you wish to define a new function for and press Enter.

5 • Use the arrow key to select Device Functions.

6 • Press Insert to add the new device function.

7 • Enter the function name.

8 • Use the arrow keys to move to the Escape Sequence field.

9 • Enter a valid printer code as defined by the printer's manufacturer.

10 • Optional. Repeat steps 8–11 for each additional print code you wish to define.

11 • When you have finished defining device functions, press Escape four times to return to the main menu or press Alt-F10 to exit PRINTDEF entirely.

TIP

Always check the PDF files provided with NetWare to see if there is one for your printer before defining a new print function. If no PDF file exists, see if your printer emulates another printer that a PDF file is provided for. This could save you hours of work.

NOTE

Most printer manuals include the printer codes recognized by that particular printer. If your printer manual does not include these codes and there is no NetWare provided PDF file, contact the manufacturer.

SWIFT TRACK

Creating Device Modes

> Access Key: S
> PRINTDEF/Print Devices/Edit Print Devices/Device Modes

I • Run the PRINTDEF utility from the DOS command line by typing:

```
PRINTDEF
```

2 • Use the arrow keys to select Print Devices and press Enter.

3 • Use the arrow keys to select Edit Print Devices and press Enter.

4 • Use the arrow keys to select the print device you wish to define a new mode for and press Enter.

5 • Select Device modes and press Enter.

6 • Press Insert to add the new device mode.

7 • Enter the mode name and press Enter.

8 • Press Insert and select the printer functions that make up this mode of printing. Use the F5 key to mark multiple items.

9 • When you have finished marking the printer functions, press Enter.

10 • Optional. Repeat steps 6–9 for each additional device mode you wish to define.

II • When you have finished defining device modes, press Escape five times to return to the main menu or press Alt-F10 to exit PRINTDEF entirely.

TIP

Always check the **PDF** files provided with **NetWare** to see if there is one for your printer before defining a new print device mode. If no **PDF** file exists, see if your printer emulates another printer that a **PDF** file is provided for. This could save you hours of work.

NOTE

Most printer manuals include the printer codes recognized by that particular printer. If your printer manual does not include these codes and there is no **NetWare** provided **PDF** file, contact the manufacturer.

Creating Forms

**SWIFT
TRACK**

> **Access Key: S**
> **PRINTDEF/Forms**

1 • Run the PRINTDEF utility from the DOS command line by typing:

    PRINTDEF

2 • Use the arrow keys to select Forms and press Enter.

3 • Press the Insert key to define a new form.

4 • Enter a descriptive name for the form and press Enter.

5 • Assign a form number from 0–255 and press Enter.

6 • Enter the length of the form and press Enter.

7 • Enter the width of the form and press Enter.

8 • Press Escape and answer Yes to save changes.

9 • Press Escape once to return to the main menu or press Alt-F10 to exit PRINTDEF entirely.

The length and width parameters of the form definition are for information only and do not have an effect on the formatting of a job.

NOTE

Using Print Devices in Print Job Configurations

SWIFT TRACK

Access Key: S, U

PRINTCON/Edit Job Configurations

I • Run the PRINTCON utility from the DOS command line by typing:

```
PRINTCON
```

2 • Use the arrow keys to select Edit Print Job Configurations and press Enter

3 • Select the print job configuration you wish to use a defined print device with and press Enter. Or press the Insert key to add a new print job configuration (refer to the Adding a Print Job Configuration Swift Track).

4 • Use the arrow keys to move to the Device field and press Enter.

5 • Select the device you wish to use and press Enter.

6 • Use the arrow keys to move to the Mode field and press Enter.

7 • Select the default mode for your printer and press Enter.

8 • Press Escape and answer Yes to save the changes.

9 • Press Escape two times to return to the main menu or press Alt-F10 to exit PRINTCON entirely.

Before a print device can be selected in PRINTCON, it must first be defined in PRINTDEF.

NOTE

SWIFT
TRACK

Using Print Forms in Print Job Configurations

Access Key: S, U

PRINTCON/Edit Print Job Configurations

1 • Run the PRINTCON utility from the DOS command line by typing:

PRINTCON

2 • Use the arrow keys to select Edit Print Job Configurations and press Enter

3 • Select the print job configuration you wish to use a defined print form with and press Enter. Or press the Insert key to add a new print job configuration (refer to the Adding a Print Job Configuration Swift Track).

4 • Use the arrow keys to move to the Form Name field and press Enter.

5 • Select the form you wish to use and press Enter.

6 • Press Escape and answer Yes to save the changes.

7 • Press Escape two times to return to the main menu or press Alt-F10 to exit PRINTCON entirely.

Before a print device can be selected in PRINTCON, it must first be defined in PRINTDEF.

NOTE

Managing a NetWare 3 Print System

SWIFT
TRACK

Checking a Printer's Status

> Access Key: S, U
>
> PCONSOLE/Print Server Information/Print Server Status Control/
>
> Printer Status

I • Run the PCONSOLE utility from the DOS command line by typing:

PCONSOLE

2 • Use the arrow keys to select Print Server Information and press Enter.

3 • Select the print server where the printer is defined and press Enter.

4 • Select Print Server Status/Control and press Enter.

5 • Select Printer Status and press Enter.

6 • Select the printer whose status you wish to view and press Enter.

7 • When you have finished viewing the printer's status, press Escape five times to return to the main menu or press Alt-F10 to exit PCONSOLE entirely.

The Print Server Status/Control option will only be displayed if the print server is up and running.

WARNING

SWIFT TRACK

Mounting a Form

Access Key: S, PSO
PCONSOLE/Print Server Information/Print Server Status Control/
Printer Status

1 • Run the PCONSOLE utility from the DOS command line by typing:

PCONSOLE

2 • Use the arrow keys to select Print Server Information and press Enter.

3 • Select the print server where the printer is defined and press Enter.

4 • Select Print Server Status/Control and press Enter.

5 • Select Printer Status and press Enter.

6 • Select the printer that you wish to mount the new form on and press Enter.

7 • Use the arrow keys to move to the Mounted Form field and enter the PRINTDEF form number you wish to mount and press Enter.

8 • Press Escape five times to return to the main menu or press Alt-F10 to exit PCONSOLE entirely.

WARNING

The Print Server Status/Control option will only be displayed if the print server is up and running.

NOTE

Be sure to define a form in PRINTDEF before attempting to mount it.

SWIFT
TRACK

Pausing a Printer

> Access Key: S, PSO
> PCONSOLE/Print Server Information/Print Server Status Control/
> Printer Status/Printer Control

1 • Run the PCONSOLE utility from the DOS command line by typing:

 PCONSOLE

2 • Use the arrow keys to select Print Server Information and press Enter.

3 • Select the print server where the printer is defined and press Enter.

4 • Select Print Server Status/Control and press Enter.

5 • Select Printer Status and press Enter.

6 • Select the printer that you wish to pause and press Enter.

7 • Use the arrow keys to move to the Printer Control field and press Enter.

8 • Select Pause Printer and press Enter.

9 • Press Escape five times to return to the main menu or press Alt-F10 to exit PCONSOLE entirely.

Once a printer is paused in PCONSOLE, no printing will take place until the printer is restarted again.

WARNING

The Print Server Status/Control option will only be displayed if the print server is up and running.

WARNING

SWIFT TRACK

Restarting a Paused Printer

> Access Key: S, PSO
>
> PCONSOLE/Print Server Information/Print Server Status Control/
> Printer Status/Printer Control

1 • Run the PCONSOLE utility from the DOS command line by typing:

  PCONSOLE

2 • Use the arrow keys to select Print Server Information and press Enter.

3 • Select the print server where the printer is defined and press Enter.

4 • Select Print Server Status/Control and press Enter.

5 • Select Printer Status and press Enter.

6 • Select the printer that you wish to restart and press Enter.

7 • Use the arrow keys to move to the Printer Control field and press Enter.

8 • Select Start Printer and press Enter.

9 • Press Escape five times to return to the main menu or press Alt-F10 to exit PCONSOLE entirely.

The Print Server Status/Control option will only be displayed if the print server is up and running.

WARNING

**SWIFT
TRACK**

Aborting a Print Job

Access Key: S, PSO
PCONSOLE/Print Server Information/Print Server Status Control/
Printer Status/Printer Control

I • Run the PCONSOLE utility from the DOS command line by typing:

PCONSOLE

2 • Use the arrow keys to select Print Server Information and press Enter.

3 • Select the print server where the printer is defined and press Enter.

4 • Select Print Server Status/Control and press Enter.

5 • Select Printer Status and press Enter.

6 • Select the printer that you wish to abort the print job on and press Enter.

7 • Use the arrow keys to move to the Printer Control field and press Enter.

8 • Select Abort Print Job and press Enter.

9 • Press Escape five times to return to the main menu or press Alt-F10 to exit PCONSOLE entirely.

The Print Server Status/Control option will only be displayed if the print server is up and running.

WARNING

SWIFT
TRACK

Issuing a Form Feed

Access Key: S, PSO
PCONSOLE/Print Server Information/Print Server Status Control/
Printer Status/Printer Control

1 • Run the PCONSOLE utility from the DOS command line by typing:

PCONSOLE

2 • Use the arrow keys to select Print Server Information and press Enter.

3 • Select the print server where the printer is defined and press Enter.

4 • Select Print Server Status/Control and press Enter.

5 • Select Printer Status and press Enter.

6 • Select the printer that you wish to issue a form feed on and press Enter.

7 • Use the arrow keys to move to the Printer Control field and press Enter.

8 • Select Form Feed and press Enter.

9 • Press Escape five times to return to the main menu or press Alt-F10 to exit PCONSOLE entirely.

The Print Server Status/Control option will only be displayed if the print server is up and running.

WARNING

SWIFT TRACK

Aligning a Form

> Access Key: S, PSO
>
> PCONSOLE/Print Server Information/Print Server Status Control/
>
> Printer Status/Printer Control

1 • Run the PCONSOLE utility from the DOS command line by typing:

    PCONSOLE

2 • Use the arrow keys to select Print Server Information and press Enter.

3 • Select the print server where the printer is defined and press Enter.

4 • Select Print Server Status/Control and press Enter.

5 • Select Printer Status and press Enter.

6 • Select the printer that you wish to align a form on and press Enter.

7 • Use the arrow keys to move to the Printer Control field and press Enter.

8 • Select Mark Top of Form and press Enter.

9 • Press Escape five times to return to the main menu or press Alt-F10 to exit PCONSOLE entirely.

WARNING

The Print Server Status/Control option will only be displayed if the print server is up and running.

SWIFT
TRACK

Rewinding a Printer

| Access Key: S, PSO |
| PCONSOLE/Print Server Information/Print Server Status Control/ |
| Printer Status/Printer Control |

1 • Run the PCONSOLE utility from the DOS command line by typing:

PCONSOLE

2 • Use the arrow keys to select Print Server Information and press Enter.

3 • Select the print server where the printer is defined and press Enter.

4 • Select Print Server Status/Control and press Enter.

5 • Select Printer Status and press Enter.

6 • Select the printer that you wish to rewind print job pages on and press Enter.

7 • Use the arrow keys to move to the Printer Control field and press Enter.

8 • Select Rewind Printer and press Enter.

9 • Enter the number of pages you wish to rewind or the page number you wish to reprint and press Enter.

10 • Press Escape six times to return to the main menu or press Alt-F10 to exit PCONSOLE entirely.

The Print Server Status/Control option will only be displayed if the print server is up and running.

WARNING

SWIFT TRACK

Stopping a Printer

Access Key: S, PSO
PCONSOLE/Print Server Information/Print Server Status Control/
Printer Status/Printer Control

1 • Run the PCONSOLE utility from the DOS command line by typing:

PCONSOLE

2 • Use the arrow keys to select Print Server Information and press Enter.

3 • Select the print server where the printer is defined and press Enter.

4 • Select Print Server Status/Control and press Enter.

5 • Select Printer Status and press Enter.

6 • Select the printer that you wish to stop and press Enter.

7 • Use the arrow keys to move to the Printer Control field and press Enter.

8 • Select Stop Printer and press Enter.

9 • Press Escape five times to return to the main menu or press Alt-F10 to exit PCONSOLE entirely.

The Print Server Status/Control option will only be displayed if the print server is up and running.

WARNING

Once a printer has been stopped, no printing will occur on that printer until it has been restarted again.

WARNING

SWIFT
TRACK

Loading a Remote Printer

> **Access Key: S, U**
>
> From the workstation with the printer attached, type:
>
> RPRINTER PrintServerName PrinterNumber

I • Verify that the workstation's NET.CFG file contains the following line:

```
SPX CONNECTIONS = 60
```

If necessary, use a text editor to add this line.

2 • Load the NetWare Client software at the workstation to attach to the server where the printer is defined.

3 • Verify that the workstation has access to the following files:

```
IBMRUN.OVL

RPRINTER.EXE

RPRINTER.HLP

SYS$HELP.DAT

SYS$MSG.DAT

SYS$ERR.DAT
```

These files are located in the SYS:PUBLIC directory of the NetWare server, so they can be accessed by logging in to the server or they can be copied to a local directory on the workstation.

4 • Load the remote printer software by typing the following from the DOS command line:

```
RPRINTER PrintServerName PrinterNumber
```

For example:

```
RPRINTER SLCII_PS 2
```

NOTE

For a printer to attach to a print server, the print server must be running before RPRINTER is loaded.

SWIFT
TRACK

Disconnecting a Remote Printer

Access Key: S, U

From the workstation with the remote printer attached, type:

RPRINTER PrintServerName PrinterNumber -r

1 • Go to the workstation with the remote printer attached.

2 • From the DOS command line, enter the following command:

```
RPRINTER PrintServerName PrinterNumber -r
```

For example:

```
RPRINTER SLCII_PS 2 -r
```

Making a Remote Printer Private

SWIFT TRACK

> Access Key: S, U
>
> From the workstation with the remote printer attached, type:
>
> PSC PS=PrintServerName P=PrinterNumber PRI

1 • Go to the workstation with the remote printer attached.

2 • From the DOS command line, enter the following command:

```
PSC PS=PrintServerName P=PrinterNumber PRI
```

For example:

```
PSC PS=SLCII_PS P=2 PRI
```

WARNING

Once a remote network printer has been made private, it can no longer be used by other network users until the PSC command has been reissued with the SHared parameter.

**SWIFT
TRACK**

Returning a Remote Printer to Shared Mode

Access Key: S, U

From the workstation with the remote printer attached, type:

PSC PS=PrintServerName P=PrinterNumber SH

I • Go to the workstation with the remote printer attached.

2 • From the DOS command line, enter the following command:

PSC PS=*PrintServerName* P=*PrinterNumber* SH

For example:

PSC PS=SLCII_PS P=2 SH

SWIFT TRACK

Placing a Print Job on Hold

> Access Key: S, PQO, U
> PCONSOLE/Print Queue Information/Current Print Job Entries/
> User or Operator Hold

I • Run the PCONSOLE utility from the DOS command line by typing:

```
PCONSOLE
```

2 • Use the arrow keys to select Print Queue Information and press Enter.

3 • Select the print queue that contains the job you wish to place on hold and press Enter.

4 • Select Current Print Job Entries and press Enter.

5 • Select the print job you wish to place a hold on and press Enter.

6 • Use the arrow keys to move to the User Hold field if you are the job owner or the Operator Hold field if you are a SUPERVISOR or Print Queue Operator.

7 • Type a Y for "yes" and press Enter.

8 • Press Escape four times to return to the main menu or press Alt-F10 to exit PCONSOLE entirely.

Deferring a Print Job

SWIFT TRACK

> Access Key: S, PQO, U
> PCONSOLE/Print Queue Information/Current Print Job Entries/
> Defer Printing

1 • Run the PCONSOLE utility from the DOS command line by typing:
PCONSOLE

2 • Use the arrow keys to select Print Queue Information and press Enter.

3 • Select the print queue that contains the job you wish to defer the printing of and press Enter.

4 • Select Current Print Job Entries and press Enter.

5 • Select the print job you wish to defer and press Enter.

6 • Use the arrow keys to move to the Defer Printing field.

7 • Type a Y for "yes" and press Enter.

8 • Use the arrow keys to move down one field and enter the date that you want the job to print on.

9 • Use the arrow keys to move down one field and enter the time that you want the job to print.

10 • Press Escape four times to return to the main menu or press Alt-F10 to exit PCONSOLE entirely.

Checking a Print Job's Status

Access Key: S, PQO, U
PCONSOLE/Print Queue Information/Current Print Job Entries

1 • Run the PCONSOLE utility from the DOS command line by typing:

   PCONSOLE

2 • Use the arrow keys to select Print Queue Information and press Enter.

3 • Select the print queue that contains the job you wish to check the status of and press Enter.

4 • Select Current Print Job Entries and press Enter.

5 • View the status of the job in the queue.

6 • Press Escape three times to return to the main menu or press Alt-F10 to exit PCONSOLE entirely.

SWIFT
TRACK

Modifying a Print Job's CAPTURE Parameters

> Access Key: S, PQO, U
> PCONSOLE/Print Queue Information/Current Print Job Entries

1 • Run the PCONSOLE utility from the DOS command line by typing:

PCONSOLE

2 • Use the arrow keys to select Print Queue Information and press Enter.

3 • Select the print queue that contains the job you wish to change the CAPTURE parameters for and press Enter.

4 • Select Current Print Job Entries and press Enter.

5 • Select the print job you wish to modify and press Enter.

6 • Modify the parameters as desired.

7 • When you have finished modifying the CAPTURE parameters, press Escape four times to return to the main menu or press Alt-F10 to exit PCONSOLE entirely.

Assigning Print Queue Users

Access Key: S, PQO
PCONSOLE/Print Queue Information/Queue Users

1 • Run the PCONSOLE utility from the DOS command line by typing:

   PCONSOLE

2 • Use the arrow keys to select Print Queue Information and press Enter.

3 • Select the print queue that you wish to assign users for and press Enter.

4 • Select Queue Users and press Enter.

5 • Press the Insert key to add queue users (or Delete to remove a queue user)

6 • Select the users you wish to use this queue from the list. The F5 key can be used to mark multiple users.

7 • When you have finished marking the users, press Enter.

8 • Press Escape three times to return to the main menu or Alt-F10 to exit PCONSOLE entirely.

**SWIFT
TRACK**

Assigning Print Queue Operators

1 • Run the PCONSOLE utility from the DOS command line by typing:

PCONSOLE

2 • Use the arrow keys to select Print Queue Information and press Enter.

3 • Select the print queue that you wish to assign an operator for and press Enter.

4 • Select Queue Operators and press Enter.

5 • Press the Insert key to add queue operators (or Delete to remove a queue Operator)

6 • Select the user you wish to be an Operator for the queue from the list. The F5 key can be used to mark multiple users.

7 • When you have finished marking the users, press Enter.

8 • Press Escape three times to return to the main menu or Alt-F10 to exit PCONSOLE entirely.

SWIFT TRACK

Disabling the Servicing of Print Jobs in a Queue

> Access Key: S, PQO
> PCONSOLE/Print Queue Information/Current Queue Status

I • Run the PCONSOLE utility from the DOS command line by typing:

    PCONSOLE

2 • Use the arrow keys to select Print Queue Information and press Enter.

3 • Select the print queue on which you wish to disable the servicing of print jobs and press Enter.

4 • Select Current Queue Status and press Enter.

5 • If you do not want users to be able to place jobs in the queue, type an N for "no" in the first field. If you want jobs to go to the queue but not be serviced, type an N for "no" in the second field.

6 • When you have finished, press Escape three times to return to the main menu or Alt-F10 to exit PCONSOLE entirely.

▶ · ◀

SWIFT
TRACK

Downing a Print Server through PCONSOLE

Access Key: S, PSO
PCONSOLE/Print Server Information/Print Server Status Control/
Server Info/Down

1 • Run the PCONSOLE utility from the DOS command line by typing:

    PCONSOLE

2 • Use the arrow keys to select Print Server Information and press Enter.

3 • Select the print server that you wish to take down and press Enter.

4 • Select Print Server Status/Control and press Enter.

5 • Select Server and press Enter.

6 • Select Current Server Status and press Enter.

7 • Use the arrow keys to move to Down if you wish for the print server to
go down immediately or Going Down after current jobs if you want the
print server to finish servicing the jobs in the queue. When you have
finished, press Enter.

8 • Press Escape five times to return to the main menu or press Alt-F10 to
exit PCONSOLE entirely.

WARNING

**The Print Server Status/Control option will only be displayed if the
print server is up and running.**

SWIFT
TRACK

Enabling **CAPTURE** from the **DOS** Command Line

Access Key: S, U
CAPTURE Options ...

I • From the DOS command line of a workstation, issue the Capture command using the following syntax:

```
CAPTURE OPTION OPTION...
```

For example:

```
CAPTURE Q=HP4_Q L=2 NB NFF TI=20
```

Enabling CAPTURE through User Login Scripts

> Access Key: S, U
> SYSCON/User Information/Login Script

1 • Run the SYSCON utility from the DOS command line by typing:

```
SYSCON
```

2 • Use the arrow keys to select User Information and press Enter.

3 • Select the user whose login script you wish to modify and press Enter.

4 • Select Login Script.

5 • Enter the CAPTURE statement with the following syntax:

```
#CAPTURE OPTION OPTION...
```

For example:

```
#CAPTURE Q=HP4_Q L=2 NB NFF TI=20
```

6 • Press Escape and answer Yes to save changes.

7 • Press Escape twice to return to the main menu or press Alt-F10 to exit SYSCON entirely.

SWIFT
TRACK

Enabling CAPTURE through the System Login Script

Access Key: S
SYSCON/Supervisor Options/System Login Script

I • Run the SYSCON utility from the DOS command line by typing:

   SYSCON

2 • Use the arrow keys to select Supervisor Options Information and press Enter.

3 • Select System Login Script and press Enter.

4 • Enter the CAPTURE statement with the following syntax:

   #CAPTURE *OPTION OPTION...*

   For example:

   #CAPTURE Q=HP4_Q L=2 NB NFF TI=20

5 • Press Escape and answer Yes to save changes.

6 • Press Escape once to return to the main menu or press Alt-F10 to exit SYSCON entirely.

SWIFT TRACK

Enabling CAPTURE through Windows 95

> Access Key: S, U
>
> WIN95/Network Neighborhood/File/Capture Printer Port

1 • From the Windows 95 Desktop, double-click on Network Neighborhood.

2 • Double-click the file server on which the printer is defined.

3 • Click once on the printer you wish to capture.

4 • From the menu bar select File and the Capture Printer Port.

5 • In the device field, select the printer port you wish to capture.

6 • Click on OK.

Creating a Basic NetWare 4 Print System

Creating a Print Queue—PCONSOLE

SWIFT
TRACK

> **Access Key: S**
>
> **PCONSOLE/Print Queues**

1 • Run the PCONSOLE utility from the DOS command line by typing:

PCONSOLE

2 • Verify the context shown at the top of the screen. If necessary, select Change Context and press Enter. Use the Insert key to browse the directory tree for the context you wish to create the print queue in and press F10 or Escape to save.

3 • From the PCONSOLE main menu, use the arrow keys to select Print Queues and press Enter.

4 • From the print queue list, press the Insert key to add a new print queue.

5 • Assign a descriptive name for the queue from 1 to 45 characters and press Enter.

6 • Press Escape to return to the PCONSOLE main menu or AltALT-F10 to exit PCONSOLE entirely.

For this print queue to be functional, you must assign a print server and printer to service this queue, and the print server must be running.

NOTE

**SWIFT
TRACK**

Creating a Print Queue—NWAdmin

Access Key: S

Object/Create/Print Queue

1 • From Windows, run NWAdmin by double-clicking the icon or selecting it from the Start menu (Windows 95).

2 • Use the mouse to navigate through the directory tree to find the desired container you wish to create a print queue in. Double-clicking on a container object moves you deeper into the tree.

3 • Highlight the container you wish to create the print queue in and press Insert or select Object/Create from the menu bar. If you are using the NetWare 4.11 version of NWAdmin, you may also click on the Create Print Queue button from the toolbar.

4 • From the New Object dialog box, select Print Queue and click OK.

5 • Enter a descriptive name for the print queue.

6 • Select the volume you wish to create the print queue ion by clicking the browse button to the right of the Print Queue Volume field.

7 • Using the Directory Context dialog box, browse the directory tree for the print queue volume. Double-clicking the yellow up arrow moves you up the directory tree. Double-clicking a container object moves you into that container.

8 • When you locate the print queue volume, select it by single clicking the object in the Objects dialog box and click OK.

9 • From the Create Print Queue dialog box, click Create.

NOTE

For this print queue to be functional, you must assign a print server and printer to service this queue, andqueue and the print server must be running.

Creating a Print Server—PCONSOLE

SWIFT
TRACK

Access Key: A
PCONSOLE/Print Servers

1 • Run the PCONSOLE utility from the DOS command line by typing:

PCONSOLE

2 • Verify the context shown at the top of the screen. If necessary, select Change Context and press Enter. Use the Insert key to browse the directory tree for the context you wish to create the print queue in and press F10 or Escape to save.

3 • From the PCONSOLE main menu, use the arrow keys to select Print Servers and press Enter.

4 • From the print server list, press the Insert key to add a new print server.

5 • Assign a descriptive name for the print server from 1 to 64 characters and press Enter.

6 • Press Escape to return to the PCONSOLE main menu or AltALT-F10 to exit PCONSOLE entirely.

For this print server to be functional, you must configure at least one printer and assign a queue to be serviced and the print server must be running.

NOTE

Creating a Print Server—NWAdmin

SWIFT
TRACK

> **Access Key: A**
>
> Object/Create/Print Server

1 • From Windows, run NWAdmin by double-clicking the icon or selecting it from the Start menu (Windows 95).

2 • Use the mouse to navigate through the directory tree to find the desired container you wish to create a print server in. Double-clicking on a container object moves you deeper into the tree.

3 • Highlight the container you wish to create the print server in and press Insert, or select Object/Create from the menu bar. If you are using the NetWare 4.11 version of NWAdmin, you may also click on the Create Object button from the toolbar.

4 • From the New Object dialog box, select Print Server and click OK.

5 • Enter a descriptive name for the print server.

6 • To save this print server, click on Create.

For this print server to be functional, you must configure at least one printer and assign a queue to be serviced and the print server must be running.

NOTE

SWIFT
TRACK

Creating Printers—PCONSOLE

> Access Key: A, PSO
> PCONSOLE/Printers

1 • Run the PCONSOLE utility from the DOS command line by typing:

   PCONSOLE

2 • Verify the context shown at the top of the screen. If necessary, select Change Context and press Enter. Use the Insert key to browse the directory tree for the context you wish to create the print queue in and press F10 or Escape to save.

3 • From the PCONSOLE main menu, use the arrow keys to select Printers and press Enter.

4 • From the printer list, press the Insert key to add a new printer.

5 • Assign a descriptive name for the print server from 1 to 64 characters and press Enter.

6 • Select the printer by pressing Enter.

7 • Select the printer type and press Enter.

8 • Press Enter on Configuration and enter the specifics about this printer (see Part I, Chapter 3 for details).

9 • Enter the remaining printer configuration information (see Part I, Chapter 3 for details) and press Enter.

10 • When the printer's configuration is complete, press Escape.

11 • Press Escape to return to the PCONSOLE main menu or AltALT-F10 to exit PCONSOLE entirely.

NOTE

For this printer to be functional, you must assign it to service at least one print queue, andqueue and the print server must be running. If a remote printer was defined, **RPRINTER.EXE** must be loaded at the workstation with the printer attached.

Creating Printers—NWAdmin

SWIFT TRACK

> Access Key: A, PSO
> Object/Create/Printer

1 • From Windows, run NWAdmin by double-clicking the icon or selecting it from the Start menu (Windows 95).

2 • Use the mouse to navigate through the directory tree to find the desired container you wish to create a printer in. Double-clicking on a container object moves you deeper into the tree.

3 • Highlight the container you wish to create the printer in and press Insert or select Object/Create from the menu bar. If you are using the NetWare 4.11 version of NWAdmin, you may also click on the Create Object button from the toolbar.

4 • From the New Object dialog box, select Printer and click OK.

5 • Enter a descriptive name for the printer.

6 • To save the printer object, click Create.

NOTE

For this printer to be functional, you must assign it to service at least one print queue, andqueue and the print server must be running. If a remote printer was defined, RPRINTER.EXE must be loaded at the workstation with the printer attached.

SWIFT
TRACK

Assigning Queues to be Serviced by Printer—PCONSOLE

> Access Key: A, PSO
>
> PCONSOLE/Printers/Print Queues Assigned

1 • Run the PCONSOLE utility from the DOS command line by typing:

PCONSOLE

2 • Verify the context shown at the top of the screen. If necessary, select Change Context and press Enter. Use the Insert key to browse the directory tree for the context you wish to create the print queue in and press F10 or Escape to save.

3 • From the PCONSOLE main menu, use the arrow keys to select Printers and press Enter.

4 • From the printer list, select the printer you wish to assign a queue to and press Enter.

5 • Select Print queues assigned and press Enter.

6 • Press the Insert key and browse the directory tree for the print queue you wish to assign this printer to. When you have located the printer, press F10 or Enter to select the printer.

7 • Optional. Repeat step 6 for each additional print queue you would like this printer to service.

8 • When you have finished selecting print queues, press Escape three3 times to return to the PCONSOLE main menu or press AltALT-F10 to exit PCONSOLE entirely.

For the printer and print queue to be functional, the print server must be running.

NOTE

SWIFT
TRACK

Assigning Queues to be Serviced by Printer— NWAdmin

Access Key: A, PSO

Printer Object/Details/Assignments/Add

1 • From Windows, run NWAdmin by double-clicking the icon or selecting it from the Start menu (Windows 95).

2 • Use the mouse to navigate through the directory tree to find the container that the printer resides in. Double-clicking on a container object moves you deeper into the tree.

3 • Select the printer object by double-clicking on it. If you are using the NetWare 4.11 version of NWAdmin, you may also click on the View Modify Object Properties button from the toolbar.

4 • From the printer's details page, click Assignments.

5 • From the print queue dialog, click Add.

6 • From the Select Object screen, browse the directory tree for the print queue you wish for this printer to service. Double-clicking the yellow up arrow in the Directory Context dialog box moves you up the directory tree. Double-clicking a container object moves you into that container.

7 • When you locate the print queue, select it by clicking on the object once in the Objects dialog and click OK to save.

8 • Optional. Repeat steps 5–7 for each additional print you wish for this printer to service.

9 • When you have finished, click OK to save.

For the printer and print queue to be functional, the print server must be running.

NOTE

▶ . . . . ◀

Using Quick Setup to Creating Printing Components—PCONSOLE

SWIFT
TRACK

> Access Key: A
>
> PCONSOLE/Quick Setup

1 • Run the PCONSOLE utility from the DOS command line by typing:

   PCONSOLE

2 • Verify the context shown at the top of the screen. If necessary, select Change Context and press Enter. Use the Insert key to browse the directory tree for the context you wish to create the print queue in and press F10 or Escape to save.

3 • From the PCONSOLE main menu, use the arrow keys to select Quick Setup and press Enter.

4 • Accept the default names or use the arrow keys to select and modify the names of the print objects.

5 • Use the arrow keys to move down to Print queue volume.

6 • If the default volume is not correct, press Enter and then Insert to browse the directory tree for the correct volume. When you have found the volume, highlight it and press F10 or Enter to select it.

7 • In the Banner type field, select the type of printing your printer supports and press Enter.

8 • Enter the printer type and configuration (see Part I, Chapter 3 for details).

9 • When you have finished configuring the print system, press Escape and Enter to save the changes.

NOTE

In order for this printing system to be functional, the print server must be loaded and remote printers must be attached.

▶ · ◀

SWIFT
TRACK

Using Quick Setup to Creating Printing Components—NWAdmin (NetWare 4.11 only)

> Access Key: A
>
> Tools/Print Services Quick Setup

1 • In Windows, run NWAdmin by double-clicking the icon or by selecting it from the Start menu (Windows 95).

2 • Use the mouse to navigate through the directory tree to find the desired container where you want to create printing objects. Double-clicking on a container object moves you deeper into the tree.

3 • Highlight the container where you want to create the objects and select Tools/Print Services Quick Setup from the menu bar.

4 • In the Print Services Quick Setup dialog box, enter a new print server name or browse the directory tree to select an existing print server.

5 • Enter a name for the printer you want to create and the associated configuration information.

6 • Enter a print queue name.

7 • Use the browse button to the right of the Volume field to browse the tree for the volume where you want this print queue to be created.

8 • When you finish, click Create to create the objects and have all necessary assignments made.

For this printing system to be functional, the print server must be loaded and remote printers must be attached.

NOTE

Starting the Print Server—PSERVER.NLM

> Access Key: A, PSO, U
>
> At the server console, type: LOAD PSERVER

1 • Go to the console of the file server you wish to load the print server on or establish an RCONSOLE session from a workstation by running RCONSOLE.EXE and choosing the server you wish to load the print server on.

2 • From the server console prompt type:

```
LOAD PSERVER <Enter>
```

3 • Press enter to browse the directory tree for the print server you wish to load. When you locate the print server, press Enter to select it.

4 • Enter the print server's password (if one has been assigned) and press Enter.

NOTE

To establish an **RCONSOLE** session with a file server, you must first load **REMOTE.NLM** and **RSPX.NLM** at the server's console.

NOTE

For remote printers to attach to the print server, you must load **NPRINTER.EXE** at the workstations with the printers attached.

WARNING

Because a regular user can load a print server, it is important that all print servers be assigned a password to prevent an unauthorized user from loading it.

SWIFT TRACK

Connecting Remote Printers—File Server Attached—NPRINTER.NLM

> Access Key: A, PSO, U
>
> From the server console, type:
>
> LOAD NPRINTER printservername printername

I • Go to the console of the file server you wish to load the NPRINTER on or establish an RCONSOLE session from a workstation by running RCONSOLE.EXE and choosing the server you wish to load NPRINTER.NLM on.

2 • From the server console prompt, type:

```
LOAD NPRINTER printservername printername
```

For example:

```
LOAD NPRINTER SLCII_PS 1
```

NOTE

For a printer to attach to a print server, the print server must be running before NPRINTER is loaded.

SWIFT TRACK

Connecting Remote Printers—Workstation Attached

> Access Key: A, PSO, U
>
> From the workstation with the printer attached, type:
>
> NPRINTER PrintServerName PrinterNumber

1 • Verify that the workstation's NET.CFG file contains the following line:

```
SPX CONNECTIONS = 60
```

If necessary, use a text editor to add this line.

2 • Load the NetWare Client software at the workstation to attach to the server where the printer is defined.

3 • Log in to the server.

4 • Load the remote printer software by typing the following from the DOS command line:

```
NPRINTER PrintServerName PrinterNumber
```

For example:

```
NPRINTER SLCII_PS 2
```

Or use the following NDS syntax:

```
NPRINTER
.CN=printername.OU=OrganizationalUnit.O=Organization
```

For example:

```
NPRINTER .CN=P1.OU=SLCII.O=AIRPORTS
```

NOTE

For a printer to attach to a print server, the print server must be running before NPRINTER is loaded.

Creating Print Job Configurations—PRINTCON

> Access Key: A, U
>
> PRINTCON/Edit Print Job Configurations

1 • Run the PRINTCON utility from the DOS command line by typing:

```
PRINTCON
```

2 • Verify the user object shown at the top of the screen. If this is not the user you wish to create a print job configuration for, select Change Current Object and press Enter. Use the insert key to browse the directory tree. When you have located the desired user, select the object by highlighting it and pressing Enter or F10. Press Escape to return to the PRINTCON main menu.

3 • From the main menu, use the arrow keys to select Edit Print Job Configurations and press Enter.

4 • Press Insert to add a new print job configuration.

5 • Enter a unique descriptive name for this job configuration and press Enter.

6 • Press Enter to select the job configuration and edit the print job configuration's parameters by using the arrow keys to move through the fields.

7 • Press Escape twice to return to the main menu or press AltALT-F10 to exit PRINTCON entirely.

SWIFT TRACK

Creating Print Job Configurations—NWAdmin

> Access Key: A, U
>
> User or Container/Details/Print Job Configuration/New

1 • From Windows, run NWAdmin by double-clicking the icon or selecting it from the Start menu (Windows 95).

2 • Use the mouse to navigate through the directory tree to find the object you wish to create a job configuration for. Double-clicking on a container object moves you deeper into the tree.

3 • Select the object by double-clicking on it, or if it is a container object, select Object/Details from the menu bar. If you are using the NetWare 4.11 version of NWAdmin, you may also click on the View Modify Object Properties button from the toolbar.

Using the right mouse button also enables you to access the Details page.

TIP

4 • From the Details page, click Print Job Configuration.

5 • Click New to add a new job configuration.

6 • Enter a descriptive name for the job configuration.

7 • Use the mouse or the tab key to move through the remaining fields and make the desired modifications.

8 • When you have finished modifying the parameters, click OK to save.

9 • From the Details page, click OK to save the changes to this object.

**SWIFT
TRACK**

Setting a Default Print Job Configuration—PRINTCON

> Access Key: A, U
> PRINTCON/Select Default Print Job Configuration

1 • Run the PRINTCON utility from the DOS command line by typing:

    PRINTCON

2 • Verify the user object shown at the top of the screen. If this is not the user you wish to set the default print job configuration for, select Change Current Object and press Enter. Use the Insert key to browse the directory tree. When you have located the desired user, select the object by highlighting it and pressing Enter or F10. Press Escape to return to the PRINTCON main menu.

3 • From the main menu, use the arrow keys to select Select Default Print Job Configuration and press Enter.

4 • Highlight the job configuration you wish to make the default and press Enter.

5 • Press Escape once to return to the main menu or press AltALT-F10 to exit PRINTCON entirely.

Setting a Default Print Job Configuration—NWAdmin

SWIFT
TRACK

> Access Key: A, U
>
> User or Container/Details/Print Job Configuration/Default

1 • From Windows, run NWAdmin by double-clicking the icon or selecting it from the Start menu (Windows 95).

2 • Use the mouse to navigate through the directory tree to find the object you wish to set the default job configuration for. Double-clicking on a container object moves you deeper into the treedeeper in the tree.

3 • Select the object by double-clicking on it, or if it is a container object, select Object/Details from the menu bar. If you are using the NetWare 4.11 version of NWAdmin, you may also click on the View Modify Object Properties button from the toolbar.

Using the right mouse button also enables you to access the Details page.

TIP

4 • From the Details page, click Print Job Configuration.

5 • Click on the job configuration you wish to make the default and click Default.

6 • Click OK to save the changes to this object.

SWIFT
TRACK

Importing Print Devices (*.PDFs)—PRINTDEF

> Access Key: A
> PRINTDEF/Print Devices/Import Print Devices

1 • Run the PRINTDEF utility from the DOS command line by typing:

   PRINTDEF

2 • Verify the context shown at the top of the screen. If this is not the container you wish to import print devices to, select Change Current Context and press Enter. Use the Insert key to browse the directory tree for the desired context. Select the context by highlighting it and pressing Enter and then Escape to save.

3 • From the main menu, use the arrow keys to select Print Devices and press Enter.

4 • Use the arrow keys to select Import Print Devices and press Enter.

5 • Enter the source directory by typing:

   SYS:PUBLIC <Enter>

   Or, if the PDF file you wish to import is in another location, press the Insert key and browse through the directory structure until you find the desired directory and press Enter.

6 • Use the arrow keys to select the appropriate PDF file for your printer and press Enter.

7 • Press Escape once to return to the main menu or press AltALT-F10 to exit PRINTDEF entirely.

Importing Print Devices (*.PDFs)—NWAdmin

SWIFT
TRACK

Access Key: A

Container Object/Details/Print Devices/Import

I • From Windows, run NWAdmin by double-clicking the icon or selecting it from the Start menu (Windows 95).

2 • Use the mouse to navigate through the directory tree to find the container object you wish to import print devices to. Double-clicking on a container object moves you deeper into the treedeeper in the tree.

3 • Select the container and choose Object/Details from the menu bar. If you are using the NetWare 4.11 version of NWAdmin, you may also click on the View Modify Object Properties button from the toolbar.

Using the right mouse button also enables you to access the Details page.

TIP

4 • From the Details page, click Print Devices.

5 • To import a print device, click Import.

6 • Select the default PDF directory of SYS:PUBLIC by clicking OK, or use the Directories dialog to browse the file system for the directory that contains the PDF file you wish to import and click OK.

7 • From the Files dialog box, choose the appropriate PDF file for your printer and click OK.

8 • From the Details page, click OK to save the changes to this object.

**SWIFT
TRACK**

Creating a Print Device—PRINTDEF

> Access Key: A
> PRINTDEF/Print Devices/Edit Print Devices

I • Run the PRINTDEF utility from the DOS command line by typing:

PRINTDEF

2 • Verify the context shown at the top of the screen. If this is not the context you wish to create a new print device in, select Change Current Context and press Enter. Use the Insert key to browse the directory tree for the desired context. Select the context by highlighting it and pressing Enter and then Escape to save.

3 • From the main menu, use the arrow keys to select Print Devices and press Enter.

4 • Use the arrow keys to select Edit Print Devices and press Enter.

5 • To add a new print device press Insert.

6 • Enter the new device name.

7 • Select the new device by pressing Enter.

8 • Define the device functions and modes for your printer.

9 • When you have finished defining device functions and modes, press Escape three times to return to the main menu or press AltALT-F10 to exit PRINTDEF entirely.

TIP

Always check the PDF files provided with NetWare to see if one exists for your printer before defining a new print device. If no PDF file exists, see if your printer emulates another printer that a PDF file is provided for. This could save you hours of work.

NOTE

Most printer manuals include the printer codes recognized by that particular printer. If your printer manual does not include these codes and NetWare provides no **PDF** file, contact the manufacturer.

Creating a Print Device—NWAdmin

Access Key: A
Container Object/Details/Print Devices/Create

1 • From Windows, run NWAdmin by double-clicking the icon or selecting it from the Start menu (Windows 95).

2 • Use the mouse to navigate through the directory tree to find the container object you wish to create the new print device in. Double-clicking on a container object moves you deeper into the treedeeper in the tree.

3 • Select the container and choose Object/Details from the menu bar. If you are using the NetWare 4.11 version of NWAdmin, you may also click on the View Modify Object Properties button from the toolbar.

Using the right mouse button also enables you to access the Details page.

TIP

4 • From the Details page, click Print Devices.

5 • To create a new print device, click Create.

6 • Enter a name for the new device.

7 • Define the device functions and modes for your printer.

8 • When you have finished, click OK to save the new print device.

9 • From the Details page, click OK to save the changes to the container object.

TIP

Always check the PDF files provided with NetWare to see if one exists for your printer before defining a new print device. If no PDF file exists, see if your printer emulates another printer that a PDF file is provided for. This could save you hours of work.

NOTE

Most printer manuals include the printer codes recognized by that particular printer. If your printer manual does not include these codes and NetWare provides no PDF file, contact the manufacturer.

SWIFT
TRACK

Creating Device Functions—PRINTDEF

> Access Key: A
> PRINTDEF/Print Devices/Edit Print Devices/Device Functions

1 • Run the PRINTDEF utility from the DOS command line by typing:

PRINTDEF

2 • Verify the context shown at the top of the screen. If this is not the context you wish to create a new device function in, select Change Current Context and press Enter. Use the Insert key to browse the directory tree for the desired context. Select the context by highlighting it and pressing Enter and then Escape to save.

3 • From the main menu, use the arrow keys to select Print Devices and press Enter.

4 • Use the arrow keys to select Edit Print Devices and press Enter.

5 • Use the arrow keys to select the print device you wish to define a new function for and press Enter.

6 • Use the arrow key to select Device Functions and press Enter.

7 • Press Insert to add the new device function.

8 • Enter the function name.

9 • Use the arrow keys to move to the Control Sequence field.

10 • Enter a valid printer code as defined by the printer's manufacturer.

11 • Optional. Repeat steps 7–9 for each additional print code you wish to define.

12 • When you have finished defining device functions, press Escape four times to return to the main menu or press AltALT-F10 to exit PRINTDEF entirely.

TIP

Always check the PDF files provided with NetWare to see if one exists for your printer before defining a new print function. If no PDF file exists, see if your printer emulates another printer that a PDF file is provided for. This could save you hours of work.

NOTE

Most printer manuals include the printer codes recognized by that particular printer. If your printer manual does not include these codes and NetWare provides no PDF file, contact the manufacturer.

Creating Device Functions—NWAdmin

SWIFT TRACK

Access Key: A
Container Object/Details/Print Devices/Modify/Create Function

1 • From Windows, run NWAdmin by double-clicking the icon or selecting it from the Start menu (Windows 95).

2 • Use the mouse to navigate through the directory tree to find the container object you wish to create the device function for. Double-clicking on a container object moves you deeper into the treedeeper in the tree.

3 • Select the container and choose Object/Details from the menu bar. If you are using the NetWare 4.11 version of NWAdmin, you may also click on the View Modify Object Properties button from the toolbar.

TIP

Using the right mouse button also enables you to access the Details page.

4 • From the Details page, click Print Devices.

5 • Select the print device you wish to add the new function for and click on Modify.

6 • To add a new function for this print device, click Create Function.

7 • Enter the function name.

8 • Press tab or use the mouse to move to the Control Sequence field.

9 • Enter a valid printer code as defined by the printer's manufacturer.

10 • Optional. Repeat steps 6–9 for each additional print code you wish to define.

11 • When you have finished, click OK to save the changes to this print device.

12 • From the Details page, click OK to save the changes to the container object.

TIP

Always check the PDF files provided with NetWare to see if one exists for your printer before defining a new print device. If no PDF file exists, see if your printer emulates another printer that a PDF file is provided for. This could save you hours of work.

NOTE

Most printer manuals include the printer codes recognized by that particular printer. If your printer manual does not include these codes and NetWare provides no PDF file, contact the manufacturer.

SWIFT TRACK

Creating Device Modes—PRINTDEF

> **Access Key: A**
>
> PRINTDEF/Print Devices/Edit Print Devices/Device Modes

1 • Run the PRINTDEF utility from the DOS command line by typing:

PRINTDEF

2 • Verify the context shown at the top of the screen. If this is not the context you wish to create a new device mode in, select Change Current Context and press Enter. Use the Insert key to browse the directory tree for the desired context. Select the context by highlighting it and pressing Enter and then Escape to save.

3 • From the main menu, use the arrow keys to select Print Devices and press Enter.

4 • Use the arrow keys to select Edit Print Devices and press Enter.

5 • Use the arrow keys to select the print device you wish to define a new mode for and press Enter.

6 • Select Device Modes and press Enter.

7 • Press Insert to add the new device mode.

8 • Enter the mode name and press Enter.

9 • Press Enter to select the device mode and then Insert to select the printer functions that make up this mode of printing. Use the F5 key to mark multiple items.

10 • When you have finished marking the printer functions, press Enter.

11 • Optional. Repeat steps 7–10 for each additional device mode you wish to define.

12 • When you have finished defining device modes, press Escape five times to return to the main menu or press AltALT-F10 to exit PRINTDEF entirely.

Always check the PDF files provided with NetWare to see if one exists for your printer before defining a new print device mode. If no PDF file exists, see if your printer emulates another printer that a PDF file is provided for. This could save you hours of work.

TIP

Most printer manuals include the printer codes recognized by that particular printer. If your printer manual does not include these codes and NetWare provides no PDF file, contact the manufacturer.

NOTE

Creating Device Modes—NWAdmin

| Access Key: A |
| Container Object/Details/Print Devices/Modify/Create Mode |

I • From Windows, run NWAdmin by double-clicking the icon or selecting it from the Start menu (Windows 95).

2 • Use the mouse to navigate through the directory tree to find the container object you wish to create the device mode for. Double-clicking on a container object moves you deeper into the treedeeper in the tree.

3 • Select the container and choose Object/Details from the menu bar. If you are using the NetWare 4.11 version of NWAdmin, you may also click on the View Modify Object Properties button from the toolbar.

Using the right mouse button also enables you to access the Details page.

TIP

4 • From the Details page, click Print Devices.

5 • Select the print device you wish to add the new print mode for and click on Modify.

6 • To add a new mode for this print device, click Create Mode.

7 • Enter the mode name and click OK.

8 • With the new mode selected, click Modify.

9 • Use the mouse to select the device functions that make up this mode of printing. Click Add Above to insert the function above the highlighted function. Click Add Below to insert the function below the highlighted function. Refer to your printer's manual for the proper functions and their order for a specific mode of printing.

10 • When you have finished selecting the device functions, click OK to save this print mode.

11 • Optional. Repeat steps 6–10 for each additional print mode you wish to define.

12 • When you have finished, click OK to save the changes to this print device.

13 • From the Details page, click OK to save the changes to the container object.

TIP

Always check the PDF files provided with NetWare to see if one exists for your printer before defining a new print device. If no PDF file exists, see if your printer emulates another printer that a PDF file is provided for. This could save you hours of work.

NOTE

Most printer manuals include the printer codes recognized by that particular printer. If your printer manual does not include these codes and NetWare provides no PDF file, contact the manufacturer.

Creating Forms—PRINTDEF

SWIFT TRACK

Access Key: A
PRINTDEF/Printer Forms

1 • Run the PRINTDEF utility from the DOS command line by typing:

PRINTDEF

2 • Verify the context shown at the top of the screen. If this is not the context you wish to create a new form in, select Change Current Context and press Enter. Use the Insert key to browse the directory tree for the desired context. Select the context by highlighting it and pressing Enter and then Escape to save.

3 • From the main menu, use the arrow keys to select Printer Forms and press Enter.

4 • Press the Insert key to define a new form.

5 • Enter a descriptive name for the form and press Enter.

6 • Assign a form number from 0 to –255 and press Enter.

7 • Enter the length of the form and press Enter.

8 • Enter the width of the form and press Enter.

9 • Press Escape and answer Yes to save changes.

10 • Press Escape once to return to the main menu or press AltALT-F10 to exit PRINTDEF entirely.

NOTE The length and width parameters of the form definition are for information only and do not have an affect on the formatting of a job.

SWIFT
TRACK

Creating Forms—NWAdmin

> Access Key: A
> Container Object/Details/Printer Forms/Create

1 • From Windows, run NWAdmin by double-clicking the icon or selecting it from the Start menu (Windows 95).

2 • Use the mouse to navigate through the directory tree to find the container object you wish to create the printer form for. Double-clicking on a container object moves you deeper into the treedeeper in the tree.

3 • Select the container and choose Object/Details from the menu bar. If you are using the NetWare 4.11 version of NWAdmin, you may also click on the View Modify Object Properties button from the toolbar.

Using the right mouse button also enables you to access the Details page.

TIP

4 • From the Details page, click Printer Forms.

5 • To add a new form, click Create.

6 • Enter a descriptive name for the form.

7 • Use the tab key or the mouse to move to the Number field and enter a form number.

8 • Move to the Length and Width fields and enter the length and width of this form.

9 • When you have finished, click OK to save the changes to this form.

10 • From the Details page, click OK to save the changes to this container object.

NOTE

The length and width parameters of the form definition are for information only and do not have an affect on the formatting of a job.

▶ · ◀

SWIFT
TRACK

Using Print Devices in Print Job Configurations— PRINTCON

Access Key: A, U

PRINTCON/Edit Job Configurations

I • Run the PRINTCON utility from the DOS command line by typing:

PRINTCON

2 • Verify the user object shown at the top of the screen. If this is not the user you wish to use a print device for, select Change Current Object and press Enter. Use the insert key to browse the directory tree. When you have located the desired user, select the object by highlighting it and pressing Enter or F10. Press Escape to return to the PRINTCON main menu.

3 • From the main menu, use the arrow keys to select Edit Print Job Configurations and press Enter.

4 • Select the print job configuration you wish to use a defined print device with and press Enter. Or press the Insert key to add a new print job configuration (refer to the Adding a Print Job Configuration Quick Path).

5 • Use the arrow keys to move to the Device field and press Enter.

6 • Select the device you wish to use and press Enter.

7 • Use the arrow keys to move to the Mode field and press Enter.

8 • Select the default mode for your printer and press Enter.

9 • Press Escape and answer Yes to save the changes.

10 • Press Escape two times to return to the main menu or press AltALT-F10 to exit PRINTCON entirely.

· · · · ·

NOTE

Before a print device can be selected in **PRINTCON**, it must first be defined in **PRINTDEF.**

SWIFT
TRACK

Using Print Devices in Print Job Configurations—NWAdmin

> Access Key: A, U
>
> User or Container/Details/Print Job Configuration/Modify

1 • From Windows, run NWAdmin by double-clicking the icon or selecting it from the Start menu (Windows 95).

2 • Use the mouse to navigate through the directory tree to find the user or container object you wish to use the print device for. Double-clicking on a container object moves you deeper into the treedeeper in the tree.

3 • Select the object by double-clicking on it, or if it is a container object, select Object/Details from the menu bar. If you are using the NetWare 4.11 version of NWAdmin, you may also click on the View Modify Object Properties button from the toolbar.

Using the right mouse button also enables you to access the Details page.

TIP

4 • From the Details page, click Print Job Configuration.

5 • Select the job configuration you wish to use the device with and click Modify.

6 • Click on the Device field and select the print device you wish to use with the job configuration.

7 • Click on the Mode field and select the default mode for this printer.

8 • Click on OK to save the changes to this job configuration.

9 • From the Details page, click OK to save the changes to this object.

NOTE

Before a print device can be selected in a print job configuration, it must first be defined.

SWIFT
TRACK

Using Print Forms in Print Job Configurations— PRINTCON

> ### Access Key: A, U
> ### PRINTCON/Edit Print Job Configurations

1 • Run the PRINTCON utility from the DOS command line by typing:

`PRINTCON`

2 • Verify the user object shown at the top of the screen. If this is not the user you wish to use a print form for, select Change Current Object and press Enter. Use the Insert key to browse the directory tree. When you have located the desired user, select the object by highlighting it and pressing Enter or F10. Press Escape to return to the PRINTCON main menu.

3 • From the main menu, use the arrow keys to select Edit Print Job Configurations and press Enter.

4 • Select the print job configuration you wish to use a defined print form with and press Enter. Or press the Insert key to add a new print job configuration (refer to the Adding a Print Job Configuration Quick Path).

5 • Use the arrow keys to move to the Form name field and press Enter.

6 • Select the form you wish to use and press Enter.

7 • Press Escape and answer Yes to save the changes.

8 • Press Escape two times to return to the main menu or press AltALT-F10 to exit PRINTCON entirely.

NOTE

Before a print form can be selected in **PRINTCON**, it must first be
defined in **PRINTDEF.**

SWIFT TRACK

Using Print Forms in Print Job Configurations— NWAdmin

> Access Key: A, U
>
> User or Container/Details/Print Job Configuration/Modify

1 • From Windows, run NWAdmin by double-clicking the icon or selecting it from the Start menu (Windows 95).

2 • Use the mouse to navigate through the directory tree to find the user or container object you wish to use the print form for. Double-clicking on a container object moves you deeper into the treedeeper in the tree.

3 • Select the object by double-clicking on it, or if it is a container object, select Object/Details from the menu bar. If you are using the NetWare 4.11 version of NWAdmin, you may also click on the View Modify Object Properties button from the toolbar.

TIP

Using the right mouse button also enables you to access the Details page.

4 • From the Details page, click Print Job Configuration.

5 • Select the job configuration you wish to use the form with and click Modify.

6 • Click on the Form Name field and select the form you wish to use with this job configuration.

7 • Click on OK to save the changes to this job configuration.

8 • From the Details page, click OK to save the changes to this object.

NOTE

Before a print form can be selected in NWAdmin, it must first be defined.

Managing a NetWare 4 Print System

SWIFT TRACK

Checking a Printer's Status—PCONSOLE

> Access Key: A, U
>
> PCONSOLE/Printers/Printer Status

1 • Run the PCONSOLE utility from the DOS command line by typing:

PCONSOLE

2 • Verify the context shown at the top of the screen. If necessary, select Change Context and press Enter. Use the Insert key to browse the directory tree for the context the printer is located in and press F10 or Escape to save.

3 • From the PCONSOLE main menu, use the arrow keys to select Printers and press Enter.

4 • Select the printer you wish to check the status of and press Enter.

5 • Select Printer Status and press Enter.

6 • When you have finished viewing the printer's status, press Escape three times to return to the main menu or press Alt-F10 to exit PCONSOLE entirely.

Checking a Printer's Status—NWAdmin

> Access Key: A, U
>
> Object/Details/Printer Status

1 • From Windows, run NWAdmin by double-clicking the icon or selecting it from the Start menu (Windows 95).

2 • Use the mouse to navigate through the directory tree to find the container the printer is located in. Double-clicking on a container object moves you deeper into the tree.

3 • Highlight the printer you wish to view the status of and double-click or select Object/Details from the menu bar. If you are using the NetWare 4.11 version of NWAdmin, you may also click on the View Modify Object Properties button from the toolbar.

Using the right mouse button also enables you to access the Details page.

TIP

4 • From the Details page, click Printer Status.

5 • When you have finished viewing this printer's status, click Cancel.

SWIFT
TRACK

Checking a Printer's Status—Print Server

Access Key: A, U

Print Server Console/Printer Status

1 • Go to the console of the file server the print server is running on or establish an RCONSOLE session from a workstation by running RCONSOLE.EXE and choosing the file server the print server is running on.

2 • Press Alt-Esc (Alt-F3 if you are using RCONSOLE) until the Print Server Console is the active screen.

3 • From the Print Server Console Available Options menu, select Printer Status.

4 • From the Printer List screen, choose the printer you wish to view the status of by using the arrow keys to highlight it and press Enter.

5 • View the Current Status field for the status of the printer.[MDW1]

6 • When you have finished viewing the printer status, press Escape two times to return to the print server main menu.

Mounting a Form—PCONSOLE

> Access Key: A, PSO
> PCONSOLE/Printers/Printer Status/Mounted Form

1 • Run the PCONSOLE utility from the DOS command line by typing:

PCONSOLE

2 • Verify the context shown at the top of the screen. If necessary, select Change Context and press Enter. Use the Insert key to browse the directory tree for the context the printer is located in and press F10 or Escape to save.

3 • From the PCONSOLE main menu, use the arrow keys to select Printers and press Enter.

4 • Select the printer you wish to mount a form on and press Enter.

5 • Select Printer Status and press Enter.

6 • Use the arrow keys to move to the Mounted Form field and enter the form number you wish to mount and press Enter.

7 • Press Escape three times to return to the main menu or press Alt-F10 to exit PCONSOLE entirely.

Be sure to define a form in PRINTDEF or NWAdmin before attempting to mount it.

NOTE

Mounting a Form—NWAdmin

> Access Key: A, PSO
>
> Object/Details/Printer Status/Mount Form

1 • From Windows, run NWAdmin by double-clicking the icon or selecting it from the Start menu (Windows 95).

2 • Use the mouse to navigate through the directory tree to find the container the printer is located in. Double-clicking on a container object moves you deeper into the tree.

3 • Highlight the printer you wish to mount a form on and double-click or select Object/Details from the menu bar. If you are using the NetWare 4.11 version of NWAdmin, you may also click on the View Modify Object Properties button from the toolbar.

Using the right mouse button also enables you to access the Details page.

TIP

4 • From the Details page, click Printer Status.

5 • From the Printer Status Dialog Box, click on Mount Form.

6 • Enter the form number you wish to mount and click OK.

7 • When you have finished mounting the form, click Cancel from the printer's Details page to return to the NWAdmin main menu.

Be sure to define a form in PRINTDEF or NWAdmin before attempting to mount it.

NOTE

SWIFT
TRACK

Mounting a Form—Print Server

Access Key: A, PSO
Print Server Console/Printer Status/Mounted Form

1 • Go to the console of the file server print server is running on or establish an RCONSOLE session from a workstation by running RCONSOLE.EXE and choosing the file server the print server is running on.

2 • Press Alt-Esc (Alt-F3 if you are using RCONSOLE) until the Print Server Console is the active screen.

3 • From the Print Server Console Available Options menu, select Printer Status.

4 • From the Printer List screen, choose the printer you wish to mount the form on by using the arrow keys to highlight it and press Enter.

5 • Use the arrow keys to move to the Mounted Form field and enter the form number you wish to mount and press Enter.

6 • When you have finished, press Escape two times to return to the print server main menu.

Be sure to define a form in PRINTDEF or NWAdmin before attempting to mount it.

NOTE

SWIFT
TRACK

Pausing a Printer—PCONSOLE

> Access Key: A, PSO
> PCONSOLE/Printers/Printer Status/Printer Control/Pause

I • Run the PCONSOLE utility from the DOS command line by typing:

PCONSOLE

2 • Verify the context shown at the top of the screen. If necessary, select Change Context and press Enter. Use the Insert key to browse the directory tree for the context the printer is located in and press F10 or Escape to save.

3 • From the PCONSOLE main menu, use the arrow keys to select Printers and press Enter.

4 • Select the printer you wish to pause and press Enter.

5 • Select Printer Status and press Enter.

6 • Use the arrow keys to move to the Printer Control field and press Enter.

7 • Select Pause Printer and press Enter.

8 • Press Escape three times to return to the main menu or press Alt-F10 to exit PCONSOLE entirely.

WARNING

Once a printer is paused in PCONSOLE, no printing can take place until the printer is restarted again.

SWIFT
TRACK

Pausing a Printer—NWAdmin

> Access Key: A, PSO
> Object/Details/Printer Status/Pause

1 • From Windows, run NWAdmin by double-clicking the icon or selecting it from the Start menu (Windows 95).

2 • Use the mouse to navigate through the directory tree to find the container the printer is located in. Double-clicking on a container object moves you deeper into the tree.

3 • Highlight the printer you wish to pause and double-click or select Object/Details from the menu bar. If you are using the NetWare 4.11 version of NWAdmin, you may also click on the View Modify Object Properties button from the toolbar.

TIP

Using the right mouse button also enables you to access the Details page.

4 • From the Details page, click Printer Status.

5 • From the Printer Status Dialog Box, click on Pause.

6 • When you have finished pausing the printer, click Cancel from the printer's Details page to return to the NWAdmin main screen.

WARNING

Once a printer is paused, no printing can take place until the printer is restarted again.

SWIFT TRACK

Pausing a Printer—Print Server

Access Key: A, PSO

Print Server Console/Printer Status/Printer Control/Pause Printer

1 • Go to the console of the file server print server is running on or establish an RCONSOLE session from a workstation by running RCONSOLE.EXE and choosing the file server the print server is running on.

2 • Press Alt-Esc (Alt-F3 if you are using RCONSOLE) until the Print Server Console is the active screen.

3 • From the Print Server Console Available Options menu, select Printer Status.

4 • From the Printer List screen, choose the printer you wish to pause by using the arrow keys to highlight it and press Enter.

5 • Use the arrow keys to move to the Printer Control field and press Enter.

6 • Select Pause Printer and press Enter.

7 • When you have finished, press Escape two times to return to the print server main menu.

Once a printer is paused, no printing can take place until the printer is restarted again.

WARNING

SWIFT
TRACK

Restarting a Paused Printer—PCONSOLE

Access Key: A, PSO

PCONSOLE/Printers/Printer Status/Printer Control/Start

1 • Run the PCONSOLE utility from the DOS command line by typing:

PCONSOLE

2 • Verify the context shown at the top of the screen. If necessary, select Change Context and press Enter. Use the Insert key to browse the directory tree for the context the printer is located in and press F10 or Escape to save.

3 • From the PCONSOLE main menu, use the arrow keys to select Printers and press Enter.

4 • Select the printer you wish to restart and press Enter.

5 • Select Printer Status and press Enter.

6 • Use the arrow keys to move to the Printer Control field and press Enter.

7 • Select Start Printer and press Enter.

8 • Press Escape three times to return to the main menu or press Alt-F10 to exit PCONSOLE entirely.

SWIFT TRACK

Restarting a Paused Printer—NWAdmin

Access Key: A, PSO
Object/Details/Printer Status/Start

1 • From Windows, run NWAdmin by double-clicking the icon or selecting it from the Start menu (Windows 95).

2 • Use the mouse to navigate through the directory tree to find the container the printer is located in. Double-clicking on a container object moves you deeper into the tree.

3 • Highlight the printer you wish to restart and double-click or select Object/Details from the menu bar. If you are using the NetWare 4.11 version of NWAdmin, you may also click on the View Modify Object Properties button from the toolbar.

TIP

Using the right mouse button also enables you to access the Details page.

4 • From the Details page, click Printer Status.

5 • From the Printer Status Dialog Box, click on Start.

6 • When you have finished, click Cancel from the printer's Details page to return to the NWAdmin main screen.

SWIFT TRACK

Restarting a Paused Printer—Print Server

Access Key: A, PSO

Print Server Console/Printer Status/Printer Control/Start Printer

1 • Go to the console of the file server print server is running on or establish an RCONSOLE session from a workstation by running RCONSOLE.EXE and choosing the file server the print server is running on.

2 • Press Alt-Esc (Alt-F3 if you are using RCONSOLE) until the Print Server Console is the active screen.

3 • From the Print Server Console Available Options menu, select Printer Status.

4 • From the Printer List screen, choose the printer you wish to restart by using the arrow keys to highlight it and press Enter.

5 • Use the arrow keys to move to the Printer Control field and press Enter.

6 • Select Start Printer and press Enter.

7 • When you have finished, press Escape two times to return to the print server main menu.

SWIFT TRACK

Aborting a Print Job—PCONSOLE

> Access Key: A, PSO
> PCONSOLE/Printers/Printer Status/Printer Control/Abort Print Job

I • Run the PCONSOLE utility from the DOS command line by typing:

    PCONSOLE

2 • Verify the context shown at the top of the screen. If necessary, select Change Context and press Enter. Use the Insert key to browse the directory tree for the context the printer is located in and press F10 or Escape to save.

3 • From the PCONSOLE main menu, use the arrow keys to select Printers and press Enter.

4 • Select the printer you wish to abort the print job on and press Enter.

5 • Select Printer Status and press Enter.

6 • Use the arrow keys to move to the Printer Control field and press Enter.

7 • Select Abort Print Job and press Enter.

8 • Press Escape three times to return to the main menu or press Alt-F10 to exit PCONSOLE entirely.

Aborting a Print Job—NWAdmin

SWIFT
TRACK

> Access Key: A, PSO
> Object/Details/Printer Status/Abort Job

I • From Windows, run NWAdmin by double-clicking the icon or selecting it from the Start menu (Windows 95).

2 • Use the mouse to navigate through the directory tree to find the container the printer is located in. Double-clicking on a container object moves you deeper into the tree.

3 • Highlight the printer you wish to pause and double-click or select Object/Details from the menu bar. If you are using the NetWare 4.11 version of NWAdmin, you may also click on the View Modify Object Properties button from the toolbar.

TIP

Using the right mouse button also enables you to access the Details page.

4 • From the Details page, click Printer Status.

5 • From the Printer Status Dialog Box, click on Abort Job.

6 • When you have finished aborting the print job, click Cancel from the printer's Details page to return to the NWAdmin main screen.

Aborting a Print Job—Print Server

Access Key: A, PSO
Print Server Console/Printer Status/Printer Control/Abort Print Job

1 • Go to the console of the file server print server is running on or establish an RCONSOLE session from a workstation by running RCONSOLE.EXE and choosing the file server the print server is running on.

2 • Press Alt-Esc (Alt-F3 if you are using RCONSOLE) until the Print Server Console is the active screen.

3 • From the Print Server Console Available Options menu, select Printer Status.

4 • From the Printer List screen, choose the printer you wish to abort the print job on by using the arrow keys to highlight it and press Enter.

5 • Use the arrow keys to move to the Printer Control field and press Enter.

6 • Select Abort Print Job and press Enter.

7 • When you have finished, press Escape two times to return to the print server main menu.

**SWIFT
TRACK**

Issuing a Form Feed—PCONSOLE

Access Key: A, PSO
PCONSOLE/Printers/Printer Status/Printer Control/Form Feed

1 • Run the PCONSOLE utility from the DOS command line by typing:

PCONSOLE

2 • Verify the context shown at the top of the screen. If necessary, select Change Context and press Enter. Use the Insert key to browse the directory tree for the context the printer is located in and press F10 or Escape to save.

3 • From the PCONSOLE main menu, use the arrow keys to select Printers and press Enter.

4 • Select the printer you wish to issue a form feed on and press Enter.

5 • Select Printer Status and press Enter.

6 • Use the arrow keys to move to the Printer Control field and press Enter.

7 • Select Form Feed and press Enter.

8 • Press Escape three times to return to the main menu or press Alt-F10 to exit PCONSOLE entirely.

SWIFT
TRACK

Issuing a Form Feed—NWAdmin

> Access Key: A, PSO
> Object/Details/Printer Status/Eject Page

1 • From Windows, run NWAdmin by double-clicking the icon or selecting it from the Start menu (Windows 95).

2 • Use the mouse to navigate through the directory tree to find the container the printer is located in. Double-clicking on a container object moves you deeper into the tree.

3 • Highlight the printer you wish to issue a form feed on and double-click or select Object/Details from the menu bar. If you are using the NetWare 4.11 version of NWAdmin, you may also click on the View Modify Object Properties button from the toolbar.

TIP

Using the right mouse button also enables you to access the Details page.

4 • From the Details page, click Printer Status.

5 • From the Printer Status Dialog Box, click on Eject Page.

6 • When you have finished, click Cancel from the printer's Details page to return to the NWAdmin main screen.

**SWIFT
TRACK**

Issuing a Form Feed—Print Server

> Access Key: A, PSO
> Print Server Console/Printer Status/Printer Control/Form Feed

1 • Go to the console of the file server print server is running on or establish an RCONSOLE session from a workstation by running RCONSOLE.EXE and choosing the file server the print server is running on.

2 • Press Alt-Esc (Alt-F3 if you are using RCONSOLE) until the Print Server Console is the active screen.

3 • From the Print Server Console Available Options menu, select Printer Status.

4 • From the Printer List screen, choose the printer you wish to issue the form feed on by using the arrow keys to highlight it and press Enter.

5 • Use the arrow keys to move to the Printer Control field and press Enter.

6 • Select Form Feed and press Enter.

7 • When you have finished, press Escape two times to return to the print server main menu.

Aligning a Form—PCONSOLE

> Access Key: A, PSO
>
> PCONSOLE/Printers/Printer Status/Printer Control/Mark top of form[MDW2]

1 • Run the PCONSOLE utility from the DOS command line by typing:

   PCONSOLE

2 • Verify the context shown at the top of the screen. If necessary, select Change Context and press Enter. Use the Insert key to browse the directory tree for the context the printer is located in and press F10 or Escape to save.

3 • From the PCONSOLE main menu, use the arrow keys to select Printers and press Enter.

4 • Select the printer you wish to align and press Enter.

5 • Select Printer Status and press Enter.

6 • Use the arrow keys to move to the Printer Control field and press Enter.

7 • Select Mark top of form[MDW3] and press Enter.

8 • Press Escape three times to return to the main menu or press Alt-F10 to exit PCONSOLE entirely.

**SWIFT
TRACK**

Aligning a Form—Print Server

> Access Key: A, PSO
>
> Print Server Console/Printer Status/Printer Control/Mark top of Form[MDW4]

1 • Go to the console of the file server print server is running on or establish an RCONSOLE session from a workstation by running RCONSOLE.EXE and choosing the file server the print server is running on.

2 • Press Alt-Esc (Alt-F3 if you are using RCONSOLE) until the Print Server Console is the active screen.

3 • From the Print Server Console Available Options menu, select Printer Status.

4 • From the Printer List screen, choose the printer you wish to align a form on by using the arrow keys to highlight it and press Enter.

5 • Use the arrow keys to move to the Printer Control field and press Enter.

6 • Select Mark top of Form[MDW5] and press Enter.

7 • When you have finished, press Escape two times to return to the print server main menu.

Rewinding a Printer—PCONSOLE

Access Key: A, PSO
PCONSOLE/Printers/Printer Status/Printer Control/Rewind
Printer

1 • Run the PCONSOLE utility from the DOS command line by typing:

PCONSOLE

2 • Verify the context shown at the top of the screen. If necessary, select Change Context and press Enter. Use the Insert key to browse the directory tree for the context the printer is located in and press F10 or Escape to save.

3 • From the PCONSOLE main menu, use the arrow keys to select Printers and press Enter.

4 • Select the printer you wish to rewind and press Enter.

5 • Select Printer Status and press Enter.

6 • Use the arrow keys to move to the Printer Control field and press Enter.

7 • Select Rewind Printer and press Enter.

8 • Enter the number of bytes you wish to rewind and the print job copy number you wish to rewind to and press Enter.

9 • Press Escape and answer Yes to save changes.

10 • Press Escape three times to return to the main menu or press Alt-F10 to exit PCONSOLE entirely.

SWIFT TRACK

Stopping a Printer—PCONSOLE

> Access Key: A, PSO
> PCONSOLE/Printers/Printer Status/Printer Control/Stop Printer

1 • Run the PCONSOLE utility from the DOS command line by typing:

   PCONSOLE

2 • Verify the context shown at the top of the screen. If necessary, select Change Context and press Enter. Use the Insert key to browse the directory tree for the context the printer is located in and press F10 or Escape to save.

3 • From the PCONSOLE main menu, use the arrow keys to select Printers and press Enter.

4 • Select the printer you wish to stop and press Enter.

5 • Select Printer Status and press Enter.

6 • Use the arrow keys to move to the Printer Control field and press Enter.

7 • Select Stop Printer and press Enter.

8 • Press Escape three times to return to the main menu or press Alt-F10 to exit PCONSOLE entirely.

WARNING

Once a printer has been stopped, no printing can occur on that printer until it has been restarted again.

SWIFT TRACK

Stopping a Printer—Print Server

> Access Key: A, PSO
>
> Print Server Console/Printer Status/Printer Control/Stop Printer

1 • Go to the console of the file server print server is running on or establish an RCONSOLE session from a workstation by running RCONSOLE.EXE and choosing the file server the print server is running on.

2 • Press Alt-Esc (Alt-F3 if you are using RCONSOLE) until the Print Server Console is the active screen.

3 • From the Print Server Console Available Options menu, select Printer Status.

4 • From the Printer List screen, choose the printer you wish to stop by using the arrow keys to highlight it and press Enter.

5 • Use the arrow keys to move to the Printer Control field and press Enter.

6 • Select Stop Printer and press Enter.

7 • When you have finished, press Escape two times to return to the print server main menu.

Once a printer has been stopped, no printing can occur on that printer until it has been restarted again.

WARNING

SWIFT TRACK

Connecting Remote Printers—File Server Attached—NPRINTER.NLM

Access Key: A, PSO, U

From the server console, type:

LOAD NPRINTER printservername printername

I • Go to the console of the file server you wish to load the NPRINTER on or establish an RCONSOLE session from a workstation by running RCONSOLE.EXE and choosing the server you wish to load NPRINTER.NLM on.

2 • From the server console prompt type:

LOAD NPRINTER *printservername printername*

For example:

LOAD NPRINTER SLCII_PS 1

NOTE

For a printer to attach to a print server, the print server must be running before NPRINTER is loaded.

SWIFT TRACK

Connecting Remote Printers—Workstation Attached

> Access Key: A, PSO, U
>
> From the workstation with the printer attached, type:
>
> NPRINTER PrintServerName PrinterNumber

1 • Verify that the workstation's NET.CFG file contains the following line:

```
SPX CONNECTIONS = 60
```

If necessary, use a text editor to add this line.

2 • Load the NetWare Client software at the workstation to attach to the server where the printer is defined.

3 • Log in to the server.

4 • Load the remote printer software by typing the following from the DOS command line:

```
NPRINTER PrintServerName PrinterNumber
```

For example:

```
  RPRINTER SLCII_PS 2
```

Or use the following NDS syntax:

```
NPRINTER .CN=printername.OU=OrganizationalUnit.O=Organization
```

For example:

```
NPRINTER .CN=P1.OU=SLCII.O=AIRPORTS
```

For a printer to attach to a print server, the print server must be running before NPRINTER is loaded.

NOTE

SWIFT
TRACK

Disconnecting a Remote Printer

Access Key: A, U

From the workstation with the remote printer attached, type:

RPRINTER PrintServerName PrinterNumber -r

I • Go to the workstation with the remote printer attached.

2 • From the DOS command line, enter the following command:

```
RPRINTER PrintServerName PrinterNumber -r
```

For example:

```
RPRINTER SLCII_PS 2 -r
```

SWIFT TRACK

Making a Remote Printer Private

> Access Key: A, U
>
> From the workstation with the remote printer attached, type:
>
> PSC PS=PrintServerName P=PrinterNumber PRI

1 • Go to the workstation with the remote printer attached.

2 • From the DOS command line, enter the following command:

```
PSC PS=PrintServerName P=PrinterNumber PRI
```

For example:

```
PSC PS=SLCII_PS P=2 PRI
```

WARNING

Once a remote network printer has been made private, it can no longer be used by other network users until the PSC command has been reissued with the SHared[MDW6] parameter.

SWIFT TRACK

Returning a Remote Printer to Shared Mode

Access Key: A, U

From the workstation with the remote printer attached, type:

PSC PS=PrintServerName P=PrinterNumber SH

1 • Go to the workstation with the remote printer attached.

2 • From the DOS command line, enter the following command:

PSC PS=*PrintServerName* P=*PrinterNumber* SH

For example:

PSC PS=SLCII_PS P=2 SH

SWIFT TRACK

Placing a Print Job on Hold—PCONSOLE

> Access Key: A, PQO, U
>
> PCONSOLE/Print Queues/Print Jobs/User or Operator Hold

1 • Run the PCONSOLE utility from the DOS command line by typing:

PCONSOLE

2 • Verify the context shown at the top of the screen. If necessary, select Change Context and press Enter. Use the Insert key to browse the directory tree for the context the print queue is located in and press F10 or Escape to save.

3 • Use the arrow keys to select Print Queue and press Enter.

4 • Select the print queue that contains the job you wish to place on hold and press Enter.

5 • Select Print Jobs and press Enter.

6 • Select the print job you wish to place a hold on and press Enter.

7 • Use the arrow keys to move to the User Hold field if you are the job owner or the Operator Hold field if you are an ADMIN or Print Queue Operator.

8 • Type a Y for "yes" and press Enter.

9 • Press Escape four times to return to the main menu or press Alt-F10 to exit PCONSOLE entirely.

SWIFT
TRACK

Placing a Print Job on Hold—NWAdmin

> Access Key: A, PQO, U
> Object/Details/Job List

I • From Windows, run NWAdmin by double-clicking the icon or selecting it from the Start menu (Windows 95).

2 • Use the mouse to navigate through the directory tree to find the container the print queue is located in. Double-clicking on a container object moves you deeper into the tree.

3 • Highlight the print queue the job is located in and double-click or select Object/Details from the menu bar. If you are using the NetWare 4.11 version of NWAdmin, you may also click on the View Modify Object Properties button from the toolbar.

TIP

Using the right mouse button also enables you to access the Details page.

4 • From the Details page, click Job List.

5 • From the Job List dialog box, highlight the job you wish to place on hold and click on Hold Job. To release the hold, click on Resume.

6 • When you have finished, click Cancel from the print queue's Details page to return to the NWAdmin main screen.

SWIFT
TRACK

Deferring a Print Job—PCONSOLE

> Access Key: A, PQO, U
> PCONSOLE/Print Queues/Print Jobs/Defer Printing

1 • Run the PCONSOLE utility from the DOS command line by typing:

   PCONSOLE

2 • Verify the context shown at the top of the screen. If necessary, select Change Context and press Enter. Use the Insert key to browse the directory tree for the context the print queue is located in and press F10 or Escape to save.

3 • Use the arrow keys to select Print Queues and press Enter.

4 • Select the print queue that contains the job you wish to defer the printing of and press Enter.

5 • Select Print Jobs and press Enter.

6 • Select the print job you wish to defer and press Enter.

7 • Use the arrow keys to move to the Defer Printing field.

8 • Type a Y for "yes" and press Enter.

9 • Use the arrow keys to move down one field and enter the date that you want the job to print on.

10 • Use the arrow keys to move down one field and enter the time that you want the job to print.

11 • Press Escape four times to return to the main menu or press Alt-F10 to exit PCONSOLE entirely.

SWIFT
TRACK

Deferring a Print Job—NWAdmin

Access Key: A, PQO, U

Object/Details/Job List/Job Details/Defer Printing

1 • From Windows, run NWAdmin by double-clicking the icon or selecting it from the Start menu (Windows 95).

2 • Use the mouse to navigate through the directory tree to find the container the print queue is located in. Double-clicking on a container object moves you deeper into the tree.

3 • Highlight the print queue the job is located in and double-click or select Object/Details from the menu bar. If you are using the NetWare 4.11 version of NWAdmin, you may also click on the View Modify Object Properties button from the toolbar.

 Using the right mouse button also enables you to access the Details page.

TIP

4 • From the Details page, click Job List.

5 • From the Job List dialog box, highlight the job you wish to defer the printing of and click Job Details.

6 • From the Print Job Detail dialog box click the Defer Printing box in the lower right hand portion of the screen.

7 • Use the up and down arrows next to the Target Date and Time fields to select the desired printing date and time. When you have finished, click OK to save the changes.

8 • When you have finished deferring printing, click Cancel from the print queue's Details page to return to the NWAdmin main screen.

SWIFT
TRACK

Checking a Print Job's Status—PCONSOLE

> Access Key: A, PQO, U
>
> PCONSOLE/Print Queues/Print Jobs

1 • Run the PCONSOLE utility from the DOS command line by typing:

`PCONSOLE`

2 • Verify the context shown at the top of the screen. If necessary, select Change Context and press Enter. Use the Insert key to browse the directory tree for the context the print queue is located in and press F10 or Escape to save.

3 • Use the arrow keys to select Print Queues and press Enter.

4 • Select the print queue that contains the job you wish to check the status of and press Enter.

5 • Select Print Jobs and press Enter.

6 • View the status of the job in the queue.

7 • Press Escape three times to return to the main menu or press Alt-F10 to exit PCONSOLE entirely.

Checking a Print Job's Status—NWAdmin

SWIFT
TRACK

Access Key: A, PQO, U
Object/Details/Job List/Job Details

1 • From Windows, run NWAdmin by double-clicking the icon or selecting it from the Start menu (Windows 95).

2 • Use the mouse to navigate through the directory tree to find the container the print queue is located in. Double-clicking on a container object moves you deeper into the tree.

3 • Highlight the print queue the job is located in and double-click or select Object/Details from the menu bar. If you are using the NetWare 4.11 version of NWAdmin, you may also click on the View Modify Object Properties button from the toolbar.

Using the right mouse button also enables you to access the Details page.

TIP

4 • From the Details page, click Job List.

5 • From the Job List dialog box, highlight the job you wish to view the status of and click Job Details.

6 • From the Print Job Detail dialog box, view the Status field.

7 • When you have finished viewing the print job's status, click Cancel from the print queue's Details page to return to the NWAdmin main screen.

SWIFT
TRACK

Modifying a Print Job's CAPTURE Parameters— PCONSOLE

> **Access Key: A, PQO, U**
> **PCONSOLE/Print Queues/Print Jobs**

1 • Run the PCONSOLE utility from the DOS command line by typing:

PCONSOLE

2 • Verify the context shown at the top of the screen. If necessary, select Change Context and press Enter. Use the Insert key to browse the directory tree for the context the print queue is located in and press F10 or Escape to save.

3 • Use the arrow keys to select Print Queues and press Enter.

4 • Select the print queue that contains the job you wish to change the CAPTURE parameters for and press Enter.

5 • Select Print Jobs and press Enter.

6 • Select the print job you wish to modify and press Enter.

7 • Modify the parameters as desired.

8 • When you have finished modifying the CAPTURE parameters, press Escape three times to return to the main menu or press Alt-F10 to exit PCONSOLE entirely.

SWIFT TRACK

Modifying a Print Job's CAPTURE Parameters— NWAdmin

Access Key: A, PQO, U
Object/Details/Job List/Job Details

1 • From Windows, run NWAdmin by double-clicking the icon or selecting it from the Start menu (Windows 95).

2 • Use the mouse to navigate through the directory tree to find the container the print queue is located in. Double-clicking on a container object moves you deeper into the tree.

3 • Highlight the print queue the job is located in and double-click or select Object/Details from the menu bar. If you are using the NetWare 4.11 version of NWAdmin, you may also click on the View Modify Object Properties button from the toolbar.

TIP

Using the right mouse button also enables you to access the Details page.

4 • From the Details page, click Job List.

5 • From the Job List dialog box, highlight the job you wish to change the CAPTURE parameters for and click Job Details.

6 • From the Print Job Detail dialog box, change the desired CAPTURE parameter fields.

7 • When you have finished, click Cancel from the print queue's Details page to return to the NWAdmin main screen.

SWIFT
TRACK

Assigning Print Queue Users—PCONSOLE

Access Key: A, PQO
PCONSOLE/Print Queues/Users

1 • Run the PCONSOLE utility from the DOS command line by typing:

PCONSOLE

2 • Verify the context shown at the top of the screen. If necessary, select Change Context and press Enter. Use the Insert key to browse the directory tree for the context the print queue is located in and press F10 or Escape to save.

3 • Use the arrow keys to select Print Queues and press Enter.

4 • Select the print queue that you wish to assign users for and press Enter.

5 • Select Users and press Enter.

6 • Press the Insert key to add queue users (or delete to remove a queue user).

7 • Browse the directory tree and select the users you wish to use the queue by highlighting them and pressing Enter. The F5 key can be used to mark multiple users.

8 • When you have finished marking the users, press Enter.

9 • Press Escape three times to return to the main menu or Alt-F10 to exit PCONSOLE entirely.

Assigning Print Queue Users—NWAdmin

SWIFT TRACK

> Access Key: A, PQO
> Object/Details/Users/Add

1 • From Windows, run NWAdmin by double-clicking the icon or selecting it from the Start menu (Windows 95).

2 • Use the mouse to navigate through the directory tree to find the container the print queue is located in. Double-clicking on a container object moves you deeper into the tree.

3 • Highlight the print queue you wish to add users to and double-click or select Object/Details from the menu bar. If you are using the NetWare 4.11 version of NWAdmin, you may also click on the View Modify Object Properties button from the toolbar.

TIP

Using the right mouse button also enables you to access the Details page.

4 • From the Details page, click Users.

5 • From the Users dialog box, click Add. To remove a user, highlight the user in the list and click Delete.

6 • From the Select Object dialog box, browse the directory tree for the user or users you wish to add. Double-clicking the yellow up arrow in the Directory Context box moves you up the directory tree. Double-clicking a container object moves you into that container.

7 • When you have located the user you wish to add, click on the user in the Objects box and then click OK. Multiple users can be selected at once by holding down the Shift key and clicking on the user objects.

8 • When you have finished adding users, click OK to save the new user list and return to the NWAdmin main screen.

Assigning Print Queue Operators—PCONSOLE

SWIFT
TRACK

> Access Key: A
> PCONSOLE/Print Queues/Operators

1 • Run the PCONSOLE utility from the DOS command line by typing:

   PCONSOLE

2 • Verify the context shown at the top of the screen. If necessary, select Change Context and press Enter. Use the Insert key to browse the directory tree for the context the print queue is located in and press F10 or Escape to save.

3 • Use the arrow keys to select Print Queues and press Enter.

4 • Select the print queue that you wish to assign an operator for and press Enter.

5 . Select Operators and press Enter.

6 • Press the Insert key to add queue operators (or delete to remove a queue operator).

7 • Browse the directory tree and select the user you wish to be an operator for this queue. The F5 key can be used to mark multiple users.

8 • When you have finished marking the users, press Enter.

9 • Press Escape three times to return to the main menu or Alt-F10 to exit PCONSOLE entirely.

Assigning Print Queue Operators—NWAdmin

SWIFT
TRACK

> Access Key: A
> Object/Details/Operators/Add

1 • From Windows, run NWAdmin by double-clicking the icon or selecting it from the Start menu (Windows 95).

2 • Use the mouse to navigate through the directory tree to find the container the print queue is located in. Double-clicking on a container object moves you deeper into the tree.

3 • Highlight the print queue you wish to add an operator for and double-click or select Object/Details from the menu bar. If you are using the NetWare 4.11 version of NWAdmin, you may also click on the View Modify Object Properties button from the toolbar.

Using the right mouse button also enables you to access the Details page.

TIP

4 • From the Details page, click Operator.

5 • From the Operator dialog box, Click Add. To remove an operator, highlight the user in the list and click Delete.

6 • From the Select Object dialog box, browse the directory tree for the user or users you wish to add. Double-clicking the yellow up arrow in the Directory Context box moves you up the directory tree. Double-clicking a container object moves you into that container.

7 • When you have located the user you wish to add, click on the user in the Objects box and then click OK. Multiple users can be selected at once by holding down the Shift key and clicking on the user objects.

8 • When you have finished adding operators, click OK to save the new operator list and return to the NWAdmin main screen.

SWIFT TRACK

Disabling the Servicing of Print Jobs in a Queue— PCONSOLE

> Access Key: A, PQO
>
> PCONSOLE/Print Queues/Status

1 • Run the PCONSOLE utility from the DOS command line by typing:

PCONSOLE

2 • Verify the context shown at the top of the screen. If necessary, select Change Context and press Enter. Use the Insert key to browse the directory tree for the context the print queue is located in and press F10 or Escape to save.

3 • Use the arrow keys to select Print Queues and press Enter.

4 • Select the print queue in which you wish to disable the servicing of print jobs and press Enter.

5 • Select Status and press Enter.

6 • If you do not want users to be able to place jobs in the queue, type an N for "no" in the first field. If you want jobs to go to the queue but not be serviced, type an N for "no" in the second field.

7 • When you have finished, press Escape three times to return to the main menu or Alt-F10 to exit PCONSOLE entirely.

Disabling the Servicing of Print Jobs in a Queue—NWAdmin

SWIFT
TRACK

> Access Key: A, PQO
> Object/Details

1 • From Windows, run NWAdmin by double-clicking the icon or selecting it from the Start menu (Windows 95).

2 • Use the mouse to navigate through the directory tree to find the container the print queue is located in. Double-clicking on a container object moves you deeper into the tree.

3 • Highlight the print queue you wish to disable and double-click or select Object/Details from the menu bar. If you are using the NetWare 4.11 version of NWAdmin, you may also click on the View Modify Object Properties button from the toolbar.

Using the right mouse button also enables you to access the Details page.

TIP

4 • From the Details page, click the Operator Status Flags you desire. If you do not want users to be able to place jobs in the queue, click the first field. If you want jobs to go to the queue but not be serviced, click the second field.

5 • When you have finished, click OK to save the changes and return to the NWAdmin main screen.

SWIFT
TRACK

Downing a Print Server through PCONSOLE

Access Key: A, PSO

PCONSOLE/Print Servers/Information and Status/Down

1 • Run the PCONSOLE utility from the DOS command line by typing:

PCONSOLE

2 • Verify the context shown at the top of the screen. If necessary, select Change Context and press Enter. Use the Insert key to browse the directory tree for the context the print server is located in and press F10 or Escape to save.

3 • Use the arrow keys to select Print Servers and press Enter.

4 • Select the print server you wish to take down and press Enter.

5 • Select Information and Status and press Enter.

6 • Select Current Server Status and press Enter.

7 • Use the arrow keys to move to Down if you wish for the print server to go down immediately or Going Down after current jobs if you want the print server to finish servicing the jobs in the queue. When you have finished, press Enter.[MDW7]

8 • Press Escape three times to return to the main menu or press Alt-F10 to exit PCONSOLE entirely.

Downing a Print Server through NWAdmin

Access Key: A, PSO
Object/Details/Unload

I • From Windows, run NWAdmin by double-clicking the icon or selecting it from the Start menu (Windows 95).

2 • Use the mouse to navigate through the directory tree to find the container the print server is located in. Double-clicking on a container object moves you deeper into the tree.

3 • Highlight the print server you wish to take down and double-click or select Object/Details from the menu bar. If you are using the NetWare 4.11 version of NWAdmin, you may also click on the View Modify Object Properties button from the toolbar.

Using the right mouse button also enables you to access the Details page.

TIP

4 • From the Details page, click Unload.

5 • If you want the print server to go down immediately, click Unload Print Server Immediately and click OK. If you would like the current print jobs to finish before the print server goes down, select Unload After Current Print Jobs and click OK.

6 • When you have finished, click Cancel from the Print Server's Details page to return to the NWAdmin main screen.

SWIFT TRACK

Downing a Print Server from the Server Console

> Access Key: A, PSO
>
> Print Server Console/Print Server Information/Current Status/Down

1 • Go to the console of the file server print server is running on or establish an RCONSOLE session from a workstation by running RCONSOLE.EXE and choosing the file server the print server is running on.

2 • Press Alt-Esc (Alt-F3 if you are using RCONSOLE) until the Print Server Console is the active screen.

3 • From the Print Server Console Available Options menu, select Print Server Information.

4 • Use the arrow keys to move to the Current Status and press Enter.

5 • Use the arrow keys to move to Unload and press Enter if you wish for the print server to go down immediately, or go to Unload after Active Print Jobs and press Enter if you want the print server to finish servicing the jobs in the queue.

6 • When you have finished, press Escape two times to return to the print server main menu.

SWIFT TRACK

Searching for Printers—NETADMIN

> Access Key: A, U
> NETADMIN/Search

I • Run the NETADMIN utility from the DOS command line by typing:

NETADMIN

2 • Use the arrow keys to select Search and press Enter.

3 • Enter the context you wish to search from by pressing Enter to browse the tree. Or to search the entire tree, type the following in the Context field:

[ROOT]

4 • Move to the Search Depth field and specify whether you wish to search all containers or only the current container and press Enter.

5 • In the class field, press Enter and select Printer as the class you wish to search.

6 • If you wish to search for all printers in the tree, press F10 to begin the search. If you wish to search based on specific criteria, go to step 7.

7 • If you wish to search based on specific criteria, press Enter in the property field and select the property you wish to search on. For example, to search for all printers called HP4, select the name property.

8 • In the Operator field, press Enter to select a search operator. For example, select Equal to search for a property that is equal to the value specified.

9 • Specify the data value you wish to search for. For example, enter HP4 to search for all printers named HP4.

10 • When you have finished specifying the search criteria, press F10 to begin the search.

11 • When you have finished searching, press Escape two times to return to the main menu or press Alt-F10 to exit NETADMIN entirely.

Searching for Printers—NWAdmin

> Access Key: A, U
> Object/Search

1 • From Windows, run NWAdmin by double-clicking the icon or selecting it from the Start menu (Windows 95).

2 • From the menu bar, select Object and then Search. If you are using the NetWare 4.11 version of NWAdmin, you may also click the Search button from the toolbar.

3 • In the Start From field, enter the context you wish to begin the search from, or to search the entire tree, type [Root]. You may also browse the tree for the context you desire by clicking on the Browse button to the right of the field. Double-clicking the yellow up arrow moves you up the directory tree. Double-clicking a container object moves you into that container.

4 • If you wish to search all containers within the context being searched, click the Search Entire Subtree box.

5 • In the Search for field click once and move though the list to select Printer as the object type you wish to search for. If you wish to search for all printers in the tree, click OK to begin the search. If you wish to search for specific printers, go to the next step.

6 • If you wish to search for specific printers, click in the property box and choose the property you wish to search for. For example, to search for all printers named HP4, choose the Name property.

7 • In the next field, choose the search operator. In the preceding example, the search operator of Equal to[MDW8] should be chosen.

8 • To the right of the search operator field, enter the data value you wish to search for. In the preceding example, the data value would be HP4.

9 • When you have finished entering the search parameters, click OK to begin the search.

10 • When you have finished viewing the search results, close the box to return to the NWAdmin main screen.

SWIFT
TRACK

Enabling **CAPTURE** from the DOS Command Line

Access Key: A, U

CAPTURE Options ...

I • From the DOS command line of a workstation, issue the CAPTURE command using the following syntax:

```
CAPTURE OPTION OPTION...
```

For example:

```
CAPTURE Q=.CN=HP4_Q.OU=SLC_II.OU=Airports.O=Skydive
L=2 NB NFF TI=20
```

Or, if the print queue is in your current context,

```
CAPTURE Q=HP4_Q L=2 NB NFF TI=20
```

SWIFT TRACK

Enabling CAPTURE through User Login Scripts—NETADMIN

> Access Key: A, U
>
> NETADMIN/Manage Object/View Edit Properties of this Object/Login Script

1 • Run the NETADMIN utility from the DOS command line by typing:

NETADMIN

2 • Verify the context shown at the top of the screen. If necessary, select Change Context and press Enter. Use the Insert key to browse the directory tree for the context the user is located in and press F10 or Escape to save.

3 • Use the arrow keys to select Manage Objects and press Enter.

4 • Select the user whose login script you wish to modify and press Enter.

5 • Select View or Edit Properties of this Object and press Enter.

6 • Select Login Script and press Enter.

7 • Enter the CAPTURE statement with the following syntax:

#CAPTURE *OPTION OPTION...*

For example:

#CAPTURE Q=.CN=HP4_Q.OU=SLC_II.OU=Airports.O=Skydive
L=2 NB NFF TI=20

Or, if the print queue is in the user's current context:

#CAPTURE Q=HP4_Q L=2 NB NFF TI=20

8 • Press Escape and answer Yes to save changes.

9 • Press Escape three times to return to the main menu or press Alt-F10 to exit NETADMIN entirely.

SWIFT TRACK

Enabling CAPTURE through User Login Scripts— NWAdmin

> **Access Key: A, U**
> **Object/Details/Login Script**

1 • From Windows, run NWAdmin by double-clicking the icon or selecting it from the Start menu (Windows 95).

2 • Use the mouse to navigate through the directory tree to find the container the user is located in. Double-clicking on a container object moves you deeper into the tree.

3 • Highlight the user you wish to edit the login script for and double-click or select Object/Details from the menu bar. If you are using the NetWare 4.11 version of NWAdmin, you may also click on the View Modify Object Properties button from the toolbar.

TIP

Using the right mouse button also enables you to access the Details page.

4 • From the Details page, click Login Script.

5 • Enter the CAPTURE statement with the following syntax:

```
#CAPTURE OPTION OPTION...
```

For example:

```
#CAPTURE Q=.CN=HP4_Q.OU=SLC_II.OU=Airports.O=Skydive
L=2 NB NFF TI=20
```

Or, if the print queue is in the user's current context:

```
#CAPTURE Q=HP4_Q L=2 NB NFF TI=20
```

6 • When you have finished modifying the user's login script, click OK to save the changes and return to the NWAdmin main screen.

· ◄

**SWIFT
TRACK**

Enabling CAPTURE through Container Login Scripts—NETADMIN

> Access Key: A
>
> NETADMIN/Manage Object/View Edit Properties of this Object/
> Login Script

I • Run the NETADMIN utility from the DOS command line by typing:

```
NETADMIN
```

2 • Verify the context shown at the top of the screen. If necessary, select Change Context and press Enter. Use the Insert key to browse the directory tree for the context the container is located in and press F10 or Escape to save.

3 • Use the arrow keys to select Manage Objects and press Enter.

4 • Select the container whose login script you wish to modify and press F10.

5 • Select View or Edit Properties of this Object and press Enter.

6 • Select Login Script and press Enter.

7 • Enter the CAPTURE statement with the following syntax:

```
#CAPTURE OPTION OPTION...
```

For example:

```
#CAPTURE Q=.CN=HP4_Q.OU=SLC_II.OU=Airports.O=Skydive
L=2 NB NFF TI=20
```

Or, if the print queue is in the user's current context:

```
#CAPTURE Q=HP4_Q L=2 NB NFF TI=20
```

8 • Press Escape and answer Yes to save changes.

9 • Press Escape three times to return to the main menu or press Alt-F10 to exit NETADMIN entirely.

SWIFT TRACK

Enabling CAPTURE through Container Login Scripts—NWAdmin

Access Key: A
Object/Details/Login Script

I • From Windows, run NWAdmin by double-clicking the icon or selecting it from the Start menu (Windows 95).

2 • Use the mouse to navigate through the directory tree to find the desired container. Double-clicking on a container object moves you deeper into the tree.

3 • Highlight the container you wish to edit the login script for and select Object/Details from the menu bar. If you are using the NetWare 4.11 version of NWAdmin, you may also click on the View Modify Object Properties button from the toolbar.

TIP

Using the right mouse button also enables you to access the Details page.

4 • From the Details page, click Login Script.

5 • Enter the CAPTURE statement with the following syntax:

```
#CAPTURE OPTION OPTION...
```

For example:

```
#CAPTURE Q=.CN=HP4_Q.OU=SLC_II.OU=Airports.O=Skydive
L=2 NB NFF TI=20
```

Or, if the print queue is in the user's current context:

```
#CAPTURE Q=HP4_Q L=2 NB NFF TI=20
```

6 • When you have finished modifying the container's login script, click OK to save the changes and return to the NWAdmin main screen.

SWIFT
TRACK

Enabling CAPTURE through Profile Login Scripts— NETADMIN

> Access Key: A, U
>
> NETADMIN/Manage Object/View Edit Properties of this Object/
>
> Login Script

1 • Run the NETADMIN utility from the DOS command line by typing:

```
NETADMIN
```

2 • Verify the context shown at the top of the screen. If necessary, select Change Context and press Enter. Use the Insert key to browse the directory tree for the context the profile is located in and press F10 or Escape to save.

3 • Use the arrow keys to select Manage Objects and press Enter.

4 • Select the profile whose login script you wish to modify and press Enter, or to create a new profile, press the Insert key.

5 • Select View or Edit Properties of this Object and press Enter.

6 • Select Login Script and press Enter.

7 • Enter the CAPTURE statement with the following syntax:

```
#CAPTURE OPTION OPTION...
```

For example:

```
#CAPTURE Q=.CN=HP4_Q.OU=SLC_II.OU=Airports.O=Skydive
L=2 NB NFF TI=20
```

Or, if the print queue is in the user's current context:

```
#CAPTURE Q=HP4_Q L=2 NB NFF TI=20
```

8 • Press Escape and answer Yes to save changes.

9 • Press Escape three times to return to the main menu or press Alt-F10 to exit NETADMIN entirely.

**SWIFT
TRACK**

Enabling CAPTURE through Profile Login Scripts— NWAdmin

Access Key: A

Object/Details/Login Script

1 • From Windows, run NWAdmin by double-clicking the icon or selecting it from the Start menu (Windows 95).

2 • Use the mouse to navigate through the directory tree to find the container the profile object is located in. Double-clicking on a container object moves you deeper into the tree.

3 • Highlight the profile you wish to edit the login script for and select Object/Details from the menu bar. If you are using the NetWare 4.11 version of NWAdmin, you may also click on the View Modify Object Properties button from the toolbar.

TIP

Using the right mouse button also enables you to access the Details page.

4 • From the Details page, click Login Script.

5 • Enter the CAPTURE statement with the following syntax:

```
#CAPTURE OPTION OPTION...
```

For example:

```
#CAPTURE Q=.CN=HP4_Q.OU=SLC_II.OU=Airports.O=Skydive
L=2 NB NFF TI=20
```

Or, if the print queue is in the user's current context:

```
#CAPTURE Q=HP4_Q L=2 NB NFF TI=20
```

6 • When you have finished modifying the profile's login script, click OK to save the changes and return to the NWAdmin main screen.

SWIFT
TRACK

Enabling **CAPTURE** through Windows 95

Access Key: A, U

WIN95/Network Neighborhood/File/Capture Printer Port

1 • From the Windows 95 Desktop, double-click on Network Neighborhood.

2 • Double-click the file server or directory tree the printer is defined on.

3 • Click once on the printer you wish to capture.

4 • From the Menu Bar, select File and then Capture Printer Port.

5 • In the device field, select the printer port you wish to capture.

6 • Click OK.

SWIFT TRACK

Enabling CAPTURE through NETUSER

> Access Key: A, U
>
> NETUSER/Printing/LPTlx/Change Printers

1 • Run the NETUSER utility from the DOS command line by typing:

NETUSER

2 • Verify the context shown at the top of the screen. If necessary, select Change Context and press Enter. Use the Insert key to browse the directory tree for the context the printer or print queue is located in and press F10 or Escape to save.

3 • Use the arrow keys to select Printing and press Enter.

4 • Choose the LPT port you wish to capture and press Enter.

5 • Select Change Printers and press Enter.

6 • Choose the printer or print queue you wish to capture and press Enter.

7 • Press Escape two times to return to the main menu or press Alt-F10 to exit NETUSER entirely.

Troubleshooting

If you have a network printing problem, the following table can help. Scan the two columns on the left for the symptom you're experiencing and possible causes. The third column gives solutions, and the fourth column lists cross references to this book's chapters where each problem is covered.

SYMPTOM	POSSIBLE CAUSES	SOLUTION	FOR MORE INFORMATION SEE
Can't print from a workstation to a network printer.	LPT port not captured.	Type CAPTURE SH at the workstation's DOS prompt to view current CAPTURE settings. If the LPT port is not currently captured, issue the appropriate CAPTURE command.	Chapter 2, Chapter 3.
LPT port is CAPTURED but print jobs do not make it to the print queue.	Print queue has been placed on hold.	Set the "Allow users to submit print jobs" flag to "yes."	Chapter 6, Chapter 7.
	LPT port has been captured to the wrong print queue.	Use CAPTURE SH to verify CAPTURE settings.	Chapter 2, Chapter 3.
User cannot CAPTURE to the desired printer or print queue.	User is not an authorized print queue user.	Add the user to the print queue user list.	Chapter 6, Chapter 7.
Print Jobs go to the queue but are not serviced by print server.	Print server not assigned to service the queue.	Verify the print layout configuration and make the necessary printer/ print queue and printer/ print server assignments.	Chapter 2, Chapter 3.
	An operator flag has been set on the print queue.	Set the "Allow print servers to service queue" flag to "yes."	Chapter 6, Chapter 7.
	Print server is waiting for a new form to be mounted at the printer.	Mount the form being requested by the first job in the queue.	Chapter 6, Chapter 7.
	Print server is not running.	Load the print server software.	Chapter 2, Chapter 3.

SYMPTOM	POSSIBLE CAUSES	SOLUTION	FOR MORE INFORMATION SEE
Users can't print to a workstation-attached shared network printer.	Remote printer software has not been loaded.	Load NPRINTER.EXE (NetWare 4) or RPRINTER.EXE (NetWare 3) at the workstation.	Chapter 2, Chapter 3.
	PSC has been used to make the printer PRIvate.	Use PSC to return the printer to Shared mode.	Chapter 2, Chapter 3.
Can't print from a workstation to a locally attached printer.	Printer is off or unplugged.	Turn the printer on or verify that it has power.	
	Printer cable is loose or disconnected.	Ensure that all printer cables are securely attached.	
Print job is interrupted by another job in the queue.	The Time Out value is too low.	Increase the $TI=$ value in the CAPTURE statement.	Chapter 2, Chapter 3.
Print output is garbled.	Incorrect print driver is being used.	Contact the printer manufacturer for an updated driver or use a NetWare-provided print device.	Chapter 2, Chapter 3.
Print jobs do not print until the user exits from his or her application.	The Autoendcap Time Out value has been set to 0 (default).	Increase the $TI=$ value in the CAPTURE statement.	Chapter 2, Chapter 3.
Print Server prompts for a password when no password exists.	The incorrect print server name is being used.	Verify the name of the print server and reload it using the proper name.	Chapter 2, Chapter 3.

(continued)

SYMPTOM	POSSIBLE CAUSES	SOLUTION	FOR MORE INFORMATION SEE
When loading the print server, you cannot see the print server you created.	You need to load the print server from a different context (NetWare 4).	When context shows during the PSERVER load, backspace over all the text and press Enter. You can then browse and find the proper container.	Chapter 3.
Windows 95 does not show any print devices when you attempt to print from an application	You need to create a local printer under Windows 95 before you can print to the network.	Obtain the Windows 95 CD or floppies and install a printer device for the network printer you need to print to.	Chapter 7.
When CAPTURE is executed (in a script or manually), the "No default Queue" error message appears.	A print job configuration has not been created either for the container or the user.	Create a print job configuration and make it the default either for the container or the user.	Chapter 3.
	A queue name or printer name wasn't specified when the CAPTURE command was executed.	Specify a queue name or a printer name when CAPTUREing. Use full names if possible under NetWare 4 (such as *queue.container. container.org*).	Chapter 7.
A job appears to print, but never comes out of the printer, or is missing the last page.	A Form Feed needs to be executed after the print job (typical on some printers with some applications).	When CAPTUREing, use the / FF (Form Feed) flag option or under a print job configuration, select Form Feed.	Chapter 2, Chapter 3.

SYMPTOM	POSSIBLE CAUSES	SOLUTION	FOR MORE INFORMATION SEE
Using a third-party printer acting as a print device, the print server doesn't service jobs after working successfully for some time.	If under NetWare 4, check the *Bindery Context* settings under SERVMAN. If the third-party device does not support NDS (only through Bindery Emulation) then a change to the Bindery Context would prevent the printer from seeing print jobs.	Load SERVMAN.NLM at the server and check the Bindery Context relative to where the print objects reside in NDS. Make sure that a context entry corresponds to where those devices exist. You can also do this using the SET command at the server console. **Note:** You can have multiple entries for Bindery Contexts under NetWare 4.1.	Chapter 8.
Print jobs are not accepted into a queue. An error message is returned.	The volume that hosts the print queue is full. If this is NetWare 3.x, you need to delete some files under volume SYS (SYS is the only volume that can host queues).	NetWare 3: Delete some files on the SYS volume or move them somewhere else.	Chapter 2.
	Under NetWare 4, you can re-create the queue on a different volume, or delete some files on the host volume. Doing so re-enables print services.	NetWare 4: Delete some files on the host volume (the problem could be something other than SYS) or re-create the queue on another volume and update the other print objects (printers, print servers) accordingly.	Chapter 3.

(continued)

SYMPTOM	POSSIBLE CAUSES	SOLUTION	FOR MORE INFORMATION SEE
A third-party device acting as a remote printer fails to attach to the print server.	The printer's name and the NetWare-defined printer name do not match.	Under NWAdmin, locate the printer name, select it, and choose Rename from the File menu. Rename it to match the printer name for the remote device. You can obtain the device's name using the utility provided with the device (such as JetAdmin with HP Printers).	Chapter 8.

Disk Installation Instructions

Print Utilities

The following steps install the print utilities onto your hard drive:

1. Copy the BC450RTL.DLL file to the C:\WINDOWS directory on your hard drive.

2. Copy the file PTRSNAP.DLL to the C:\WINDOWS directory on your hard drive.

3, Open the NWADMIN.INI file found in the C:\WINDOWS directory and add the following lines:

```
[Snapin Object DLLs]

PTRSNAP=PTRSNAP.DLL
```

If the header already exists, just add the second line under it.

4. Choose Save from the File menu to save the file and then exit from Notepad. The next time you start NWAdmin, you'll notice two new options under the Tools section: Capture Selected Printer and End Printer Capture.

5. To use the Capture option, select a Print Queue and choose Tools. Choose Capture and double-click on the selected port.

6. To end the Capture, choose the End Capture option on the toolbar. Select one or more ports to stop the capture on and then click on OK.

NOTE

The capture feature was created to allow search and capture under NWAdmin. To search and capture, start a search from the Object/Search menu option. Find the queues that match the criteria and select Capture Selected Printer on the toolbar.

Novell Application Notes

Two self-extracting files on the disk contain Novell Application Notes. The files in APPNOTE1.EXE are in WordPerfect format. The files in APPNOTE2.EXE are in Microsoft Word format. Copy the appropriate file to your hard drive and double-click on it in Windows Explorer. The files will be extracted to your hard drive. You can read them by double-clicking each filename or by opening them through WordPerfect or Word.

Index

T

U

W

X

(b) You may not reverse engineer, decompile, or disassemble the Software. You may transfer the Software and user documentation on a permanent basis, provided that the transferee agrees to accept the terms and conditions of this Agreement and you retain no copies. If the Software is an update or has been updated, any transfer must include the most recent update and all prior versions.

4. <u>**Restrictions on Use of Individual Programs**</u>. You must follow the individual requirements and restrictions detailed for each individual program in Appendix B of this Book. These limitations are contained in the individual license agreements recorded on the disk(s)/CD-ROM. These restrictions include a requirement that after using the program for the period of time specified in its text, the user must pay a registration fee or discontinue use. By opening the Software packet(s), you will be agreeing to abide by the licenses and restrictions for these individual programs. None of the material on this disk(s) or listed in this Book may ever be distributed, in original or modified form, for commercial purposes.

5. <u>**Limited Warranty**</u>.

(a) IDGB warrants that the Software and disk(s)/CD-ROM are free from defects in materials and workmanship under normal use for a period of sixty (60) days from the date of purchase of this Book. If IDGB receives notification within the warranty period of defects in materials or workmanship, IDGB will replace the defective disk(s)/CD-ROM.

(b) IDGB AND THE AUTHOR OF THE BOOK DISCLAIM ALL OTHER WARRANTIES, EXPRESS OR IMPLIED, INCLUDING WITHOUT LIMITATION IMPLIED WARRANTIES OF MERCHANTABILITY AND FITNESS FOR A PARTICULAR PURPOSE, WITH RESPECT TO THE SOFTWARE, THE PROGRAMS, THE SOURCE CODE CONTAINED THEREIN, AND/OR THE TECHNIQUES DESCRIBED IN THIS BOOK. IDGB DOES NOT WARRANT THAT THE FUNCTIONS CONTAINED IN THE SOFTWARE WILL MEET YOUR REQUIREMENTS OR THAT THE OPERATION OF THE SOFTWARE WILL BE ERROR FREE.

(c) This limited warranty gives you specific legal rights, and you may have other rights which vary from jurisdiction to jurisdiction.

6. **Remedies**.

(**a**) IDGB's entire liability and your exclusive remedy for defects in materials and workmanship shall be limited to replacement of the Software, which is returned to IDGB at the address set forth below with a copy of your receipt. This Limited Warranty is void if failure of the Software has resulted from accident, abuse, or misapplication. Any replacement Software will be warranted for the remainder of the original warranty period or thirty (30) days, whichever is longer.

(**b**) In no event shall IDGB or the author be liable for any damages whatsoever (including without limitation damages for loss of business profits, business interruption, loss of business information, or any other pecuniary loss) arising out of the use of or inability to use the Book or the Software, even if IDGB has been advised of the possibility of such damages.

(**c**) Because some jurisdictions do not allow the exclusion or limitation of liability for consequential or incidental damages, the above limitation or exclusion may not apply to you.

7. **U.S. Government Restricted Rights**. Use, duplication, or disclosure of the Software by the U.S. Government is subject to restrictions stated in paragraph (c) (1) (ii) of the Rights in Technical Data and Computer Software clause of DFARS 252.227-7013, and in subparagraphs (a) through (d) of the Commercial Computer—Restricted Rights clause at FAR 52.227-19, and in similar clauses in the NASA FAR supplement, when applicable.

8. **General**. This Agreement constitutes the entire understanding of the parties, and revokes and supersedes all prior agreements, oral or written, between them and may not be modified or amended except in a writing signed by both parties hereto which specifically refers to this Agreement. This Agreement shall take precedence over any other documents that may be in conflict herewith. If any one or more provisions contained in this Agreement are held by any court or tribunal to be invalid, illegal or otherwise unenforceable, each and every other provision shall remain in full force and effect.

IDG BOOKS WORLDWIDE, INC.
END-USER LICENSE AGREEMENT

<u>Read This</u>. You should carefully read these terms and conditions before opening the software packet(s) included with this book ("Book"). This is a license agreement ("Agreement") between you and IDG Books Worldwide, Inc. ("IDGB"). By opening the accompanying software packet(s), you acknowledge that you have read and accept the following terms and conditions. If you do not agree and do not want to be bound by such terms and conditions, promptly return the Book and the unopened software packet(s) to the place you obtained them for a full refund.

1. **License Grant**. IDGB grants to you (either an individual or entity) a nonexclusive license to use one copy of the enclosed software program(s) (collectively, the "Software") solely for your own personal or business purposes on a single computer (whether a standard computer or a workstation component of a multi-user network). The Software is in use on a computer when it is loaded into temporary memory (i.e., RAM) or installed into permanent memory (e.g., hard disk, CD-ROM or other storage device). IDGB reserves all rights not expressly granted herein.

2. **Ownership**. IDGB is the owner of all right, title and interest, including copyright, in and to the compilation of the Software recorded on the disk(s)/CD-ROM. Copyright to the individual programs on the disk(s)/CD-ROM is owned by the author or other authorized copyright owner of each program. Ownership of the Software and all proprietary rights relating thereto remain with IDGB and its licensors.

3. <u>Restrictions On Use and Transfer</u>.

    (a) You may only (i) make one copy of the Software for backup or archival purposes, or (ii) transfer the Software to a single hard disk, provided that you keep the original for backup or archival purposes. You may not (i) rent or lease the Software, (ii) copy or reproduce the Software through a LAN or other network system or through any computer subscriber system or bulletin-board system, or (iii) modify, adapt or create derivative works based on the Software.

IDG BOOKS WORLDWIDE REGISTRATION CARD

RETURN THIS REGISTRATION CARD FOR FREE CATALOG

Title of this book: **Novell's Guide to NetWare® Printing**

My overall rating of this book: ❑ Very good [1] ❑ Good [2] ❑ Satisfactory [3] ❑ Fair [4] ❑ Poor [5]

How I first heard about this book:

❑ Found in bookstore; name: [6]

❑ Advertisement: [8]

❑ Word of mouth; heard about book from friend, co-worker, etc.: [10]

❑ Book review: [7]

❑ Catalog: [9]

❑ Other: [11]

What I liked most about this book:

What I would change, add, delete, etc., in future editions of this book:

Other comments:

Number of computer books I purchase in a year: ❑ 1 [12] ❑ 2-5 [13] ❑ 6-10 [14] ❑ More than 10 [15]

I would characterize my computer skills as: ❑ Beginner [16] ❑ Intermediate [17] ❑ Advanced [18] ❑ Professional [19]

I use ❑ DOS [20] ❑ Windows [21] ❑ OS/2 [22] ❑ Unix [23] ❑ Macintosh [24] ❑ Other: [25]_____

(please specify)

I would be interested in new books on the following subjects:

(please check all that apply, and use the spaces provided to identify specific software)

❑ Word processing: [26]

❑ Data bases: [28]

❑ File Utilities: [30]

❑ Networking: [32]

❑ Other: [34]

❑ Spreadsheets: [27]

❑ Desktop publishing: [29]

❑ Money management: [31]

❑ Programming languages: [33]

I use a PC at (please check all that apply): ❑ home [35] ❑ work [36] ❑ school [37] ❑ other: [38] _____

The disks I prefer to use are ❑ 5.25 [39] ❑ 3.5 [40] ❑ other: [41]_____

I have a CD ROM: ❑ yes [42] ❑ no [43]

I plan to buy or upgrade computer hardware this year: ❑ yes [44] ❑ no [45]

I plan to buy or upgrade computer software this year: ❑ yes [46] ❑ no [47]

Name: _____ Business title: [48] _____ Type of Business: [49] _____

Address (❑ home [50] ❑ work [51] /Company name: _____)

Street/Suite# _____

City [52] /State [53] /Zipcode [54]: _____ Country [55] _____

❑ **I liked this book!** You may quote me by name in future IDG Books Worldwide promotional materials.

My daytime phone number is _____

IDG BOOKS

THE WORLD OF COMPUTER KNOWLEDGE

❑ YES!

Please keep me informed about IDG's World of Computer Knowledge.
Send me the latest IDG Books catalog.